KU-484-632

PENGUIN BOOKS

# ADAM, EVE, AND THE SERPENT

Elaine Pagels is the Harrington Spear Paine Professor of Religion at Princeton University. She is the author of the award-winning *The Gnostic Gospels* as well as of *The Johannine Gospel in Gnostic Exegesis* and *The Gnostic Paul*.

# ADAM, EVE,
## AND THE
# SERPENT

## ELAINE PAGELS

PENGUIN BOOKS

### PENGUIN BOOKS

Published by the Penguin Group
27 Wrights Lane, London W8 5TZ, England
Viking Penguin Inc., 40 West 23rd Street, New York, New York 10010, USA
Penguin Books Australia Ltd, Ringwood, Victoria, Australia
Penguin Books Canada Ltd, 2801 John Street, Markham, Ontario, Canada L3R 1B4
Penguin Books (NZ) Ltd, 182–190 Wairau Road, Auckland 10, New Zealand

Penguin Books Ltd, Registered Offices: Harmondsworth, Middlesex, England

First published in Great Britain by Weidenfeld and Nicolson 1988
Published in Penguin Books 1990
1 3 5 7 9 10 8 6 4 2

Grateful acknowledgement is made to the following for permission
to reprint previously published material:

*Harvard Theological Review:* Excerpts from "Christian Apologists
and the 'Fall of the Angels': An Attack on Roman Imperial Power?"
by Elaine Pagels, which appeared in *Harvard Theological Review* 78, 3–4 (1985),
pp. 301–325; and "The Politics of Paradise: Augustine's Exegesis of
Genesis 1–3 Versus That of John Chrysostom," by Elaine Pagels,
which appeared in *Harvard Theological Review* 78, 1–2 (1985), pp. 67–95.
Copyright © 1985 by the President and Fellows of Harvard College.
Reprinted by permission.

Hendrickson Publishers, Inc.: Excerpts from "Exegesis and Exposition of
the Genesis Creation Accounts in Selected Texts from Nag Hammadi,"
by Elaine Pagels, in *Nag Hammadi, Gnosticism, and Early Christianity*, edited by
C. Hedrick and R. Hodgson, pp. 257–286. Used by permission of
Hendrickson Publishers, Inc., Peabody, Mass.

T&T Clark Ltd: Excerpts by Elaine Pagels from *The New Testament
and Gnosis: Essays in Honour of R. McL. Wilson*, edited by A. H. B. Logan
and A. J. M. Wedderburn (Edinburgh, Scotland, 1983), pp. 146–175.

National Council of the Churches of Christ in the USA: Scripture quotations
are from the Revised Standard Version Bible. Copyright 1946, 1952, © 1971
by the Division of Christian Education of the National Council of the
Churches of Christ in the USA. Used by permission.

Made and printed in Great Britain by
Cox & Wyman Ltd, Reading, Berks.

TO OUR BELOVED SON, MARK,
WHO FOR SIX AND A HALF YEARS
GRACED OUR LIVES WITH HIS PRESENCE

*October 26, 1980–April 10, 1987*

# ACKNOWLEDGMENTS

THIS BOOK is based upon research originally presented, for the most part, in scholarly publications (cited at the beginning of each chapter's footnotes), and revised to make it more generally accessible. During the eight years of research and writing, I have consulted with many scholars and friends. I am especially grateful to those who read the entire manuscript and helped me with corrections, criticism, and encouragement: Thomas Bos-looper, Peter Brown, Elizabeth Clark, Linda Hess, Martha Himmelfarb, Bentley Layton, Wayne Meeks, William Meninger, O.C.S.O., Alan Segal, S. David Sperling, and Robert Wilken; and to those who offered comments and criticism on portions of the work as it was in progress, especially Harry Attridge, Glen Bowersock, Bernadette Brooten, Mary Douglas, Theodor H. Gaster, John Gager, Marilyn Harran, Dennis MacDonald, Birger Pearson, Gilles Quispel, Morton Smith, and Lewis Spitz. Helmut Koester, formerly my thesis adviser, remains for me, as for many others, a respected and loved mentor and friend. I owe special thanks, too, to those friends and fellow writers who not only shared to some extent in the process of the work, but also read the manuscript and helped me with their criticism: Lydia Bronte, Elizabeth Diggs, Nick Herbert, Ralph Hiesey, my brother, Emily McCulley, Richard Ogust, and Sharon Olds.

Soon after I had begun the research for this book, the John D. and Catherine T. MacArthur Foundation astonished me with the award of a MacArthur Prize Fellowship, which gave me the most welcome and unexpected gift of all—time for research and writing. For this, and for the continuing work of the foundation on behalf of other recipients, I will always be grateful. Ellen Futter, president of Barnard College, and Charles Olton, then dean of the faculty, graciously arranged the first year of leave from full-time teaching and chairing the Department of Religion, so that I could devote the time to this research. I wish to thank my present colleagues in the Department of Religion at Princeton University, both for conversations that have contributed much to the process, and for their considerable grace during the years of research and writing, and also to thank the students, both graduate and undergraduate, who have struggled through these texts with me.

There are certain people without whose participation I cannot imagine having written this book. I have enjoyed working with Jason Epstein as editor, and deeply appreciate the insight, wit, and passion for clarity he has brought to this process, along with his enthusiastic support. My colleague Tom Boslooper has participated in the entire process of research and the preparation of the manuscript with an equanimity, generosity, and wisdom that always amaze me. John Brockman and Katinka Matson have seen the project through from the beginning, and have contributed in innumerable ways with sage advice and encouragement. I am very grateful to William T. Golden, who has lent me the use of an office for research and writing, which has proven to be a haven from the noises of New York: much of this book was written there. I wish to thank Richard Lim, too, for his prompt and increasingly expert assistance in finding research materials, and Dotty Holliger and Carol Shookhoff for their conscientious typing of parts of the manuscript.

Finally, I am grateful to those many friends whose presence and personal support in ways known to each of them have helped see me through these years, and mention in particular my parents, Louise and William M. Hiesey; Edith Davis; Jean Da Silva; Lita A. Hazen and Joseph H. Hazen; Betsy Herbert; Rev. Jane Henderson and Rev. Hugh Hildesley; Lucy and Robert Mann, Barbara Munsell, Richard Olney, and Katy Smith.

My most personal thanks I owe to my husband, Heinz Pagels, not only for reading the manuscript and offering excellent criticism while he was working on his own most recent book, but much more, of course, for his constant and loving presence during these years that included the lifetime and the death of our son, Mark, and the arrival of our daughter, Sarah.

# THE BOOK OF GENESIS

## CHAPTERS 1–3
### (Revised Standard Version)

IN THE BEGINNING God created the heavens and the earth. ²The earth was without form and void, and darkness was upon the face of the deep; and the Spirit of God was moving over the face of the waters.

3 And God said, "Let there be light"; and there was light. ⁴And God saw that the light was good; and God separated the light from the darkness. ⁵God called the light Day, and the darkness he called Night. And there was evening and there was morning, one day.

6 And God said, "Let there be a firmament in the midst of the waters, and let it separate the waters from the waters." ⁷And God made the firmament and separated the waters which were under the firmament from the waters which were above the firmament. And it was so. ⁸And God called the firmament Heaven. And there was evening and there was morning, a second day.

9 And God said, "Let the waters under the heavens be gathered together into one place, and let the dry land appear." And it was so. ¹⁰God called the dry land Earth, and the waters that were gathered together he called Seas. And God saw that it was good. ¹¹And God said, "Let the earth put forth vegetation, plants yielding seed, and fruit trees bearing fruit in which is their seed, each according to its kind, upon the earth." And it was so. ¹²The earth brought forth vegetation, plants yielding seed according to their own kinds, and trees bearing fruit in which is their seed, each according to its kind. And God saw that it was good. ¹³And there was evening and there was morning, a third day.

14 And God said, "Let there be lights in the firmament of the heavens to separate the day from the night; and let them be for signs and for seasons and for days and years, ¹⁵and let them be lights in the firmament of the heavens to give light upon the earth." And it was so. ¹⁶And God made the two great lights, the greater light to rule the day, and the lesser light to rule the night; he made the stars also. ¹⁷And God set them in the firmament of the heavens to give light upon the earth, ¹⁸to rule over the day and over the night, and to separate the light from the darkness. And God saw that it was good. ¹⁹And there was evening and there was morning, a fourth day.

20 And God said, "Let the waters bring forth swarms of living creatures,

and let birds fly above the earth across the firmament of the heavens." 21So God created the great sea monsters and every living creature that moves, with which the waters swarm, according to their kinds, and every winged bird according to its kind. And God saw that it was good. 22And God blessed them, saying, "Be fruitful and multiply and fill the waters in the seas, and let birds multiply on the earth." 23And there was evening and there was morning, a fifth day.

24 And God said, "Let the earth bring forth living creatures according to their kinds: cattle and creeping things and beasts of the earth according to their kinds." And it was so. 25And God made the beasts of the earth according to their kinds and the cattle according to their kinds, and everything that creeps upon the ground according to its kind. And God saw that it was good.

26 Then God said, "Let us make man in our image, after our likeness; and let them have dominion over the fish of the sea, and over the birds of the air, and over the cattle, and over all the earth, and over every creeping thing that creeps upon the earth." 27So God created man in his own image, in the image of God he created him; male and female he created them. 28And God blessed them, and God said to them, "Be fruitful and multiply, and fill the earth and subdue it; and have dominion over the fish of the sea and over the birds of the air and over every living thing that moves upon the earth." 29And God said, "Behold, I have given you every plant yielding seed which is upon the face of all the earth, and every tree with seed in its fruit; you shall have them for food. 30And to every beast of the earth,

and to every bird of the air, and to everything that creeps on the earth, everything that has the breath of life, I have given every green plant for food." And it was so. 31And God saw everything that he had made, and behold, it was very good. And there was evening and there was morning, a sixth day.

2 Thus the heavens and the earth were finished, and all the host of them. 2And on the seventh day God finished his work which he had done, and he rested on the seventh day from all his work which he had done. 3So God blessed the seventh day and hallowed it, because on it God rested from all his work which he had done in creation.

4 These are the generations of the heavens and the earth when they were created.

In the day that the Lord God made the earth and the heavens, 5when no plant of the field was yet in the earth and no herb of the field had yet sprung up—for the Lord God had not caused it to rain upon the earth, and there was no man to till the ground; 6but a mist went up from the earth and watered the whole face of the ground— 7then the Lord God formed man of dust from the ground, and breathed into his nostrils the breath of life; and man became a living being. 8And the Lord God planted a garden in Eden, in the east; and there he put the man whom he had formed. 9And out of the ground the Lord God made to grow every tree that is pleasant to the sight and good for food, the tree of life also in the midst of the garden, and the tree of the knowledge of good and evil.

10 A river flowed out of Eden to water the garden, and there it divided

and became four rivers. <sup>11</sup>The name of the first is Pishon; it is the one which flows around the whole land of Hav'-ilah, where there is gold; <sup>12</sup>and the gold of that land is good; bdellium and onyx stone are there. <sup>13</sup>The name of the second river is Gihon; it is the one which flows around the whole land of Cush. <sup>14</sup>And the name of the third river is Tigris, which flows east of Assyria. And the fourth river is the Euphra'tes.

15 The Lord God took the man and put him in the garden of Eden to till it and keep it. <sup>16</sup>And the Lord God commanded the man, saying, "You may freely eat of every tree of the garden; <sup>17</sup>but of the tree of the knowledge of good and evil you shall not eat, for in the day that you eat of it you shall die."

18 Then the Lord God said, "It is not good that the man should be alone; I will make him a helper fit for him." <sup>19</sup>So out of the ground the Lord God formed every beast of the field and every bird of the air, and brought them to the man to see what he would call them; and whatever the man called every living creature, that was its name. <sup>20</sup>The man gave names to all cattle, and to the birds of the air, and to every beast of the field; but for the man there was not found a helper fit for him. <sup>21</sup>So the Lord God caused a deep sleep to fall upon the man, and while he slept took one of his ribs and closed up its place with flesh; <sup>22</sup>and the rib which the Lord God had taken from the man he made into a woman and brought her to the man. <sup>23</sup>Then the man said,

"This at last is bone of my bones
    and flesh of my flesh;
she shall be called Woman,
    because she was taken out of
      Man."

<sup>24</sup>Therefore a man leaves his father and his mother and cleaves to his wife, and they become one flesh. <sup>25</sup>And the man and his wife were both naked, and were not ashamed.

3 Now the serpent was more subtle than any other wild creature that the Lord God had made. He said to the woman, "Did God say, 'You shall not eat of any tree of the garden'?" <sup>2</sup>And the woman said to the serpent, "We may eat of the fruit of the trees of the garden; <sup>3</sup>but God said, 'You shall not eat of the fruit of the tree which is in the midst of the garden, neither shall you touch it, lest you die.' " <sup>4</sup>But the serpent said to the woman, "You will not die. <sup>5</sup>For God knows that when you eat of it your eyes will be opened, and you will be like God, knowing good and evil." <sup>6</sup>So when the woman saw that the tree was good for food, and that it was a delight to the eyes, and that the tree was to be desired to make one wise, she took of its fruit and ate; and she also gave some to her husband, and he ate. <sup>7</sup>Then the eyes of both were opened, and they knew that they were naked; and they sewed fig leaves together and made themselves aprons.

8 And they heard the sound of the Lord God walking in the garden in the cool of the day, and the man and his wife hid themselves from the presence of the Lord God among the trees of the garden. <sup>9</sup>But the Lord God called to the man, and said to him, "Where are you?" <sup>10</sup>And he said, "I heard the sound of thee in the garden, and I was afraid, because I was naked; and I hid myself." <sup>11</sup>He said, "Who told you that you were naked? Have you eaten of the tree of which I commanded you not to eat?" <sup>12</sup>The man said, "The woman

whom thou gavest to be with me, she gave me fruit of the tree, and I ate." ¹³Then the Lord God said to the woman, "What is this that you have done?" The woman said, "The serpent beguiled me, and I ate." ¹⁴The Lord God said to the serpent,

"Because you have done this,
cursed are you above all cattle,
and above all wild animals;
upon your belly you shall go,
and dust you shall eat
all the days of your life.
¹⁵I will put enmity between you
and the woman,
and between your seed and her
seed;
he shall bruise your head,
and you shall bruise his heel."
¹⁶To the woman he said,

"I will greatly multiply your pain
in childbearing;
in pain you shall bring forth
children,
yet your desire shall be for your
husband,
and he shall rule over you."
¹⁷And to Adam he said,

"Because you have listened to the
voice of your wife,
and have eaten of the tree
of which I commanded you,

'You shall not eat of it,'
cursed is the ground because of you;
in toil you shall eat of it all the
days of your life;
¹⁸thorns and thistles it shall bring
forth to you;
and you shall eat the plants of
the field.
¹⁹In the sweat of your face
you shall eat bread
till you return to the ground,
for out of it you were taken;
you are dust,
and to dust you shall return."

20 The man called his wife's name Eve, because she was the mother of all living. ²¹And the Lord God made for Adam and for his wife garments of skins, and clothed them.

22 Then the Lord God said, "Behold, the man has become like one of us, knowing good and evil; and now, lest he put forth his hand and take also of the tree of life, and eat, and live for ever"— ²³therefore the Lord God sent him forth from the garden of Eden, to till the ground from which he was taken. ²⁴He drove out the man; and at the east of the garden of Eden he placed the cherubim, and a flaming sword which turned every way, to guard the way to the tree of life.

# CONTENTS

# INTRODUCTION

ABRUPT CHANGES in social attitudes have recently become commonplace, especially with respect to sexuality, including marriage, divorce, homosexuality, abortion, contraception, and gender. Whether we welcome these changes or not, they have altered the way we think of other people and ourselves, how we act, and how we respond to the actions of others. For Christians, in particular, such changes may seem to challenge not only traditional values but the very structure of human nature.

But how did these traditional patterns of gender and sexual relationship arise in the first place—patterns so obvious and "natural" to those who have accepted them that nature itself seemed to have ordained them? Reflecting on this question, I soon began to see that the sexual attitudes we associate with Christian tradition evolved in western culture at a specific time—during the first four centuries of the common era, when the Christian movement, which had begun as a defiant sect, eventually transformed itself into the religion of the Roman Empire. I saw, too, that these attitudes had not previously existed in their eventual Christian form; and that they represented a departure from both pagan practices and Jewish tradition. Many Christians of the first four centuries took pride in their sexual restraint; they eschewed polygamy and often divorce as well, which Jewish tradition allowed; and they repudiated extramarital sexual practices commonly accepted among their pagan contemporaries, practices including prostitution and homosexuality.

Certain Christian moralists of this period insisted that sexual intercourse should not be pursued for pleasure, even among those monogamously married, but should be reserved solely for procreation. Not all these attitudes were original with the Christians, who borrowed much from Jewish and philosophical, particularly Stoic, tradition; but the Christian movement emphasized and institutionalized such views, which soon became inseparable from Christian faith.

Heroic Christians went even further and embraced celibacy "for the sake of the Kingdom of Heaven," behavior which, they said, Jesus and Paul had exemplified, and which they had urged upon those capable of the "angelic life." By the beginning of the fifth century, Augustine had actually declared that spontaneous sexual desire is the proof of—and penalty for—universal original sin, an idea that would have baffled most of his Christian predecessors, to say nothing of his pagan and Jewish contemporaries.

Many pagan contemporaries of the early Christians in the Graeco-Roman society of the first four centuries pursued sexual practices that superficially may look familiar to some people in the twentieth century. The Romans, for example, legalized and taxed prostitution, both male and female; and some of them easily tolerated divorce, as well as homosexual and bisexual relationships, especially during adolescence or, in the case of married men, as a diversion from family obligations. Yet when we investigate Roman practices more closely, we find ourselves upon more unfamiliar ground; we may be dismayed to see, for example, that exposing and abandoning infants was widely and openly practiced during the first and second centuries of the common era, as was the routine sexual use and abuse of slaves. To the extent that we recoil from such practices, we reveal, whether or not we explicitly identify ourselves with religious tradition, that we too are affected by the transformation of sexual values that Christian tradition introduced into western culture.

From the first century, when the Christian movement appeared as a new and "deadly superstition" (in the words of the Roman historian Tacitus), through two centuries of persecution, during which its members were subject to arrest, torture, and execution, the movement continued to grow. Then in 313 occurred an event of incalculable significance—the conversion to Christianity of the emperor Constantine; and from that time, with only a two-year interruption during the brief reign of the neopagan emperor Julian, called the Apostate, Christianity increasingly became the official religion of the empire. Accompanying the spread of Christianity—although, as classical historians remind us, not limited to it—was a revolution in sexual attitudes and practices.

Yet when we explore Jewish and Christian writers from the first centuries of the common era, we find that they seldom talk directly about sexual behavior, and they seldom write treatises on such topics as marriage, divorce, and gender. Instead they often talk about Adam, Eve, and the serpent—the story of creation—and when they do, they tell us what they think about sexual matters. From about 200 B.C.E. (before the common era), the story of creation became, for certain Jews, and later for Christians, a primary means for revealing and defending basic attitudes and values. Our spiritual ancestors argued and speculated over how God had commanded the first man and woman to "be fruitful and multiply, and fill the earth," and how he instituted the first marriage; how Adam, after he found among the animals no "helper fit for him" (Genesis 2:20), met Eve, with well-known and disastrous consequences. Such interpretations of the first three chapters of Genesis, as we can see, engaged intensely practical concerns and articulated deeply felt attitudes.

As I investigated these Jewish and Christian sources, I found myself fascinated with the story of Adam, Eve, and the serpent, written down by members of Hebrew tribes about three thousand years ago, and probably told for generations before that. I had always assumed that this archaic story wields an extraordinary influence upon western culture, but as my work progressed I was surprised to discover how complex and extensive its effect has been.

The anthropologist Clifford Geertz defines culture as

> an historically transmitted pattern of meaning embodied in symbols; a system of inherited conceptions expressed in symbolic form, by means of which men communicate, perpetuate, and develop their knowledge about and attitudes toward life.[1]

If any of us could come to our own culture as a foreign anthropologist and observe traditional Christian attitudes toward sexuality and gender, and how we view "human nature" in relation to politics, philosophy, and psychology, we might well be astonished at attitudes that we take for granted. Augustine, one of the greatest teachers of western Christianity, derived many of these attitudes from the story of Adam and Eve: that sexual desire is sinful; that infants are infected from the moment of conception with the disease of original sin; and that Adam's sin corrupted the whole of nature itself. Even those who think of Genesis only as literature, and those who are not Christian, live in a culture indelibly shaped by such interpretations as these.

But the Genesis accounts of creation introduced into Graeco-Roman culture many values other than sexual ones—for example, the intrinsic worth of every human being, made in God's image (Genesis 1:26). Often these other values would prove immensely influential. Although the early Christians thought of this conviction of human worth in moral—not social or political—terms, Christians living more than fifteen hundred years later would invoke this idea to help transform the laws, ethics, and political institutions of the West. In 1776 the authors of the Declaration of Independence invoked the biblical account of creation to declare that "we hold these truths to be self-evident, that all men are created equal . . ."—an idea so familiar that we may have difficulty seeing that it is empirically unprovable; Aristotle, among others, would have considered it absurd. As we shall see, the idea of human moral equality flourished among converts to Christianity, many of whom, especially slaves and women, were anything but equal under Roman law.

Some Christians today, of course, invoke Genesis against the theory of evolution, criticizing the claims of scientific objectivity and the relative values they associate with "secular humanism"; many insist that the creation story validates their own social and sexual attitudes. Liberal critics accuse such interpreters of literalism; and it is true that such believers often insist that they understand perfectly well what "the Bible says," without considering that what *they* assume it means may differ entirely from what others—even their Christian predecessors—have taken it to mean. Yet such evangelical Christians intuitively understand one thing that their critics often miss: that the biblical creation story, like the creation stories of other cultures, communicates social and religious values and presents them as if they were universally valid. Many people who have—intellectually, at least—discarded the creation story as a mere folk tale nevertheless find themselves engaged with its moral implications concerning procreation, animals, work, marriage, and the human striving to "subdue" the earth and "have dominion" over all its creatures (Genesis 1:28).

This book explores, among other things, how these Christian interpretations of Genesis emerged in the first four centuries, and how Christians invoked the story of Adam and Eve to justify and establish their beliefs; how they saw their own situations, their sufferings, and their hopes mirrored in the story of the creation and the fall. I have not, by any means, written a history of early Christianity; instead, I am interested in a process of intellectual history—how these ideas of sexuality and moral equality, among others, came about; and I am interested in the hermeneutical process—how Christians read the story of Adam and Eve, and often projected themselves into it, as a way of reflecting upon such matters as sexuality, human freedom, and human nature.

As I began to explore these questions, both substantive and hermeneutical, I soon discovered that Jews and Christians in various times and places have read the creation story—and its practical implications—quite differently, sometimes even antithetically. What Christians see, or claim to see, in Genesis 1–3 changed as the church itself changed from a dissident Jewish sect to a popular movement persecuted by the Roman government, and changed further as this movement increasingly gained members throughout Roman society, until finally even the Roman emperor himself converted to the new faith and Christianity became the official religion of the Roman Empire.

During recent decades, several distinguished scholars, including Professors Robert M. Grant, Georges de Ste. Croix, Ramsay MacMullen, Wayne Meeks, and Paul Veyne, have pointed out that Christians were in many ways similar to their pagan neighbors.[2] Their works document, among other things, social, political, economic, and cultural parallels that I have not reviewed here. Instead I focus upon ways in which Christians *differed* from pagans, or claimed to differ—what made them, in other words, specifically Christian within the pagan world; I am interested, in Tertullian's words, in the "peculiarities of the Christian society."[3]

In each chapter I take up a theme that Christians attempted to understand or justify by means of the creation story. Jewish teachers of Jesus' time and earlier, as I show in Chapter 1, often invoked the story of Adam and Eve to defend Jewish sexual practices ranging from abhorrence of public nakedness (for God clothed Adam and Eve in Paradise) to marital practices designed to facilitate reproduction (for hadn't God said, "Be fruitful and multiply, and fill the earth"?). These Jewish teachers noted that Genesis contains not one but two distinct accounts of creation, of which the first begins with the opening chapter of Genesis and tells how God created the world in six days, crowning his achievement by creating *adam*—that is, humanity—in his image (Genesis 1:26). But this account ends with Genesis 2:3; and the following verse, Genesis 2:4, begins a different narrative. This second story tells how the Lord made a man out of earth, and, after making all the animals and finding none of them a suitable companion for Adam, he put Adam to sleep, brought woman out of his side, and presented her to Adam as his wife. The woman then persuaded her husband to disobey divine law and earned with him their expulsion from Paradise.

Most biblical scholars today agree that the two creation accounts, originally separate, were later joined to make up the first three chapters of Genesis. The story of Adam and Eve (Genesis 2:4f), told in the language of folklore, is considered the older of the two accounts, dating to 1000–900 B.C.E.; the account now placed first (Genesis 1:1–2:3) dates to postexilic theologians (c. 400 B.C.E.). Jewish teachers in antiquity, like many Christians after them, turned to theological ingenuity rather than historical or literary analysis to account for contradictions in the texts.

According to New Testament accounts, Jesus himself mentioned the story of Adam and Eve only once; and, like many other Jewish teachers, Jesus used Genesis to make a moral point—specifically, to answer a practical question put to him by the Pharisees, the interpreters of Jewish law, about the legitimate grounds for divorce. Jesus' reply—that what God has joined together, let no one put asunder—shocked his questioners, for instead of answering the question he had been asked about the *grounds* for divorce, he simply ruled out divorce altogether. Since procreation was assumed by many Jews to be the purpose of marriage, and since Jewish tradition had taken divorce for granted as a male prerogative—and sometimes as a necessity, in cases of a wife's infertility—Jesus' answer to the Pharisees broke with Jewish teaching. When even his own followers objected ("If such is the case of a man with his wife, it is not expedient to marry"), Jesus must have startled them even more than he had the Pharisees by suggesting that celibacy "for the sake of the Kingdom of Heaven" may, in fact, be preferable to marriage (Matthew 19:10–12). For generations—even millennia—ever since, Christians have been trying to work out the practical implications of such sayings, and those of Paul, Jesus' zealous disciple.

Paul himself, some twenty years after Jesus' death, urged an even more austere discipline upon his followers than Jesus had preached. Although Paul acknowledged that marriage was not sin (1 Corinthians 7:3), he encouraged those who were able to renounce it to do so. Paul invoked the creation account to urge Christians to avoid prostitution (1 Corinthians 6:15–20), and later to argue that women must veil their heads in church, apparently to acknowledge their subordination to men as a kind of divine order given in nature ("For man was not made from woman, but woman from man. Neither was man created for woman, but woman for man," 1 Corinthians 11:3–16). In the generations following Paul, Christians fiercely debated what the apostle meant. Some insisted that only those who "undo the sin of Adam and Eve" by practicing celibacy—even within marriage—can truly practice the gospel. Others, who were to predominate within the majority of churches, rejected such austerity and composed, in Paul's name, other letters, later incorporated into the New Testament as if Paul himself had written them, which used the story of Adam and Eve to support traditional marriage and to prove that women, being naturally gullible, are unfit for any role but raising children and keeping house (see, for example, 1 Timothy 2:11–15); thus the story of Eden was made to reinforce the patriarchal structure of community life.

But the majority of Christians, as I also show in Chapter 1, rejected the claim made by radical Christians that the sin of Adam and Eve was sexual—that the forbidden "fruit of the tree of knowledge" conveyed, above all, *carnal* knowledge. On the contrary, said Clement of Alexandria (c. 180 C.E.), conscious participation in procreation is "cooperation with God in the work of creation." Adam's sin was not sexual indulgence but disobedience; thus Clement agreed with most of his Jewish and Christian contemporaries that the real theme of the story of Adam and Eve is moral freedom and moral responsibility. Its point is to show that we are responsible for the choices we freely make—good or evil—just as Adam was.

In Chapter 2 I show how Christians also began to apply the creation account to their own precarious political situation, in which they were constantly subject to persecution by the Roman authorities. About one hundred years after Jesus' death, when many Christians lived in fear of a similar fate—arrest, torture, and execution—for refusing ordinary allegiance to the emperor and the gods, the Christian philosopher Justin invoked Genesis to argue that humankind owes allegiance only to the God who created all humanity—the God of Israel, now the God of the Christians—and not to the gods of Rome, whom Justin denounced as demons. Justin turned Genesis 6, which tells of the fall of the angels, into an indictment of the Roman emperors and their gods; for these dignitaries were, Justin said, none other than the demon offspring of the fallen angels.

About twenty years after Justin had been beheaded for refusing to worship the Roman gods, Clement of Alexandria took the statement that God had created humanity in his image as evidence of human equality—and as an indictment of the imperial cult. From such beginnings, in open defiance of the totalitarian Roman state, and often met with brutal violence, Christians forged the basis for what would become, centuries later, the western ideas of freedom and of the infinite value of each human life.

Clement realized, too, that certain inquiring and restless Christians saw in the Genesis story not only sexual and political implications but disturbing philosophical and religious ones as well. How could an all-powerful God have created the world "good" when we find in it so much suffering? Whence came the serpent? Why did God begrudge Adam and Eve the knowledge that even he admitted would make them "like one of us" (Genesis 3:22)? Such questions, and the underlying one, *unde malum* ("Whence is evil?"), were, the Christian writer Tertullian said, "the questions that make people heretics."

In Chapter 3 I explore how some of these followers of Jesus, often called gnostics, read the story of Adam and Eve in ways that dismayed and outraged orthodox Christians. For gnostic Christians declared that the story, taken literally, made no sense; thus they themselves set out to read it symbolically, often allegorically. The most radical gnostics turned the story upside down and told it, in effect, from the serpent's point of view: some said he was "wiser" than all the other animals and so tried desperately to persuade Adam and Eve to partake of the tree of knowledge, defying their jealous and hostile creator; this wise serpent, some dared say, was a manifestation of Christ himself! Other gnostics read the story of Adam and Eve as an allegory of religious experience, as relating the discovery of the authentic spiritual self (Eve) hidden within the soul (Adam). The gnostic author of the *Interpretation of the Soul* saw Eve as representing the alienated soul seeking spiritual union; the author of *Thunder: Perfect Mind* saw her as the divine energy underlying all existence, human and divine. Gnostic Christians, who disagreed with one another on almost everything else, agreed that this naïve story hid profound truths about human nature, and they vied with one another to come up with ingenious and imaginative interpretations of its deeper meaning.

Leaders of the church who called themselves orthodox (literally, "straight-thinking") Christians denounced such interpretations and accused gnostics of projecting their own bizarre fantasies upon the text. Above all, they said, gnostic Christians deny the primary reality of the Genesis account—namely, that it depicts humanity created morally free and entrusted with free will. Gnostic Christians, who denied that the human will has the power to prevent error and suffering, also denied, in effect, that baptism fully delivers us from sin and suffering and restores our moral freedom, and for this reason, among others, the gnostics were expelled by the leaders of the church and consigned to oblivion.

As the Christian movement increasingly gained converts throughout Roman society during the third and fourth centuries, some of the most ardent Christians insisted that to realize the greatest freedom one must "renounce the world" and choose poverty and celibacy. For certain Christians, celibacy was a way of rejecting Roman social life. In Genesis 1–3, where Jews—and many Christians, for that matter—traditionally saw God's endorsement of marriage and procreation, ascetic Christians saw the opposite: Adam and Eve were virgins in Paradise and should have remained so; as Gregory of Nyssa explained, God could have arranged for the human race to "multiply" in completely nonsexual ways, as angels do. But when one Roman monk, Jovinian, although himself celibate, tried to prove from the Scriptures that celibate Christians were no holier than their married sisters and brothers, Jerome, Ambrose, and Augustine, three future saints of the church, attacked him, while Pope Siricius of Rome denounced and excommunicated Jovinian for his "heresy." In Chapter 4 I explore what motivated men—and especially women—to embrace that ascetic life; and what kinds of freedom its advocates did indeed find in choosing celibacy.

From these explorations I came to see that for nearly the first four hundred years of our era, Christians regarded *freedom* as the primary message of Genesis 1–3—freedom in its many forms, including free will, freedom from demonic powers, freedom from social and sexual obligations, freedom from tyrannical government and from fate; and self-mastery as the source of such freedom. With Augustine, as I show in Chapter 5, this message changed. In the late fourth century, Augustine was living in an entirely different Christian world—one that Justin and his contemporaries could hardly have imagined—for Christianity was no longer a dissident sect. The Christian movement, having been oppressed and persecuted by Rome for some three hundred years, over several generations, with Constantine's conversion in 313, came into imperial favor and, throughout the later fourth century, consolidated its new position as the official religion of the empire. Christian bishops, once targets for arrest, torture, and execution, now received tax exemptions, gifts from the imperial treasury, prestige, and even influence at court; their churches gained new wealth, power, and prominence. Some

Christians, who once defiantly proclaimed their freedom against their persecutors, now found that their old rhetoric—and even their traditional understanding of human nature and its relation to social and political order—no longer applied to this new circumstance, which made them allies of the emperor. In a world in which Christians not only were free to follow their faith but were officially encouraged to do so, Augustine came to read the story of Adam and Eve very differently than had the majority of his Jewish and Christian predecessors. What they had read for centuries as a story of human freedom became, in his hands, a story of human bondage. Most Jews and Christians had agreed that God gave humankind in creation the gift of moral freedom, and that Adam's misuse of it brought death upon his progeny. But Augustine went further: Adam's sin not only caused our mortality but cost us our moral freedom, irreversibly corrupted our experience of sexuality (which Augustine tended to identify with original sin), and made us incapable of genuine political freedom. Furthermore, Augustine read back into Paul's letters his own teaching of the moral impotence of the human will,[4] along with his sexualized interpretation of sin.

Augustine's theory of original sin not only proved politically expedient, since it persuaded many of his contemporaries that human beings universally need external government—which meant, in their case, both a Christian state and an imperially supported church—but also offered an analysis of human nature that became, for better and worse, the heritage of all subsequent generations of western Christians and the major influence on their psychological and political thinking. Even today, many people, Catholics and Protestants alike, regard the story of Adam and Eve as virtually synonymous with original sin. During Augustine's own lifetime, as we shall see, various Christians objected to his radical theory, and others bitterly contested it; but within the next few generations, Christians who held to more traditional views of human freedom were themselves condemned as heretics.

Augustine spent the last twelve years of his life battling for his interpretation of Genesis against a young Christian bishop, Julian of Eclanum, who attacked and criticized his theory of original sin not only as an abrupt departure from orthodox Christian thought but as Manichaean heresy, the very heresy that Augustine had once admired and later attacked. When Julian challenged Augustine to define what is "nature"—human nature and nature in general—Augustine replied that mortality and sexual desire are not "natural";

both, he insists, entered into human experience only to punish Adam's sin. Chapter 6 considers this debate on the nature of nature and suggests ways in which Augustine's views—antinatural and even preposterous as they will appear to many readers—nevertheless became deeply rooted in our cultural attitudes toward suffering and death.

One of my colleagues, misunderstanding the viewpoint presented here and in my previous book, *The Gnostic Gospels,* has objected that religious ideas cannot be reduced to practical (or, in his words, political) agendas. On this I wholeheartedly agree with him. I am not saying that religious ideas are nothing but a cover for political motives, as if, for example, Christians in the fourth century first chose to join forces with the Roman state and then adopted the doctrine of original sin to justify their new political direction. Instead, I intend to show that religious insights and moral choices, in actual experience, coincide with practical ones. Scholars and theologians may separate them theoretically, but at the cost of distorting our understanding: in our actual experience—as in that of Christians in the first four centuries—moral choices often are political choices. An act of religious affirmation is always, in some sense, a practical and consequential act.

Some readers may ask, "Are you saying, then, that biblical interpretation is nothing but projection? Is *exegesis* (what one reads out of the text) merely *eisegesis* (reading into the text)?" Certainly not; but anyone concerned with the history of hermeneutics confronts the question of interpretation, a question biblical interpreters share with lawyers who debate the meaning of the Constitution, with psychiatrists as they reflect upon their interpretation of case histories, and with anthropologists and historians who ponder their data. What I am thinking of is what the anthropologist Foucault calls "the politics of truth"—that is, that what each of us perceives and acts upon as true has much to do with our situation, social, political, cultural, religious, or philosophical.

Those who are unfamiliar with biblical interpretation or cynical about it may assume that the controversies and diverging interpretations described here merely confirm what they have suspected all along: that biblical interpretation is no more than ideology under a different name. Yet those who seriously confront the Bible will realize that genuine interpretation has always required that the reader actively and imaginatively engage the texts. Through the process of interpretation, the reader's living experience comes to be woven into ancient texts, so that what was "dead letter" again comes to life.

What I intend to show in this book is how certain ideas—in particular, ideas concerning sexuality, moral freedom, and human value—took their definitive form during the first four centuries as interpretations of the Genesis creation stories, and how they have continued to affect our culture and everyone in it, Christian or not, ever since.

# Adam, Eve,
## and the
# Serpent

# (I)

# "THE KINGDOM OF GOD IS AT HAND"

J ESUS AND HIS FOLLOWERS lived at a time when the situation of the Jews was particularly turbulent and potentially explosive. The rural communities of what has come to be called the Holy Land, where Jews had practiced traditional ways of life for centuries, increasingly confronted an encroaching pagan culture that baffled and repelled them, not so much in their insulated villages, but from what they heard of city life in such places as Jerusalem.[1] Centuries of domination by foreign empires had, by the time of Jesus, brought once isolated Jewish communities into direct, often unwilling, contact with their pagan neighbors—Babylonians, Romans, Asians, Egyptians, Greeks, Africans, and Persians. Many Jews, especially the richer and more worldly ones, struggled with questions of whether, or to what extent, they should act "like the nations." Should Jews seek foreign citizenship, with its great economic and political advantages? Should they hire pagan slaves to teach their children Greek and Latin, and risk encouraging them to exercise naked in the public baths? Should they strive to enter the lively and cosmopolitan world of pagan culture and social life, abandoning ancient customs like circumcision and kosher laws that their pagan neighbors considered barbaric?

In Jesus' time, these urban Jewish communities were uneasily divided between those who accommodated pagan culture and accepted its political domination and those who resisted both pagan culture and politics. Once allies of the Romans, the Jews were now their subjects, and Judea had become a Roman province ruled by the puppet Jewish dynasty of Herod the Great for their pagan masters.

♦ 3 ♦

Even those who resisted pagan culture had been deeply affected by it; yet they held to the customs that distinguished and separated them from their pagan neighbors. Many Jews, especially poorer ones, and those who lived in the rural villages where John and Jesus preached, detested the court of the Herods, with its luxurious entertainments and extravagant palaces, which the Herods sometimes named for the emperors but financed with heavy taxes, extortion, and bribes extracted from their fellow Jews. What angered these rural people especially was the way the Herods, neglecting Jewish tradition, courted and copied the Romans.[2] Prince Herod Antipas, grandson of Herod the Great, had gone to Rome to be tutored by the same philosophers who tutored the prince Claudius, future emperor of Rome. The Jewish historian Josephus says that not long before Jesus' birth, two thousand Jews had been crucified in his native Galilee for rebelling against Rome, leaving a forest of crosses littered with rotting corpses as a warning to others.[3] Jesus himself, charged with treason against Rome, would one day suffer the same penalty. Especially among the poor, the pious, and the rural Jews, antipagan feeling ran deep; and it was among such people that Jesus found his following.

Many Jews distrusted, too, their own religious leaders who served at the Jerusalem Temple, especially the powerful and wealthy men who surrounded the high priest, for their open collusion with the Roman occupiers. Members of Jewish communities responded to this situation in a variety of ways. The most popular sect, the Pharisees, bitterly criticized these leaders for having subverted the Temple,[4] while some devout people went further and withdrew in protest from ordinary Jewish life. The Essenes, for example, during the first century B.C.E., abandoned Jerusalem, denounced the Temple worship as polluted, and formed a "pure" community in desert caves overlooking the Dead Sea. There they renounced private property to live in a monastic community; they observed the rules prescribed for holy war; and they avoided sexual contact and impure food, thoughts, and practices as they awaited the battle of Armageddon. They warned that on that day of judgment God himself would annihilate the hypocrites and evildoers and vindicate the Essenes as the righteous.

Jesus' predecessor John the Baptist, a passionate reformer who may have lived for some years with the Essenes, publicly harangued Herod Antipas, then tetrarch of Galilee, for having married his brother's ex-wife; at the instigation of Herod's wife—she was the mother of Salome—John was imprisoned and beheaded.[5] There were many people who agreed with John that the times called for radical reform. No longer was it enough merely to follow traditional Jewish patterns or to stay within the boundaries of the law. John demanded much more; he demanded, in fact, that people return not just to the letter but to the moral spirit of the law.[6] Yet for all of John's claim to speak for authentic Jewish tradition, there remained a more difficult question: Which elements of the Jewish tradition were essential and true, and which were antiquated relics of an archaic past? Which should one follow, and which discard?

Jesus of Nazareth was baptized by John and then, according to the Gospel of Mark, was driven by the spirit into the wilderness (Mark 1:12). He returned from his solitude fired with the conviction that the Kingdom of God was at hand. Like the Essenes, Jesus declared that the crisis of the times required radical sacrifice. Going from village to village near his birthplace in Galilee, Jesus warned that the coming day of judgment was about to turn the social and political world upside down. Then "many that are first will be last, and the last first" (Matthew 19:30); and the coming kingdom would be given to those who were now "despised and rejected." Jesus declared in his famous Sermon:

> *"Blessed are you poor, for yours is the kingdom of God.*
> *Blessed are you that hunger now, for you shall be satisfied.*
> *Blessed are you that weep now, for you shall laugh. . . .*
> *But woe to you that are rich, for you have received your consolation.*
> *Woe to you that are full now, for you shall hunger.*
> *Woe to you that laugh now, for you shall mourn and weep."*
>
> (LUKE 6:20–25)

Jesus disregarded—and, his accusers claimed, dismissed—strict kosher and Sabbath observance and attacked the legal casuistry that enabled people to evade responsibility for those in need. As biblical scholars generally acknowledge, the gospels of the New Testament are neither histories nor biographies in our sense of these terms; we have no independent sources with which to compare their accounts. But as they recount his life and message, Jesus demanded sacrifice and transformation, extraordinary measures to prepare for the coming new age. His message could hardly have been more radical, then or now:

> "Give to everyone who begs from you; and of him who takes your
>     goods, do not ask them again.
> "But love your enemies and do good, and lend, expecting nothing in
>     return."

(LUKE 6:30; 35)

As for the Ten Commandments:

> "You have heard that it was said to the men of old, 'You shall not kill,
> and whoever kills shall be liable to judgment.' But I say to you that
> everyone who is angry with his brother shall be liable to judgment;
> whoever insults his brother shall be liable to the council; and whoever says,
> 'You fool' shall be liable to the hell of fire.
>
> "You have heard that it was said, 'You shall not commit adultery.'
> But I say to you that every one who looks at a woman lustfully has already
> committed adultery with her in his heart."

(MATTHEW 5:21–22; 27–28)

Jesus attacked Israel's religious leaders with irony and anger:

> "The scribes and Pharisees sit in Moses' seat: so practice and observe
> whatever they tell you, but not what they do; for they preach, but do not
> practice.
>
> "Woe to you, scribes and Pharisees, hypocrites! For you tithe mint and
> dill and cumin, and have neglected the weightier matters of the law, justice
> and mercy and faith. . . . You blind guides, straining out a gnat and
> swallowing a camel!
>
> "You serpents; you brood of vipers; how are you to escape being sentenced
> to hell?"

(MATTHEW 23:2; 23–24; 33)

Jesus' passionate and powerful presence aroused enormous response,
especially when he preached among the crowds of pilgrims gathered
in Jerusalem to celebrate Passover. As the Jewish and Roman authorities well knew, tensions were high during the religious holidays
when Jewish worshipers found themselves face to face with the
Roman soldiers. Jesus' near contemporary the Jewish historian Josephus, himself a governor of Galilee, tells of a Roman soldier on
guard near the Temple who contemptuously exposed himself before
just such a crowd, an outrage that incited a riot in which twenty
thousand died.[7] When Jesus dared enter the Temple courtyard before a certain Passover, brandishing a whip, throwing down the
tables of those changing foreign money, and quoting the words of
the prophet Jeremiah to attack the Temple leaders for turning God's

house into a "den of robbers," the Gospel of Mark says, "he would not allow any one to carry anything through the temple" (Mark 11:16). But soon afterward the authorities took action to prevent this firebrand village preacher from fanning the religious and nationalistic passions already smoldering among the restless crowds. The Jewish Council, eager to keep the peace, and hoping to avoid recriminations from their Roman masters, collaborated with the Roman procurator to have Jesus arrested, tried, and hastily executed on charges of having threatened to tear down the Temple single-handed, and having conspired to rise against Rome and make himself king of the Jews (Mark 14:58–15:26).

Jesus himself, according to the New Testament, saw himself very differently, not as a revolutionary but as a man seized by the spirit that inspired Isaiah and Jeremiah—the spirit of God—as a prophet sent to warn humankind of the approaching Kingdom of God and to offer purification to those who would listen.[8] Repeatedly, according to the New Testament accounts, Jesus chose to risk death rather than allow himself to be silenced.

Leaving aside, for the moment, the religious meaning of Jesus' message, one could say from a strictly historical perspective that Jesus foresaw events accurately: in many ways the world in which he and his Jewish contemporaries lived *would* soon come to an end, less than forty years after his death, with the catastrophic Jewish war against Rome. In 66 C.E., the religious and patriotic feeling that the Jewish Council feared Jesus might ignite finally caught fire. Outbreaks of violence against the Roman occupation exploded into a civil war that finally engulfed the whole province that the Romans called Judea. Josephus, born in 37 C.E., a few years after Jesus' death, participated in that war, and described its horrifying devastation, as Titus's clanking Roman forces marched upon Jerusalem. The streets streamed with blood; the inner city was ground to rubble, and the Temple itself burned to a heap of ruins. Titus, the Roman conqueror and future emperor, annihilated Jerusalem politically as well, reestablishing in its place the colony the Romans called Aelia Capitolina, sacred to the gods of Rome.

The "new age" that followed the Roman victory challenged and split Jewish communities from Judea to Rome and throughout the world. Some Jews simply gave up and followed pagan customs, but the majority gradually came to adopt the forms in which the party of the Pharisees salvaged and recast their ancient traditions. According to Professor Jacob Neusner, the Pharisees hoped to reunite the

Jewish communities by providing a common code of law; thus they gave birth to the rabbinic movement.[9] These rabbis, or teachers, replaced the priests and the animal sacrifices that they had offered in the destroyed Jerusalem Temple—that Temple having been for many Jews the central focus of Jewish life—with the "sacrifices" of prayer, Torah study, and worship in synagogues scattered throughout the world wherever Jews lived. And the rabbis themselves, as "teachers of the law," came to replace the hereditary caste of Jewish priests who had for generations officiated in that Temple.[10]

But the radical sectarians who called themselves followers of Jesus of Nazareth went further. Having refused to fight in the Jewish war against Rome, they had already alienated themselves from the Jewish communities; now they broke with their fellow Jews and proclaimed that they themselves were the "new Israel," even the "true Israel," of this shattering new age. Some Jews who joined this Christian movement, especially those influenced by Paul's teaching, abandoned, within one or two generations of Jesus' death, the characteristic practices that had distinguished them as Jews. Many gave up circumcision, kosher laws, and Sabbath observance, claiming, in Paul's words, to be "Jews inwardly," circumcised "in the heart" (Romans 2:28–29) and not in the flesh. All converts to this new movement, whether they had once been Jews or pagans, tended to distinguish their "new Israel" from the rest of the world by insisting upon strict, even extreme, moral practices. The most controversial aspect of this new moral austerity was the sexual attitudes and practices of its adherents.[11]

This is a book not about Jesus' message but about practical elements of his message, especially as he and his followers read these elements back into the story of creation. According to the New Testament, Jesus himself mentioned the story of Adam and Eve only once, in answer to a question about the legitimate grounds for divorce. To judge by New Testament reports of his few comments concerning marriage, divorce, and celibacy, such concerns seem almost incidental to Jesus' message. But after his death, as the movement he inspired grew to include Greeks, Asians, Africans, Romans, and Egyptians, as well as Palestinian Jews, his followers struggled with questions of how to translate his spiritual teaching into the practical terms of everyday living. Should Christians marry or not? Should the roles of men and women in the community differ, and, if so, how? Should converts avoid sexual activity outside of marriage—or even within it? What about prostitution, abortion, and the sexual use of slaves? These questions, too, bore wider implications: How are Christians to understand human nature? Are slaves, for example, essentially any different from free persons?

Such questions did not, of course, originate with Christians. Jewish teachers debated such topics, and as the French scholar Paul Veyne, among others, has shown, certain pagan philosophers advocated sexual restraint similar to that adopted by Christians.[12] But the Christian movement popularized these changing attitudes with momentous consequences, especially after the fourth century, when the Roman emperor Constantine declared his own allegiance to Christ and granted Christianity not only legal but privileged status within the empire. It was from that time that Christian attitudes began to transform the consciousness, to say nothing of the moral and legal systems, that continue to form western society.

This book will explore the attitudes that Jesus and his followers took toward marriage, family, procreation, and celibacy, and thus toward "human nature" in general, and the controversies these attitudes sparked as they were variously interpreted among Christians for generations—or for millennia, depending on how one counts. It will also show how men and women who converted to Christianity often adopted attitudes toward sexuality that their families and friends considered bizarre. Moreover, I shall further speculate on how we have come to take for granted the set of attitudes about sexuality and human nature arising from "Judeo-Christian culture," attitudes that many people today take to be normal and obvious but that were, in the context of early Christian times, anything but normal and, from the anthropologically informed perspective of our own contemporaries, anything but obvious.

JESUS AND HIS FOLLOWERS, at the beginning of what came to be called the Christian Era, took up startlingly different attitudes toward divorce, procreation, and family from those that had prevailed for centuries among most of their fellow Jews. So powerful were these challenges to convention that they precipitated, or at least accompanied, the birth of a new religious movement. Despite Jesus' radical message—or perhaps because of it—the movement quickly spread throughout the Roman world and within three centuries came to dominate it.

As the Christian movement emerged within the Roman Empire, it challenged pagan converts, too, to change their attitudes and behavior. Many pagans who had been brought up to regard marriage essentially as a social and economic arrangement, homosexual relationships as an expected element of male education, prostitution, both male and female, as both ordinary and legal, and divorce, abortion, contraception, and exposure of unwanted infants as matters of practical expedience, embraced, to the astonishment of their families, the Christian message, which opposed these practices.

Certain scholars, prominently including Paul Veyne, as we have noted, have recently downplayed these differences and have pointed out that philosophical moralists such as Musonius Rufus and Plutarch advocated similar moral practices. Veyne concludes that "we must not argue in stereotypes, and imagine a conflict between pagan and Christian morality."[13] Yet as the philosopher and convert Athenagoras (c. 160 C.E.) points out in his defense of the Christians, addressed to their persecutors, the emperors, what philosophers advocate may have little or nothing to do with what actually motivates people to change, as conversion has done to many Christians.[14] Indeed, such converts as Justin, Athenagoras, Clement, and Tertullian all describe specific ways in which conversion changed their own lives and those of many other, often uneducated, believers, in matters involving sex, business, magic, money, paying taxes, and racial hatred.[15] Justin and Tertullian both relate cases in which the moral transformation accompanying a believer's conversion aroused pagan relatives to outrage and even led to legal accusations and disinheritance. Of course these Christians were writing in defense of their faith; we need not accept all their rhetoric as fact to acknowledge that they and many others certainly *did* "imagine a conflict between pagan and Christian morality" and tried to act accordingly.

Their own accounts suggest that such converts changed their attitudes toward the self, toward nature, and toward God, as well as their sense of social and political obligation, in ways that often placed them in diametric opposition to pagan culture. For the most dedicated Christians, conversion transformed both consciousness and behavior; and such converts, gathered in the increasingly popular Christian movement, would profoundly affect the consciousness of all subsequent generations as well.[16]

Other Jewish teachers of Jesus' time, and for generations before, had pronounced certain pagan sexual practices abominable. Among conscientious Jews, only the worship of pagan gods aroused more outrage than pagan sexual behavior. Generations of Jewish teachers had warned that pagans thought nothing of pederasty, promiscuity, and incest. Yet the clash with outside cultures challenged Jewish customs in turn. Many pagans found such practices as circumcision to be peculiar, antiquated, and no less barbaric than Jews found the sexual habits of pagans. Babylonians and Romans, themselves monogamous, criticized the ancient Jewish custom of polygamous marriage, practiced by such venerable patriarchs as Abraham, David, and Solomon, as well as by the wealthy few who could afford it, even in Jesus' time and later.[17] The Jewish historian Josephus, himself apparently polygamous, tried to justify to his Roman readers the ten wives of King Herod the Great (and possibly his own bigamy as well)[18] by explaining that "among us it is the custom to have many wives simultaneously."[19] Those familiar with Roman law could also question traditional Jewish divorce law, which granted to the husband (but not to the wife) the often easy right of divorce.

For centuries—indeed, for over a millennium—Jews had taught that the purpose of marriage, and therefore of sexuality, was procreation. Jewish communities had inherited their sexual customs from nomadic ancestors whose very survival depended upon reproduction, both among their herds of animals and among themselves. According to the story of Abraham told in Genesis 22, the great blessing promised through God's covenant with Israel was progeny innumerable as the sands of the sea and the stars in the sky (verse 17). To ensure the stability and survival of the nation, Jewish teachers apparently assumed that sexual activity should be committed to the primary purpose of procreation. Prostitution, homosexuality, abortion, and infanticide, practices both legal and tolerated among certain of their pagan neighbors, contradicted Jewish custom and law.

Both polygamy and divorce, on the other hand, increased opportunities for reproduction—not for women, but for the men who wrote the laws and benefited from them. Jewish law even went so far as to require that a man bound for ten years in a childless marriage should either divorce his wife and marry another, or else keep his barren wife and take a second to produce his children.[20] Jewish custom banned as "abominations" sexual acts not conducive to procreation, and the impurity laws even prohibited marital intercourse except at times most likely to result in conception.

Generations before Jesus, Jews, like so many other peoples, had begun to invoke their creation accounts, specifically in Genesis, to prove that such tribal customs as these were not barbaric or peculiar, as their pagan critics charged, but were part of the very structure of the universe itself. In their arguments from Scripture, Jewish teachers often avoided speaking directly about sexual practices but engaged in heated discussions about Adam, Eve, and the serpent, and in this metaphorical way revealed what they thought about human sexuality—and about human nature in general. The *Book of Jubilees,* for example, written about 150 years before Jesus' birth by a Palestinian Jew, retells the story of Adam and Eve to prove, among other things, that Jewish customs concerning childbirth and nakedness were not arbitrary or trivial but actually built into human nature from the beginning. As this author tells it, Adam entered Eden during the first week of creation, but Eve entered the garden only during the second week; this explains why a woman who gives birth to a male child remains ritually impure for only *one* week, while she who bears a female remains impure for two weeks.[21] The author goes on to recall that God made leather garments for Adam and Eve, and clothed them before expelling them from Paradise (Genesis 3:21); this shows that Jews must "cover their shame, and not go naked, as the Gentiles do," in public places like the baths and the gymnasia.[22] Throughout subsequent generations, what Jews and Christians read into the creation accounts of Genesis came, for better and worse, to shape what later came to be called Judeo-Christian tradition.

By the time Jesus preached, his Jewish contemporaries had no difficulty defending their ancestral emphasis upon procreation by showing from Genesis 1 that as soon as God created all living creatures, culminating with the first man and woman, he commanded them to "be fruitful and multiply, and fill the earth" (Genesis 1:28). Whatever disagreements existed between various groups of Jews (the Pharisees, for example, apparently approved of sexual pleasure within the bonds of marriage, while the Essenes practiced sexual restraint), Jewish teachers agreed that this primary and sacred obligation to procreate took precedence even over marital obligations—thus a barren marriage could be invalidated—and dictated its structure. They pointed out from Genesis that God first commanded man and woman to procreate, and only afterward, to help them do so, he brought Eve to Adam and joined them in the first marriage:

> Then the man said,
> "This at last is bone of my bones
>   and flesh of my flesh;
> she shall be called Woman,
>   because she was taken out of Man."

*Therefore a man leaves his father and his mother and cleaves to his wife, and they become one flesh.*

(GENESIS 2:23–24)

For centuries Jewish teachers built from this passage the basic laws of marital behavior. Certain rabbis actually turned these lines from Genesis into a code of sexual conduct. Rabbi Eliezer (c. 90 C.E.) took the words "Therefore a man leaves his father and his mother" to mean not only that a man must not marry his mother, but that he must also refuse to marry "her who is related to his father or to his mother" within the degrees of kinship prohibited as incest. Rabbi Akiba (c. 135 C.E.) took the next phrase, "and cleaves to his wife," to mean, in his words, "But not to his neighbor's wife, nor to a male, nor to an animal"—thus disposing of adultery, homosexuality, and bestiality. Rabbi Issi (c. 145 C.E.) among others, took the phrase "and they become one flesh" to mean, in his words, that the man "shall cleave to the place where both form one flesh," prohibiting through this euphemistic phrase what the rabbis called "unnatural intercourse"—sexual acts or positions that might inhibit conception.[23] Other Jewish teachers agreed that the purpose of marriage is to "increase and multiply"; that one must accept whatever facilitates procreation, including divorce and polygamy; and that one must reject whatever hinders procreation—even a marriage itself, in the case of an infertile wife.

Jesus radically challenged this consensus. Like other Jewish teachers, Jesus, when he speaks about marriage, goes back to the Genesis account of the first marriage; but he reads the same passage very differently than others did. Asked by conservative teachers of the law, the so-called Pharisees, about the legitimate grounds for divorce, Jesus answered that there were none:[24]

*"Have you not read that he who made them from the beginning made them male and female and said, 'For this reason a man shall leave his father and mother and be joined to his wife, and the two shall become one'? So they are no longer two but one. What therefore God has joined together, let no man put asunder."*

(MATTHEW 19:4–6)

This answer shocked his Jewish listeners and, as Matthew tells it, pleased no one. Among Jesus' Jewish contemporaries no one questioned the legitimacy of divorce. The only question was what constituted adequate grounds; and it was this question of grounds, not the legitimacy of divorce as such, that split religious schools into opposing factions. The teacher Shammai, for one, took the conservative position: the only offense serious enough to justify divorce was the wife's infidelity. Shammai's opponent Hillel, famous for his liberal judgments, argued instead that a man may divorce his wife for any reason he chooses, "even if she burn his soup!" The well-known teacher Akiba, who agreed with Hillel, added emphatically, "and even if he finds a younger woman more beautiful than she." But however various teachers disputed the grounds for divorce, no one went so far as Jesus did and prohibited it altogether. Those among his audience familiar with Jewish law demanded to know how he dared question divorce, a right—and, in some cases, an obligation—provided in Mosaic law as essential to procreation. Jesus admitted that divorce is technically legal, but he rejected the practice nevertheless. "Moses allowed you to divorce your wives, but from the beginning [i.e., from the time of creation] it was not so" (Matthew 19:8). Moses took it upon himself, Jesus says, to change what God had created and to permit divorce as a concession to "your hardness of heart."

When his own followers, offended by such vehemence, complained, "If such is the case . . . it is not expedient to marry," Jesus must have astonished them even more by agreeing that, yes, it *is* better not to marry, and praising "those who have made themselves eunuchs for the sake of the Kingdom of Heaven" (Matthew 19:12). Luke says that Jesus even praised barren women: "Blessed are . . . the wombs that never bore, and the breasts that never gave suck" (Luke 23:29), implying that the time was coming when the people who did *not* have children would be the lucky ones. Luke probably saw this as Jesus' prophecy of the coming war against Rome (66–70 C.E.); but later readers often took it as referring to the Kingdom of God. In another passage, Luke has Jesus link marriage with death, and celibacy with eternal life:

> And Jesus said to them, "The sons of this age marry and are given in marriage; but those who are accounted worthy to attain to that age and to the resurrection from the dead neither marry nor are given in marriage, for they cannot die any more, because they are equal to angels and are sons of God, being sons of the resurrection."
>
> (LUKE 20:34–36)

Such statements must have horrified Jewish traditionalists, for barren women, whom Jesus blessed, had traditionally been seen as accursed, and eunuchs, whom Jesus praised, were despised by rabbinic teachers for their sexual incapacity. Unmarried himself, Jesus praised the very persons most pitied and shunned in Jewish communities for their sexual incompleteness—those who were single and childless; for Jesus' radical message of the impending Kingdom of God left his followers no time to fulfill the ordinary obligations of everyday life. First-century Christians saw themselves participating at the birth of a revolutionary movement that they expected would culminate in the total social transformation that Jesus promised in the "age to come."

To prepare themselves for these events, Jesus commanded his followers to forget ordinary concerns about food and clothing, "sell your possessions, and give alms" (Luke 12:33), divest themselves of all property, and abandon family obligations, whether to parents, spouses, or children, for such obligations would interfere with their dedication to the apocalyptic hopes Jesus announced; the disciple must become wholly free to serve God. According to Luke, Jesus even went so far as to say, "If any one comes to me and does not hate his own father and mother and wife and children and brothers and sisters, yes, and even his own life, he cannot be my disciple" (Luke 14:26). The coming new age demands new—and total—allegiance, no longer to family and nation but to the kingdom itself. Thus Jesus urges his followers to break their merely natural relationships in favor of spiritual ones. Acknowledging that such teaching divides and disrupts family relationships, Jesus boldly declares:

> *"I came to cast fire upon the earth; and would that it were already kindled! . . . Do you think that I have come to give peace to the earth? No, I tell you, but rather division; for henceforth in one house there will be five divided, three against two and two against three; they will be divided, father against son and son against father, mother against daughter and daughter against her mother, mother-in-law against her daughter-in-law and daughter-in-law against her mother-in-law."*
>
> (LUKE 12:49–53)

Mark tells how Jesus rejected his own mother and brothers in favor of the family of his followers. When his mother and brothers came to speak with him and stood outside the crowded room where he was preaching, he refused to go to them, saying,

> *"Who are my mother and my brothers?"* And looking around on those *who sat about him, he said, "Here are my mother and my brothers! Whoever does the will of God is my brother, and sister, and mother."*
>
> (MARK 3:33–35)

Thus Jesus dismisses the family obligations considered most sacred in Jewish community life, including those to one's parents, siblings, spouse, and children. By subordinating the obligation to procreate, rejecting divorce, and implicitly sanctioning monogamous relationships, Jesus reverses traditional priorities, declaring, in effect, that other obligations, including marital ones, are now more important than procreation. Even more startling, Jesus endorses—and exemplifies—a new possibility and one he says is even better: rejecting both marriage and procreation in favor of voluntary celibacy, for the sake of following him into the new age.

Twenty years later, Jesus' zealous disciple Paul will go even further. Paul, born in the cosmopolitan Asian city of Tarsus, brought up in the strictly observant tradition of the Pharisees, was suddenly converted from bitter hostility toward Christians to become one of their leaders. While we know little of him as a person, we know from his letters, now preserved in the New Testament, that Paul was a man of intense convictions. Paul accepts Jesus' judgment that marriage is indissoluble and, like Jesus, not only subordinates but actually ignores the command to procreate. But he often speaks of marriage in negative terms, as a sop for those too weak to do what is best: renounce sexual activity altogether. Paul admits that marriage is "not sin" yet argues that it makes both partners slaves to each other's sexual needs and desires, no longer free to devote their energies "to the Lord" (1 Corinthians 7:1–35).[25] Paul sees not only marriage but even the most casual sexual encounter as a form of bondage. Shockingly, he takes the passage from Genesis traditionally used to describe the institution of marriage and applies it instead to an encounter with a prostitute: "Do you not know that he who joins himself to a prostitute becomes one body with her? For, as it is written, 'The two shall become one'" (Genesis 2:24). Paul then contrasts such sexual union with the believer's spiritual union with Christ: "But he who is united to the Lord becomes one spirit with him" (1 Corinthians 6:16–17).

Neither Jesus nor Paul, of course, invented religious celibacy. But those few Jews among their contemporaries who practiced it—some of the Essenes who lived in caves overlooking the Dead Sea, as well as Essene groups in other places, and the Therapeutae, a monastic group of men and women in Egypt—were widely considered extremists. Paul, however, declares, on the contrary, that he wishes that everyone were voluntarily celibate, for the sake of the kingdom, like himself (1 Corinthians 7:7–8). Single people, spared the anxieties and obligations that plague married people, are not only freer but, Paul says, happier. He concedes, however, that "if they cannot contain themselves, let them marry. For it is better to marry than to be aflame with passion" (1 Corinthians 7:9). Yet Paul encourages even those who are married to live as if they, too, were unmarried: "Let those who have wives live as though they had none" (1 Corinthians 7:29b).

George Bernard Shaw was wrong when he accused Paul of inventing religious celibacy, which Shaw called "this monstrous imposition upon Jesus"; and Shaw was also wrong to attribute Paul's celibacy to his "terror of sex and terror of life."[26] For Jesus and Paul, as for the Essenes, such drastic measures were not a reflection of sexual revulsion but a necessity to prepare for the end of the world, and to free oneself for the "age to come." Paul, like Jesus, encouraged celibacy not because he loathed the flesh (which in my opinion he did not) but out of his urgent concern for the practical work of proclaiming the gospel. Paul himself insisted that he did not want to place constraints upon believers, but instead, in view of "the present distress," wanted to free them from external anxieties:

> *I mean, brethren, the appointed time has grown very short. . . . I say this for your own benefit, not to lay any restraint upon you, but to promote good order and to secure your undivided devotion to the Lord.*
>
> (1 CORINTHIANS 7:29, 35)

Paul had established groups of followers among Jews and Gentiles from the Greek seaport cities of Corinth and Thessalonica to the Asian coastal cities of Galatia and Ephesus, and he jealously watched over each of these groups to keep them pure while awaiting the kingdom. He told his converts in Corinth that he saw the Christian church as Christ's "bride," and himself as a father or marriage broker anxious to preserve a young girl's virginity for her future husband:

> *I feel a divine jealousy for you, for I betrothed you to Christ to present you as a pure bride to her one husband. But I am afraid that as the serpent deceived Eve by his cunning, your thoughts will be led astray from a sincere and pure devotion to Christ.*
>
> (2 CORINTHIANS 11:2–3)

Here Paul speaks of protecting the church's virginity as a metaphor for maintaining his pure and original teaching; but certain Christians in following generations took his words literally, as an injunction to celibacy.[27]

Although Paul intended his first letter to the Christians at Corinth, and especially its seventh chapter, to settle community disputes over marital issues, the result was that he raised more questions than he answered. Some Christians took Jesus and Paul at what they believed to be their word and preached the gospel message as liberation from all worldly concerns, especially from care for family and children, which preoccupied the majority of their contemporaries. Some of Paul's converts in Corinth, both women and men, enthusiastically embraced celibacy. Although Paul specifically had advised married Christians against unilaterally refusing marital relations (1 Corinthians 7:2–5), some married Christians, prohibited by Jesus' command from divorce, chose to take Paul's advice ("Let those who have wives live as though they had none," 1 Corinthians 7:29) as if Paul had, in fact, urged sexual abstinence *within* marriage.

Within about a century of Paul's death, ascetic versions of Jesus' message were spreading rapidly, especially in the cities of Asia Minor where Paul himself once preached. What prompted this enthusiasm for renunciation is unclear, but it expressed itself in such widely popular narratives as the story of Thecla, the lovely young virgin who renounced a lucrative marriage which her mother had arranged for her, cut off her hair and dressed in men's clothes, and ran off to join the movement that Jesus and Paul had initiated. According to the *Acts of Paul and Thecla,* she was determined, in fact, to do what she believed the gospel required of her—to become, like Paul himself, a celibate evangelist, and reject her wealthy fiancé, Thamyris, who would have supported not only Thecla but her aging and impoverished mother. When Paul came to preach "the word of the virgin life"[28] in her home city of Iconium, in Asia Minor, Thecla's mother forbade her to leave the house to hear him. So Thecla sat at the window, straining to hear what Paul was saying to the crowds of young people and women pressing around him:

> "Blessed are the pure in heart, for they shall see God [Cf. Matthew 5:8]. Blessed are they who have kept the flesh pure, for they shall become a temple of God [Cf. 2 Corinthians 6:16]. Blessed are the continent, for to them God will speak. Blessed are they who have wives as if they had none, for they shall inherit God [Cf. 1 Corinthians 7:29]. Blessed are the bodies of the virgins, for they shall be well pleasing to God, and shall not lose the reward of their purity [Cf. Matthew 10:42]."[29]

Her mother, alarmed when for three days Thecla refused to leave her place even to eat or sleep, told her daughter's fiancé about the "strange man who teaches deceptive and subtle words. . . . Thamyris, this man is disturbing the city of the Iconians, and your Thecla too; for all the women and young people go in to him. 'You must,' he says, 'fear one single God only, and live in chastity.' And my daughter, too, like a spider at the window, bound by his words, is dominated by a new desire and a fearful passion; for the girl hangs upon the things he says, and is taken captive. But you go and speak to her, for she is engaged to you."[30]

But Thecla vehemently rejected Thamyris's loving pleas, as she had her mother's orders; and he, grieving and furious, immediately arranged to have Paul arrested for encouraging people to defy traditional customs and even the laws. Hearing of Paul's arrest, Thecla stole out of the house secretly at night to go to the prison, bribing the warden with her bracelets and the guard with a silver mirror to let her enter Paul's cell to talk with him privately.

The next day, when the governor, at Paul's hearing, demanded to know why Thecla refused to marry her legal fiancé, she "stood there looking steadily at Paul" and refused to answer. Her mother, enraged that Thecla would jeopardize her own future as well as her family's, burst into a violent tirade:

"Burn the lawless one! Burn her that is no bride in the middle of the amphitheater, so that all the women who have been taught by this man may be struck with terror!"[31]

The governor, shaken by Thecla's defiance and her mother's rage, ordered Paul to be beaten and driven out of town. Thecla he condemned to be burned alive for violating the laws of the city and so threatening the social order. Brought naked into the amphitheater for execution, Thecla was stretched out on a pile of wood, and the kindling lighted, but suddenly a raincloud overshadowed the amphitheater and burst. Escaping in the confusion, Thecla went searching for Paul. But a Syrian nobleman, aroused by this young woman traveling alone in Antioch, tried to rape her. To protect herself from such attacks, Thecla cut off her hair and dressed herself as a man. Thecla's story celebrates her as someone who resisted family pressure, social ostracism, rape, torture, and even execution to "follow the word of the virgin life as it was spoken by Paul." Even the apostle himself, the story says, at first would not take her seriously, refusing to baptize her or to accept her as a fellow evangelist. So she, in desperation, baptized herself, and persisted in pursuing Paul until he reluctantly granted her his blessing. Having achieved her vocation,

Thecla became a famous teacher and holy woman, revered for centuries throughout the eastern churches as a beloved saint.

Although many legends grew up around Thecla,[32] and some scholars regard her story as fiction, she may well have been an actual person.[33] Whether or not she in fact heard Paul himself preach, she—and thousands like her—welcomed such radical versions of the gospel. Following Jesus' advice, these young disciples broke with their families and refused to marry, declaring themselves now members of "God's family." Their vows of celibacy served many converts as a declaration of independence from the crushing pressures of tradition and of their families, who ordinarily arranged marriages at puberty and so determined the course of their children's lives. As early as the second century of the Christian Era, and for many generations thereafter, Christian celibates may have invoked Thecla's example to justify the right of Christian women to baptize and to preach. Even two hundred years later, Christian women who chose the way of asceticism, whether living in solitude at home or in monastic communities founded and often financed by wealthy women, called themselves "new Theclas."[34]

The enormous popularity of Thecla's story suggests how the Christian movement might have appealed to young people, to Thecla's adolescent peers. Yet other popular stories—themselves probably legends—tell how the radical message seized some of their older, married sisters and brothers and irrevocably changed their lives too. According to another widely told Christian story, the *Acts of Thomas,* the lovely Mygdonia, wife of an aristocrat in India, having heard that the Christian apostle Thomas was about to arrive in her city, was filled with curiosity and immediately set out to hear him. But as her elegant litter, carried by slaves, approached and parted the crowd surrounding Thomas, the apostle pointedly ignored Mygdonia and, turning instead to her slaves, addressed to them these vehement words:

> "This blessing and warning are *for you* who are 'heavy laden.' For although you are human beings, those who have authority over you think that you are not human beings, as they are. . . . They do not know that all people are alike before God, whether slave or free."

Mygdonia, shocked and chagrined by these words, sprang from her litter and threw herself on the ground before Thomas, acknowledging that "we act, indeed, like irrational animals," and asked him to pray for her and teach her the gospel.[35]

Thomas consented, and Mygdonia discovered through his words a sense of inner freedom and spiritual dignity she had never before experienced. Thomas persuaded her, too, that to follow the gospel she must devote herself to celibacy, even within her marriage: "This sordid communion with your husband will mean nothing if you are deprived of true communion."[36] Convinced by Thomas's words, Mygdonia turned away from her husband's anxious and loving pleas and then rejected his "shameless" sexual overtures. At first pleading headaches, she finally struck him on the face and ran naked from the bedroom, ripping down the bedroom curtains to cover herself as she escaped to sleep with her childhood nurse. Although her husband grieved, suffered, and raged, he finally yielded, and, receiving baptism himself, agreed to live with her henceforth in celibate marriage.

Such popular stories about the apostles graphically describe how some early Christian preachers, attempting to persuade men and women to "undo the sin of Adam and Eve" by choosing celibacy, disrupted the traditional order of family, village, and city, encouraging believers to reject ordinary family life for the sake of Christ.[37]

But many other Christians sharply protested. Such radical asceticism was not, they argued, the primary meaning of Jesus' gospel, and they simply ignored the more radical implications of what Jesus and Paul taught. One anonymous Christian living a generation after Paul wrote to a pagan friend that far from rejecting marriage and procreation, "Christians marry, like everyone else; they beget children; but they do not destroy fetuses."[38] His contemporary, the Christian teacher Barnabas, a convert from Judaism, assumes that Christians who follow the "way of light" act like pious Jews, abstaining only from sexual practices that violate marriage or frustrate its fulfillment in legitimate procreation.[39] Clement of Alexandria, a liberal, urbane, and sophisticated Christian teacher living in Egypt more than a hundred years after Paul (c. 180 C.E.), denounced celibates and beggars

who say that they are "imitating the Lord" who never married, nor had any possessions in the world, and who boast that they understand the gospel better than anyone else.[40]

For Clement, such extremists are arrogant, foolish and wrong.[41]

But how could such Christians as Barnabas or Clement, who

sought a more moderate message, deal with certain well-known sayings of Jesus—for example, his categorical rejection of divorce, or his statement that "if anyone does not hate his own father and mother and wife and children and brothers and sisters, yes, and even his own life, he cannot be my disciple" (Luke 14:26)? The impact of such sayings might have limited the Christian movement to only the most zealous converts. Within two generations of Jesus' death, however, some of his followers dared to change the wording of such extreme sayings and insert modifying phrases. The author of the Gospel of Matthew, for example, finding Jesus' prohibition of divorce impossibly severe, added a phrase that apparently allowed divorce in the case of the wife's infidelity: Μὴ ἐπί πορνείᾳ, "for immorality," a crucial exception that placed Jesus on the side of teacher Shammai. So according to Matthew, Jesus says, "Whoever divorces his wife, *except for immorality,* and marries another, is guilty of adultery" (Matthew 19:9). And Matthew softens what, according to Luke, Jesus had said about hating one's family: Matthew rephrases the statement so that Jesus says, "Whoever *loves* father or mother *more than* me is not worthy of me; and whoever *loves* son or daughter *more than* me is not worthy of me" (Matthew 10:37).

The author of Matthew not only apparently changes words and injects phrases but goes further, deliberately juxtaposing Jesus' more radical sayings with more moderate sayings on the same theme. According to Matthew, for example, Jesus concludes his ringing rejection of divorce—"What God has joined together, let no man put asunder"—with Matthew's modification *allowing* for divorce— "Whoever divorces his wife, except for immorality, and marries another, is guilty of adultery" (Matthew 19:9). Only a few verses later, Matthew juxtaposes Jesus' promise of great rewards to "every one that has left houses or brothers or sisters or father or mother or children or lands for my name's sake" (19:29), with Jesus' reaffirmation of the traditional commandment "Honor your father and mother" (19:19). Thus Matthew, obviously aware of such discrepancies, and perhaps embarrassed by them, implicitly discriminates between two types of saying—and two levels of discipleship. Matthew gives the reader the impression that Jesus' message and the movement he inspired need not place extreme demands upon every believer, but only upon would-be spiritual heroes—those who want to follow Jesus' command to "be perfect" (Matthew 5:48). But followers of Jesus who want to stay home with their spouses and children and continue to support their aging parents can, according to Matthew, remain committed to family life and still find their place within the Christian community.

Certain followers of Paul, concerned to make Paul's message equally accessible, and finding some statements in his first letter to the Corinthians, for example, too extreme, decided that he could not have meant what he said there, much less what enthusiastically ascetic Christians took him to mean. Thus some of Paul's followers proceeded to compose, in Paul's name, letters of their own designed to correct what they believed were dangerous misinterpretations of Paul's teaching. Several of these anonymous admirers of Paul, a generation or two after his death, forged letters, filling them with personal details of Paul's life and greetings to his friends, hoping to make them appear authentic. Many people—then and now—have assumed that these letters are genuine, and five of them were in fact incorporated into the New Testament as "letters of Paul." Even today, scholars dispute which are authentic and which are not. Most scholars, however, agree that Paul actually wrote only eight of the thirteen "Pauline" letters now included in the New Testament collection: Romans, 1 and 2 Corinthians, Galatians, Philippians, 1 Thessalonians, and Philemon. Virtually all scholars agree that Paul himself did not write 1 or 2 Timothy or Titus—letters written in a style different from Paul's and reflecting situations and viewpoints very different from those in Paul's own letters. About the authorship of Ephesians, Colossians, and 2 Thessalonians, debate continues; but the majority of scholars include these, too, among the "deutero-Pauline"—literally, secondarily Pauline—letters.[42]

Although the deutero-Pauline letters differ from one another in many ways, on *practical* matters they all agree. All reject Paul's most radically ascetic views to present instead a "domesticated Paul"[43]—a version of Paul who, far from urging celibacy upon his fellow Christians, endorses only a stricter version of traditional Jewish attitudes toward marriage and family. Just as Matthew juxtaposed Jesus' more radical sayings with modified versions of them, so the New Testament collection juxtaposes Paul's authentic letters with the deutero-Paulines, offering a version of Paul that softens him from a radical preacher into a patron saint of domestic life.

The anonymous author of 1 Timothy, for example, makes "Paul" attack as demon-inspired those "liars . . . who forbid marriage and enjoin abstinence from foods which God created" (1 Timothy 4:1–3), taking aim, presumably, at the preachers of asceticism, who depict Paul as one of themselves, indeed as their model.[44]

Denouncing the characterizations of Paul that appear in such works as the *Acts of Paul and Thecla,* the author of 2 Timothy almost goes so far as to take sides with Thecla's mother, warning people to avoid those who

> *make their way into households and capture weak women, burdened with sins and swayed by various impulses, who will listen to anybody and can never arrive at a knowledge of the truth.*
>
> (2 TIMOTHY 3:6–7)

The conservative Paul of Timothy directly contradicts the advice Paul gives in 1 Corinthians, where he urges virgins and widows to remain unmarried. According to 1 Timothy, Paul, concerned that the presence of unmarried women among the Christians may arouse suspicions and scandalous gossip, declares, "I would have the younger widows marry, bear children, rule their households, and give the enemy no occasion to revile us" (1 Timothy 5:14). Dismissing ascetic discipline as mere "bodily training" (1 Timothy 4:8), worth little for developing piety, this "Paul" warns his readers to "have nothing to do with godless and silly myths" (1 Timothy 4:7). As Dennis MacDonald persuasively shows, the author of 1 Timothy is denouncing, in all probability, such stories as those of Thecla and Mygdonia, which circulated for generations, perhaps especially among women storytellers. (See notes 33 and 34, above.) Challenging those who, like Thecla herself, claim that women have the right to teach and baptize, the author of 1 Timothy recalls Eve's sin and commands that women must

> *learn in silence with all submissiveness. I permit no woman to teach or to have authority over men; she is to keep silent. For Adam was formed first, then Eve; and Adam was not deceived, but the woman was deceived and became a transgressor. Yet woman will be saved through bearing children, if she continues in faith and love and holiness, with modesty.*
>
> (1 TIMOTHY 2:11–15)

Read this way—as it still is read by the majority of Christian churches—the story of Eve both proves woman's natural weakness and gullibility and defines her present role. Chastened by reminders of Eve's sin, deprived of all authority, women must silently submit to their husbands, grateful that they too may be saved, provided they adhere to their traditional domestic roles.[45] The "Paul" of 1 Timothy goes so far as to judge even men's leadership abilities on the basis of their domestic roles as family patriarchs:

*Now a bishop must be above reproach, the husband of one wife. . . . He must manage his own household well, keeping his children submissive and respectful . . . for if a man does not know how to manage his own household, how can he care for God's church?*

(1 TIMOTHY 3:2–5)

Thus, whereas the authentic Paul declares in his letter to the Corinthians, "I wish that all were as I myself am," voluntarily celibate, the "Paul" of 1 Timothy urges marriage and family upon men and women alike.

The Letter to the Hebrews expresses a positive reverence for marriage—and specifically for sexually active marriage: "Marriage is honorable unto all, and the marriage bed is not polluted" (Hebrews 13:4). The deutero-Pauline letter to the Ephesians calls ascetic Christians foolish, insisting that "no man ever hates his own flesh, but nourishes and cherishes it" (Ephesians 5:29). The author of Ephesians goes so far as to attribute to Paul a vision of Adam and Eve—and, consequently, of marriage itself—as symbolizing the "great mystery . . . of Christ and the church" (Ephesians 5:32). "Paul's" Christian vision of marriage confirms, this author claims, the traditional patriarchal pattern of marriage,

*for the husband is the head of the wife, as Christ is the head of the church. . . . As the church is subject to Christ, so let the wives also be subject in everything to their husbands.*

(EPHESIANS 5:23–24)

Taking his cue from Paul's saying that "the head of every man is Christ, the head of a woman is her husband" (1 Corinthians 11:3), the author of Ephesians explains that since the man, like Christ, is the head, and the woman his body, "so husbands should love their wives as their own bodies," and wives, in turn, should submit to the higher judgment of their husbands, as their "heads" (Ephesians 5:28–33).

Within thirty to fifty years of Paul's death, then, partisans of the ascetic Jesus—and of the ascetic Paul—were contending against those who advocated a much more moderate Jesus and a much more conservative Paul. Like relatives in a large family battling over the inheritance, both ascetic and nonascetic Christians laid claim to the legacies of Jesus and Paul, both sides insisting that they alone were the true heirs.

Many Christians—perhaps the majority—were more concerned to accommodate themselves to ordinary social and marital structures than to challenge them. By the end of the second century, as the majority of churches accepted as canonical the list of gospels and letters now formed into the collection we call the New Testament, the moderates could claim victory and so dominate all future Christian churches. Writers now revered as the fathers of the church seized upon the tamed and domesticated version of Paul to be found in the deutero-Paulines as a primary weapon against the ascetic extremists. Clement of Alexandria, writing more than a hundred years after Paul's death, himself far less militant and far more sympathetic toward conventional social and family life than the apostle, spoke for the majority when he argued that the ascetics had exaggerated and misunderstood Paul's teaching.[46] Clement resolved to win back for the majority the disputed territory of the gospels and Paul's letters.

Taking on his opponents' arguments point for point, Clement began by saying that although Jesus never married, he did not intend for his human followers, in this respect at least, to follow his example:

> the reason that Jesus did not marry was that, in the first place, he was already engaged, so to speak, to the church; and, in the second place, he was not an ordinary man.[47]

Ascetically inclined Christians had argued that Jesus' words prove that he advocated celibacy: why else, they asked, would he have praised women whose "wombs never bore," or men who "made themselves eunuchs for the sake of the Kingdom of Heaven"? Clement admits that such sayings are puzzling, but he avoids the issue that they raise by refusing to take them literally. He maintains that Jesus could not have meant by "eunuch" what most readers assume (a celibate man). Instead, "what Jesus meant," Clement clumsily argues, "is that a married man who has divorced his wife because of her infidelity should not *remarry.*"[48]

What about Paul, who remained, as he boasted, voluntarily celibate; or Peter, who, according to Luke 18:28, left his home to follow Jesus? Paul himself tells us, Clement could argue, that Peter, like "other apostles and the brothers of the Lord," traveled with his wife at church expense (1 Corinthians 9:5)! Then, in a passage that surely would have surprised Paul, Clement argues that Paul too was married: "The only reason he did not take [his wife] with him is that it would have been an inconvenience for his ministry."[49]

When Clement attacks ascetic interpretations of Paul's message, he finds in the deutero-Pauline letters all the ammunition he needs. For example, "to those who slander marriage," he replies by quoting the antiascetic Paul of 1 Timothy.[50] But when he confronts the authentic letters, Clement finds his task much harder. Insisting, however, that the same man wrote both groups of letters, Clement skillfully interweaves passages from the authentic and the deutero-Pauline letters. Thus Clement, and the majority of Christians ever since, can claim that Paul endorses *both* marriage and celibacy:

> In general, all the letters of the apostle teach self-control and continence, and contain numerous instructions about marriage, begetting children, and domestic life, but they nowhere exclude self-controlled marriage.[51]

Clement rejects, above all, the claim that Adam and Eve's sin was to engage in sexual intercourse—a view common among such Christian teachers as Tatian the Syrian, who taught that the fruit of the tree of knowledge conveyed *carnal* knowledge. Tatian had pointed out that after Adam and Eve ate the forbidden fruit, they became sexually aware: "Then the eyes of both were opened, and they knew that they were naked" (Genesis 3:7). Other interpreters agreed that the accuracy of this interpretation is proved in Genesis 4:1, where the Hebrew verb "to know" *('yada)* connotes sexual intercourse: "And Adam *knew* his wife, and she conceived, and bore a son." Tatian blamed Adam for inventing marriage, believing that for this sin God expelled Adam and his partner in crime from Paradise.[52] The distinguished ascetic Julius Cassianus instead blamed Satan, not Adam, for inventing sexual intercourse. According to Cassianus, Satan "borrowed this practice from the irrational animals, and persuaded Adam to have sexual union with Eve."[53] But Clement denounces all such views. Sexual intercourse, he declares, was not sinful, but part of God's original—and "good"—creation: "Nature led [Adam and Eve], like the irrational animals, to procreate";[54] "and," Clement might well have added, "when I say *nature,* I mean *God.*" Clement says that those who engage in procreation are not sinning but "cooperating with God in his work of creation."[55] Thus Clement confirms the traditional Jewish conviction, expressed in the deutero-Pauline letters, that legitimate procreation is a good work, blessed by God from the day of human creation.

If engaging in sexual intercourse was *not* the sin of Adam and Eve, what *was* that first and fatal transgression? Such fathers of the church as Clement and Irenaeus insist that the first sin was disobeying God's command. Yet even Clement and his contemporary Bishop Irenaeus of Lyons, although eager to exempt sexual desire from primary blame for the fall, admit that, as they imagined it, "man's first disobedience" and the fall did, in fact, take sexual form. Clement carefully explains that the disobedience of Adam and Eve involved not what they did, but how they did it. As Clement imagines the scene, Adam and Eve, like impatient adolescents, rushed into sexual union before they had received their Father's blessing. Irenaeus explains that Adam and Eve were, in fact, underage:

> For having been created just a short time before, they had no understanding of procreation of children. It was necessary that first they should come to adult age, and then "multiply" from that time onwards.[56]

Clement blames Adam, who, he says, "desired the fruit of marriage before the proper time, and so fell into sin. . . . they were impelled to do it more quickly than was proper because they were still young, and had been seduced by deceit."[57] Irenaeus adds that Adam's guilty response shows that he was well aware that sexual desire had incited him to sin, for he covered himself and Eve with scratchy fig leaves, "while there were many other leaves which would have irritated his body much less."[58] Thus Adam punished the very organs that had led them into sin.

The attitudes that Clement and Irenaeus helped to shape more than one hundred years after Paul's death set the standard of Christian behavior for centuries—indeed, for nearly two thousand years. What would prevail in Christian tradition was not only the stark sayings of the gospels attributed to Jesus and the encouragements to celibacy that Paul urges upon believers in 1 Corinthians, but versions of these austere teachings modified to suit the purposes of the churches of the first and second centuries. Clement and his colleagues established, too, a durable double standard that endorses marriage, but only as second best to celibacy. Clement and his fellow Christians constructed elaborate arguments, drawn primarily from the Hebrew Bible and the deutero-Pauline letters, to show that marriage, for Christians as well as for Jews, is a positive act, involving "cooperation with God's work of creation." Yet Clement can revere it as such only by going back to the consensus Jesus challenged. Clement, influenced, no doubt, by Stoic philosophers who agreed with him in principle, insisted that marriage finds its sole legitimate purpose—and sexual intercourse its only rationale—in procreation.[59] Thus even Clement, certainly the most liberal of the fathers of the church, and one who, more emphatically than any other, affirms God's blessing upon marriage and procreation, expresses deep ambivalence toward sexuality—an ambivalence that has resounded throughout Christian history for two millennia.

Clement believes that Jesus meant both to confirm and to transform traditional patterns of marriage; that he did not challenge the patriarchal structure of marriage (which for Clement expresses the natural superiority of men, as well as God's punishment upon Eve); but that Jesus did intend to eradicate such pagan sexual practices as incest, adultery, "unnatural intercourse," homosexuality, abortion, and infanticide, as well as the Hebrew practices of polygamy and divorce.

Marriage, now monogamous and indissoluble, as God originally intended it, may become, for believers, a "sacred image." But to experience it as such, the believer must be purged of the sexual passion that led Adam and Eve into sin. The married Christian must not only subordinate desire to reason but strive to annihilate desire entirely:

> Our ideal is not to experience desire at all. . . . We should do nothing from desire. Our will is to be directed only toward what is necessary. For we are children not of desire but of will. A man who marries for the sake of begetting children must practice continence so that it is not desire he feels for his wife . . . that he may beget children with a chaste and controlled will.[60]

To accomplish this, as one might imagine, is not easy. "The gospel," as Clement reads it, not only restricts sexuality to marriage but, even within marriage, limits it to specific acts intended for procreation. To engage in marital intercourse for any other reason is to "do injury to nature."[61] Clement excludes not only such counterproductive practices as oral and anal intercourse but also intercourse with a menstruating, pregnant, barren, or menopausal wife, and, for that matter, with one's wife "in the morning," "in the daytime," or "after dinner." Clement warns, indeed, that

> not even at night, although in darkness, is it fitting to carry on immodestly or indecently, but with modesty, so that whatever happens, happens in the light of reason . . . for even that union which is legitimate is still dangerous, except in so far as it is engaged in procreation of children.[62]

Even at best, however, Christian marriage remains inferior to chastity. "Chaste marriage," in which both partners devote themselves to celibacy, is better than a sexually active one. To the dedicated Christian,

> his wife, after conception, is as a sister, and is judged as if of the same father; who only recalls her husband when she looks at the children; as one destined to become a sister in reality after putting off the flesh, which separates and limits the knowledge of those who are spiritual by the specific characteristics of the sexes.[63]

Only spouses who are celibate and thereby recover, so to speak, their virginity transcend the whole structure of bodily existence and recover the spiritual equality Adam and Eve lost through the fall,

> for souls, by themselves, are equal. Souls are "neither male nor female," when "they no longer marry nor are given in marriage" [cf. Luke 20:35].[64]

Such, Clement says, was the marriage of the blessed apostles, and

> such their perfect control over their feelings even in the closest human relationships. So, too, the apostle says, "Let him who marries be as if he were not married" [cf. 1 Corinthians 7:29], requiring that marriage should not be enslaved to passion. . . . thus the soul acquires a mental disposition corresponding to the gospel in every relation of life.[65]

Like Clement, the majority of Christians for the past two thousand years have chosen to maintain simultaneously Jesus' most extreme—even shocking—sayings, such as those prohibiting divorce and encouraging renunciation, together with others that modify their severity. By the end of the second century, Christians, as we have seen, had also incorporated within the New Testament a similar double image of Paul and his message. The churches that collected Paul's letters during the second century generally included, first of all, the authentic letters, which express Paul's own complex and often ambivalent attitudes, ranging from his preference for celibacy to his admission that "the weak" are better off married than promiscuous.[66] But the majority of Christians chose the domesticated Paul over the ascetic one and tolerated contradictory statements attributed to the apostle (just as Matthew attributes contradictory statements to Jesus himself). In this way, Christians could attract into the movement those who were married—and even divorced—as well as those eager for celibacy. Clement, like most of his contemporaries, chose to subordinate Jesus' calls for radical renunciation and to endorse instead procreation within marriage—as Jesus and Paul did not—not only as the normal, but even as the sanctified, course of Christian life. But Clement and his fellows did not renounce the ascetic ideal entirely. Instead, they used the diversity of New Testament sources to establish an extraordinary view of marriage and celibacy; for Clement's views on marriage virtually ensure that anyone who takes them seriously will judge himself or herself to be deficient by their standard. And Clement goes on to invite to the "angelic life" those eager few who shun the dangerous shoals of married life. For continence and virginity are, he assumes, better still—certainly safer, and far holier.

As the Christian movement, in Clement's time and later, became more complex, gathering hundreds of thousands of converts from Rome and Greece, from Africa and Asia, and throughout the regions of Spain and Gaul, the message of Jesus and Paul, intended originally for a largely Hebrew constituency, had to be refracted through that increasingly diverse movement. Jesus' radical call to repent and purify oneself to prepare for the Kingdom of God remained, for many, the primary point of reference. Simultaneously, however, Christians developed multiple images of Jesus and Paul and multiple interpretations of their message to suit a variety of mundane and spiritual purposes.

What made such an austere message, in its many versions, attractive to so many people? How did Christianity succeed in becoming the religion of the Roman Empire? In the next chapters we take up these questions and see how, within its practical severity, many saw a new vision of human nature—one that had power to validate and transform the lives of the multitudes who heard it.

# (II)

# CHRISTIANS AGAINST THE ROMAN ORDER

I N THE PREVIOUS CHAPTER I attempted to show how Christianity
sprang up as a movement that challenged converts to break all
that bound them to their families, to their cities, to the nation—
all, in short, that conscientious people, whether Jews, Greeks,
Asians, Africans, or Romans, held most sacred—where these com-
mitments conflicted with the Christian commitment to their "brothers and sisters in Christ," fellow members of the sect that called itself
God's family.

By the end of the second century, the Christian movement had
spread through all parts of the empire, so that the North African
convert Tertullian, writing in Carthage around 200 C.E., said that

> the outcry is that the state is filled with Christians—that they are
> in the fields; in the cities; in the islands; [pagans] lament, as for
> some kind of catastrophe, that people of both sexes, every age and
> status, even those of high rank, are passing over to the profession
> of the Christian faith.[1]

In an open letter addressed to "rulers of the Roman Empire," Tertullian acknowledges that pagan critics detest the movement: "You
think that a Christian is a man of every crime, an enemy of the gods,
of the emperor, of the law, of good morals, of all nature."[2] In a sense
such critics were right; for Christians did threaten the social and
ethical system of the ancient world in ways that eventually would
alter the structure of the empire itself. Going into the marketplaces,
the shops of cobblers and carpenters, and the kitchens of great
houses, Christians offered to working people and to slaves, as well

as to anyone else who would listen,[3] a message that, as some preached it, seemed to threaten the hierarchical structure of Roman society. Yet other Christians, as we have seen, did everything they could to accommodate to that hierarchical structure and to avoid offending their pagan neighbors.[4] But what made Christians especially dangerous to the Roman order was their refusal to pay what Romans regarded as ordinary respect to their Roman rulers; and this brought some of them into direct and total opposition to the temporal as well as the divine authorities—to the emperors and to their divine patrons, the gods.[5]

A widely popular true story of the time tells of a mistress and her personal slave who were convicted as Christians after they refused to revere the emperor's image. Together they were thrown to wild animals and slaughtered in the public amphitheater in Carthage in a spectacle celebrating the emperor's birthday. The aristocratic protagonist, Vibia Perpetua, fluent in both Greek and Latin, wrote about her experiences from the time of her arrest until the evening of her execution. Perpetua, twenty-two years old, recently married, and nursing her infant son, was arrested along with her friends Saturus and Saturninus and her personal slave Felicitas and the slave Revocatus. Perpetua and her companions were thrown into a stifling and crowded African jail. After her arrest, Perpetua's father, "out of love for me," she wrote, "was trying to persuade me to change my decision."[6] Refusing his pleas to give up the name Christian, Perpetua rejected her familial name instead, although she says she grieved to see her father, mother, and brothers "suffering out of compassion for me."[7] At first, she wrote, "I was tortured with worry for my baby there," but after she gained permission for him to stay with her in prison, "at once I recovered my health, relieved as I was of my worry and anxiety for the child."[8]

Perpetua's father, anticipating that the Christians were about to be given a hearing, returned to the prison "worn with worry" to plead with Perpetua to offer sacrifice for the welfare of the emperors, kissing her hands as he spoke:

> "Daughter . . . have pity on your father, if I deserve to be called your father, if I have loved you more than all your brothers; do not abandon me. . . . Think of your brothers; think of your mother and your aunt; think of your child, who will not be able to live once you are gone. . . . Give up your pride! You will destroy all of us. None of us will ever be able to speak freely again if anything happens to you."[9]

But Perpetua refused and, she said, "he left me in great sorrow."
Then, she continued,

> one day while we were eating breakfast we were suddenly hur-
> ried off for a hearing. We arrived at the forum, and straightaway
> the story went about the neighborhood near the forum and a
> huge crowd gathered. We walked up to the prisoner's dock. All
> the others when questioned admitted their guilt. Then, when it
> came my turn, my father appeared with my son, dragged me from
> the step, and said: "Perform the sacrifice—have pity on your
> baby!"
>
> Hilarianus the governor, who had received his judicial powers
> as the successor of the late proconsul Minucius Timinianus, said
> to me: "Have pity on your father's grey head; have pity on your
> infant son. Offer the sacrifice for the welfare of the emperors."
>
> "I will not," I retorted.
>
> "Are you a Christian?" said Hilarianus. And I said: "Yes, I
> am."
>
> When my father persisted in trying to dissuade me, Hilarianus
> ordered him to be thrown to the ground and beaten with a rod.
> I felt sorry for my father, just as if I myself had been beaten. I felt
> sorry for his pathetic old age.
>
> Then Hilarianus passed sentence on all of us: we were con-
> demned to the beasts, and we returned to prison in high spirits.[10]

Even before she was sentenced, Perpetua knew that she was
going to die, for she had dreamed that she was climbing a bronze
ladder of tremendous height, bristling with daggers, swords, and
spikes, reaching all the way to the heavens. On the day before her
execution, Perpetua wrote down another vision: She dreamed that
she was led to the amphitheater, where enormous crowds waited to
see her fight with a ferocious Egyptian athlete. "My clothes were
stripped off, and suddenly I was a man." She fought and wrestled
until she got him into a headlock and so won the fight. "Then I
awoke; I realized that it was not with wild animals that I would fight,
but with the devil; but I knew that I would win the victory." Perpetua concludes her journal with the words "So much for what I did
until the evening of the contest. About what happened at the contest
itself, let whoever write about it who will."[11]

Perpetua's slave Felicitas was pregnant when she was arrested
and was in her eighth month as the execution date approached:
"Felicitas was very distressed that her martyrdom would be post-
poned because of her pregnancy; for it is against the law for pregnant

women to be executed." She feared she would have to survive her Christian companions and alone endure a later execution along with criminals.

Two days before the execution the Christians prayed for her

in one torrent of common grief, and immediately after their prayer the labor pains came upon her. She suffered a good deal in her labor because of the natural difficulty of an eight-month delivery.[12]

One of the Christian women took the infant daughter to raise as her own, leaving Felicitas free to join her companions. As Perpetua had hoped, a fellow Christian continued the story, telling two anecdotes about her imperious response to the harsh treatment to which the Christians were subjected in prison. Perpetua dared speak directly to the tribune in charge, protesting, "We are to fight on the emperor's birthday. Would it not be to your credit if we were brought forth on that day in a healthier condition?"[13] The officer, visibly disturbed, ordered improvements in the prisoners' treatment and granted increased visiting privileges for their families and friends. When the day arrived, Perpetua and Felicitas, together with their Christian brothers Revocatus, Saturninus, and Saturus, were led out of the prison to the gates of the amphitheater. The officer in charge, following the common practice, ordered the men to dress in robes of priests of the god Saturn, and the women to dress in the costumes of priestesses of the goddess Ceres, as if they were offering their deaths in sacrifice to the gods. Perpetua adamantly refused, saying,

"We came to this of our own free will, so that our liberty should not be violated. We agreed to pledge our lives in order to do no such thing [as sacrifice to the gods]. And you agreed with us to do this."[14]

Again her plea prevailed, and the officer yielded. But just as Perpetua and Felicitas were to enter the arena, they were forcibly stripped naked and placed in nets, so that

even the crowd was horrified when they saw that one was a delicate young girl, and the other woman fresh from childbirth, with milk still dripping from her breasts. And so they were brought back again and dressed in loose tunics.[15]

A mad heifer was set loose after them; Perpetua was gored and thrown to the ground. She got up and, seeing Felicitas crushed and fallen, went over to her and lifted her up, and the two stood side by side. Then, after undergoing further ordeals and seeing Saturus endure agonizing torture, Perpetua and Felicitas, along with the others, were called to the center of the arena to be slaughtered. A witness records that Perpetua "screamed as she was struck on the bone; then she took the trembling hand of the young gladiator, and guided it to her throat."[16]

Some spectators at such martyrdoms shook their heads and said, "What good was their religion to them, which they preferred even over their own lives?"[17] But others, including Tertullian himself, were sufficiently shaken by such sights to join this movement, knowing that they risked their lives by doing so.

JUSTIN THE PHILOSOPHER, born c. 110 C.E. into an affluent family in the city of Flavia Neopolis in Samaria, and having gone to Rome to practice philosophy, says that he, like Tertullian, was astonished and moved "when I saw Christians . . . fearless of death."[18] Justin had heard rumors that Christians secretly indulged in cannibalism and promiscuity; but the superhuman courage they displayed in the amphitheater as they endured torture and execution convinced him that they were possessed by an extraordinary power.

Justin began to ask himself who are these emperors—and who are these gods—in whose names government agents committed such atrocities? He knew, of course, the conventional answers—the emperors are men blessed by the gods, the powers of the universe, and divinely charged to rule over humankind—for as Justin admits, he too once worshiped the same gods as everyone else. But he was shocked by the Christians' ordeals and moved by his own subsequent conversion to see both the emperors and the gods with different eyes:

> We—who out of every race of people, used to worship Bacchus the son of Semele, and Apollo the son of Latone, who in their love affairs with human beings did such things as are shameful to mention, and Persephone and Venus, who were driven insane by love of Adonis, and whose mysteries, too, you celebrate—*we have now, through Jesus Christ, learned to despise these gods, although we be threatened with death for it.* We have dedicated ourselves to the unbegotten, impassible God, of whom we are persuaded that he was never goaded by lust for Antiope, and for Ganymede . . . we

pity those who believe such things, and we know that those who invented them are demons.[19]

Justin found among the Christians what he had vainly sought for years in philosophy. He tells us little about his background but much about his passionate longing to understand the questions that obsessed him: What is true? What makes a person happy? How can one find God? Having set out as a young man upon a philosophic search, Justin says, "First I surrendered myself to a certain Stoic." But when he complained that this teacher taught nothing about God and the Stoic replied that he did not bother with such questions, considering them irrelevant, Justin left him and joined the students of a Peripatetic philosopher with a reputation for keen intellect. After he had listened several days to this new teacher, Justin says, "he required me to settle the [tuition] fee."[20] Indignant at this request, Justin decided that since the man asked for money, "he was no philosopher at all," and abruptly departed. Finally, Justin says, he investigated Platonic philosophy, and

> then I spent as much time as possible with one who had recently arrived in our city—a wise man, holding a high position among the Platonists—and I progressed, and made the greatest improvements daily.[21]

From his Platonist teacher, Justin learned to discriminate between the appearances created by mere sense impressions and the reality that Plato says only a mind purified and disciplined by philosophy can perceive. But one day, when an older Christian philosopher whom Justin came to revere as a second Socrates challenged his Platonist assumptions, Justin admitted that his own experience of philosophic searching forced him to a conclusion that he had long resisted: that the human mind by itself cannot grasp ultimate truth. Instead, Justin came to believe, one must receive illumination through the spirit of God descending from above—the same spirit that had possessed the Christian martyrs in the amphitheater.

Once converted, and believing himself illuminated by the spirit in his baptismal initiation, Justin opened his apartment above the Baths of Timothy in Rome to philosophically minded seekers of Christian truth. But arbitrary arrests and executions of Christians, even though they occurred sporadically, reminded him that professing his newfound faith placed him in danger of being accused, arrested, and put to the test—either to make a token sacrifice to the

Roman gods or to be sentenced to torture and execution.[22] After he had described the trial and condemnation of three of his fellow Christians, Justin declared, "I, too, therefore, expect to be plotted against and crucified." Yet he decided to ignore the danger to himself, and he boldly addressed an open letter of protest directly to the emperors[23]—to Marcus Aurelius, his son Commodus, and his imperial father, Antoninus Pius. Justin initially addresses the emperors as fellow philosophers, and assures them that Christians intend to be loyal, even the best, citizens. He speaks so persuasively that the eminent historian Robert Grant has cited Justin as exemplifying "Christian devotion to the monarchy."[24] In all probability, Justin received no answer to his petition, so he addressed a second to the Senate, protesting a recent and typical case. Justin told the story of an aristocratic lady who, having converted to Christianity, refused to participate any longer with her husband in drunken sexual parties involving their household slaves. Although she wanted a divorce, her friends persuaded her to wait, hoping for a reconciliation. But when she learned that her husband, on a trip to Alexandria, had behaved worse than ever, she sued him for divorce and left. Her enraged husband accused Ptolemy, her teacher in Christianity, who was then arrested, imprisoned, and brought to trial before the judge Urbicus, who asked him only one question: "Are you a Christian?" Ptolemy said yes, whereupon Urbicus pronounced the mandatory death sentence. But as Ptolemy was being marched out to die, Lucius, one of the courtroom spectators, cried in protest:

> "What is the ground for this judgment? Why have you punished this man, not as an adulterer, nor a fornicator, nor murderer, nor thief, nor robber, nor convicted by any crime at all but who has only confessed that he is called by the name 'Christian'? This judgment of yours, Urbicus, does not become the Emperor Pius, nor the philosopher, Caesar's son Marcus Aurelius, nor the sacred Senate."[25]

Urbicus answered that Lucius himself sounded suspiciously like a Christian; when Lucius admitted as much, the prefect ordered that he and another protestor in the audience follow Ptolemy to execution. As soldiers led the condemned men from the courtroom, Lucius loudly thanked God for delivering him and his companions "from such wicked rulers" and releasing them instead to the "Father and King of the Universe."

What kinds of emperors, then, are these, Justin asked himself—

and what kinds of gods—whose laws support sexual promiscuity and private vengeance and sanction the slaughter of innocent people? Justin knew, of course, that the story he told, like the story of Perpetua and Felicitas, would raise very different questions in the minds of pagan readers. What kinds of people are these Christians, pagan critics would ask, who refuse to worship the gods and who, from the viewpoint of Roman traditionalists, are *atheists*? And why do these Christians refuse to perform ordinary token acts of loyalty, choosing to die rather than sacrifice to the emperor's divine spirit?

Justin answered that Christians had discovered a terrible secret: the powers behind the Roman magistrates—and, in particular, behind the emperors themselves—are not gods, nor are they mere appearances, as the Platonists said, but demons, active evil forces bent upon corrupting and destroying human beings, determined to blind people to the truth that there is only one God, creator of all, who made all humankind alike. Although Justin did not explicitly derive from Genesis an egalitarian view of humanity, certain other Christians did. Twenty years after Justin was beheaded by the Roman authorities, Clement of Alexandria declared that, since God made every human being "in his image,"

> I would ask you, does it not seem to you monstrous that you— human beings who are God's own handiwork—should be subjected to another master, and, even worse, serve a tyrant instead of God, the true king?[26]

Deriding the imperial cult, Clement declared that since Christ's coming, divinity now "pervades all humankind equally . . . deifying humanity,"[27] the slave equally with the master, Felicitas equally with her owner and "sister in Christ" Perpetua. Clement agreed with Justin that the worship of the emperor's *genius* (that is, his divine spirit)[28] is a lie perpetrated by demons.

Thus Christians threatened to replace the Roman pantheon of gods and goddesses, those Olympian aristocrats, with One God, creator of all humankind alike. Even worse, they threatened to replace the image of the emperor as the manifestation of divine power on earth with Jesus, a condemned criminal, whom the pagan satirist Lucian derisively called "a crucified sophist"[29]—an illiterate barbarian executed by the Romans for treason against the state! When Perpetua, Felicitas, and their companions refused to venerate the image of the emperor Geta, they did so in the name of Jesus. They insisted that although he had been defeated by the powers of Rome,

Jesus ultimately proved victorious not only over Rome but over death itself, for he was enthroned triumphant "at the right hand of God," where the martyrs confidently expected to join him after following him to their deaths in the arena.

Pagan skeptics might ridicule the Roman gods as naïve and foolish illusions; but for Justin and many of his fellow Christians these gods were real and dangerous adversaries. Justin, for example, agreed with his fellow philosopher and adversary the devout pagan emperor Marcus Aurelius that the gods embodied elemental forces at work in the universe. Marcus, however, identified himself with these powers, which he also called *providence, necessity,* and *nature,* and revered them as his divine patrons and protectors. While camped with soldiers on a military expedition, the philosopher-emperor, alone in his tent at night, wrote moral injunctions to himself:

> Providence is the source from which all things flow; and allied with it is Necessity, and the welfare of the universe. You yourself are a part of that universe. . . . Think of your procrastination, how the gods have repeatedly granted you further periods of grace. . . . It is time now to realize the nature of the universe in which you belong, and of that controlling Power whose offspring you are. . . . Hour by hour resolve fully, like a Roman and a man, to do what comes to hand with correct and natural dignity, and with humanity, independence, and justice. . . . the gods will ask nothing more.[30]

The French scholar Jean Beaujeu recently has shown that such convictions about the emperors' divinely sanctioned role had become basic to Roman political life and to Marcus himself, as well as his imperial family, his predecessors, sons, and successors. Especially since the time of Marcus Aurelius's adoptive grandfather, the great military emperor Hadrian, who rose to power from a relatively obscure Spanish family, the emperors increasingly represented themselves as the gods' agents on earth. These emperors vigorously promoted the massive imperial propaganda they had inherited from their predecessors, publicizing on coins, on stone monuments, in public entertainments from horse races and sports events to religious festivals, their claim that the gods had appointed them and their dynasty to rule over the whole human race, and over the whole known world.[31] Hadrian ordered that he himself be portrayed as a god in statues and on coins, most often represented in the form of Jupiter, "greatest of gods." Marcus Aurelius's imperial father, Antoninus, had earned from the Senate his honorific title "the Pious" for successfully lobbying to pass a decree in the Senate declaring Hadrian to be a god after his death. During his lifetime, Hadrian had scandalized conservative senators by insisting upon deifying his dead lover, Antinous, after the boy had drowned in the Nile under suspicious circumstances. When Marcus Aurelius admonished himself in his private *Meditations* to remember that he was only mortal, he was trying to keep in perspective his public role as the "greatest and most manifest of all the gods."[32]

Such propaganda involved more than personal grandiosity, and certainly more than the insane egotism that had driven the "mad emperors" Caligula and Nero one hundred years earlier to demand that their subjects worship them as incarnate gods. Belief that the emperors embodied divine powers reflected the way traditionally minded Romans already perceived the gods. For traditional religion in the Roman Empire had always held that the elemental forces of the universe—what we call natural forces—are, in fact, divine forces. The sun's energy, thunder and lightning, as well as the internal forces of passion, manifested themselves respectively in the forms of the gods Apollo, Jupiter, and Venus. Social and political experiences of power, too, could be interpreted as manifestations of those same elemental forces. Yet the much-debated question of whether educated pagans "believed in" the gods or the emperor's divinity is anachronistic, as the classicist Simon Price has pointed out.[33] Many educated pagans, like many of the empire's provincial subjects, participated in sacrifice to the gods or the emperor's *genius* as a way of demonstrating their proper relationship to the "powers that be," both human and divine. No intelligent person, the sophisticated pagan might have explained, actually *worshiped* images of the gods, or *worshiped* living emperors; instead, the gods' images—and the images of the emperors themselves—provided an accessible focus for revering the cosmic forces they represented.[34]

Yet Justin and his Christian contemporaries, far from expressing the "enlightened" or skeptical attitudes that later historians have projected upon them, usually regarded pagan practices with the utmost seriousness and recoiled from them in disgust. Justin agreed with pious pagans that the gods and emperors reflected elemental forces in the universe, but there agreement ended. For the gods that Marcus Aurelius revered as his divine patrons Justin detested as demons—evil forces manipulating the law to enforce the inequities that Christians protested and the injustices that they, among many others, suffered.

Following his conversion, Justin had been shocked to learn that the gods that he, too, once had worshiped were actually mere pretenders to divine power. Writing his open letter to the emperors, he unmasked the gods' secret identity: the patron gods of Rome were none other than the fallen angels, who, according to Genesis 6, were cast out of heaven at the beginning of time. For Justin, like many Jews and many of his fellow Christians, tended to interpret the difficulties of human life less in terms of the fall of Adam and Eve (Genesis 2–3) than in terms of the fall of the angels (Genesis 6:1–6). According to Genesis 6, the great and famous men of ancient times—those called giants—were the result of a hybrid union between God's angels and human women:

> *The sons of God [angels] saw that the daughters of men were fair;*
> *and they took to wife such of them as they chose. . . . There were*
> *giants on the earth in those days, . . . when the sons of God came*
> *in to the daughters of men, and they bore children to them, the*
> *mighty men of renown.*

> (GENESIS 6:2–4)

Justin explained that after some of the angels whom God had entrusted to administer the universe betrayed their trust by seducing women and corrupting boys (so Justin amplified the story of Genesis 6), they "begot children, who are called demons."[35] When God discovered the corruption of his administration, he expelled them from heaven. But then these exiled angels tried to compensate for their lost power by joining with their offspring, the demons, to enslave the human race. Drawing upon the supernatural powers that even disgraced angels still retain, they awed and terrified people into worshiping them instead of God. Thus, Justin said:

> The truth shall be told; since of old these evil demons, effecting
> apparitions of themselves, both polluted women and corrupted
> boys, and showed such terrifying visions to people that those who
> did not use their reason . . . were struck by terror; and being
> carried away by fear, and not knowing that these were demons,
> they called them gods.[36]

The majority of humankind fell under their power, and only an exceptional few, like Socrates and Jesus, escaped demonically induced mental slavery. This invisible network of supernatural energies proceeded, then, to promote the fortunes of their henchmen. "Taking as their ally the desire for evil in everyone," Justin explained, the demons became the patrons of powerful and ruthless men, and "instituted private and public rites in honor of those who are most powerful."[37]

Justin saw the result at every turn—above all in the vast panoply of imperial propaganda, which claimed for the Roman emperors and their governors, magistrates, and armies the power and protection of the gods. The injustice that dominated the law courts indisputably proved, according to Justin, that they were controlled by demons, who manipulated the judges to destroy anyone, from Socrates and Jesus to the present-day Christians, who opposed the demons or threatened to expose them:

> And when Socrates attempted by true reason and investigation to
> . . . deliver men from the demons, then the demons themselves,
> using men as their instruments, brought upon him death for being
> an "atheist"; and in our case, too, they do the same things.[38]

What happened in Urbicus's courtroom, where the judge protected the interests of a ruthless and immoral man while condemning a Christian teacher and his defenders to torture and death, revealed, Justin believed, this same demonic inversion of justice. As the historian Peter Brown says:

> For Justin and his contemporaries, the story of the mating of the
> angels with the daughters of men and its dire consequences for
> the peace of society was not a distant myth; it was a map on which
> they plotted the disruptions and tensions around them.[39]

What clinched the gods' identity as fallen angels was their arrogance, brutality, and licentiousness. Wherever Justin turned in Rome, he, like everyone else, encountered images of the gods; and what once he had admired as splendid, beautiful, or awesome he now saw as the leering masks of corruption and wickedness. Statues of Jupiter, often identified with the emperors, stood not only in temples but also in the public squares and government buildings and dominated the Roman amphitheater. In other cities, other gods shared the place of honor, as Saturn and Ceres did in the amphitheater at Carthage, presiding over the slaughter of Perpetua and her companions. Within these arenas, on religious holidays, actors and gladiators paraded images of the gods; often they dressed as Hercules or Attis while fighting each other to the death. Condemned criminals were forced into costume to die as if in sacrifice to the gods, as Perpetua narrowly escaped doing; her contemporary, the North African Christian Tertullian, saw in the same amphitheater men dressed as Mercury and Pluto, the gods of the dead, poking at the bodies of the dying with red-hot irons, as if the same gods who once delighted in the violence of the Trojan War now presided over the everyday brutality of slaughter for public entertainment. Images of Apollo, Mercury, Hercules, and Venus adorned the public baths, while Apollo and the Roman Dionysus, Bacchus, presided over the theaters, where actors often played out the stories of the gods on stage. Among the most popular were amorous adventures, such as those of Apollo and Daphne; Venus's affair with Mars; Zeus, whom the Romans called Jupiter, appearing in multiple forms to his human lovers—to Danae in a shower of gold, to Leda in the form of a swan, to Europa in the form of a bull, or to the boy Ganymede, whom Zeus, as an older lover, abducted and raped. Justin's student in Christianity, Tatian, charged that even the solemn festivals of religious drama offered public demonstrations of promiscuity: "Your sons and daughters see [the gods] giving lessons in adultery on stage."[40] The Christian philosopher Athenagoras said that stories such as those celebrating Zeus's rape of the boy Ganymede not only lent false glamor to those who seduce young boys but also encouraged merchants who set up "marketplaces for immorality, and establish infamous resorts for the young for every kind of corrupt pleasure."[41]

Besides the many well-known public statues, many people, as the Christian teacher Clement of Alexandria said accusingly,

> depict in their houses the unnatural passions of the demons. . . . they decorate their bedroom with paintings hung there, regarding licentiousness as religion; and lying in bed, in the midst of their embraces, they see Aphrodite locked in the embrace of her lover. . . . Such are the theologies of arrogance [*hybris*]; such are the instructions of your gods, who commit immorality with you.[42]

Clement's account is amply corroborated by the frescoes discovered at Pompeii and the annals of the court historian Suetonius, who noted, for example, that the emperor Tiberius kept in his bedroom a painting of Juno performing fellatio on Jupiter.[43]

Clement's attack upon Jupiter thinly veiled his contempt for some of the rulers themselves:

Is Jupiter, then, the good, the prophetic, the patron of hospitality, the protector of supplicants, the avenger of wrongs? No: he is instead unjust, the violator of right and law, the impious, the inhuman, the violent, the seducer, the adulterer, the incestuous . . . so given to sexual pleasures as to lust after everyone, and to indulge his lust upon everyone.[44]

Clement also attacked the cult that the emperor Hadrian had established in Clement's native city of Alexandria to honor his dead lover, the boy Antinous:

> Another new deity was added to the number with great religious pomp in Egypt, and nearby Greece as well, by the King of the Romans, who deified Antinous, whom he loved as Jupiter loved Ganymede, and whose beauty was extremely rare; for lust is not easy to restrain, being devoid of fear, as it now is; and people observe the "Sacred Nights of Antinous," the shameful nature of which the lover who spent them with him knew. Why count him among the gods—a boy honored because of impurity? . . . And why should you expand upon his beauty? Beauty damaged by corruption is horrible. . . . Now the grave of the prostituted boy is the temple of Antinous![45]

Such things happen, Clement concluded, when people worship as gods "those who themselves are only human—and often the worst of humankind!"

When Justin wrote his open letter to Hadrian's son and grandsons, some of the most distinguished emperors in Roman history, he initially addressed them respectfully, as we have seen, as "fellow philosophers and lovers of learning." But as soon as he brought up the treatment of Christians, Justin showed that he saw even Antoninus Pius and Marcus Aurelius as men dedicated to perpetuating the "violence and tyranny" of a system that treated Christians as capital criminals for refusing to worship demons. Justin darkly hinted that these emperors, too, for all their personal virtues and public rhetoric, were actually no better than a band of criminals—"robbers in a desert"[46]—who rule by force, not justice. Justin warned Antoninus, Marcus, and Commodus to "be on your guard, lest the demons whom we have been attacking deceive you, and distract you from reading and understanding what we say," for, Justin told the rulers of the world, "these demons strive to keep you as their slaves!"[47]

Had Marcus Aurelius and his colleagues bothered to listen to such diatribes, they might well have perceived at once how subversive the Christian message actually was. By publicizing his address to the emperors, Justin had launched an open attack upon the official propaganda that portrayed them as universal rulers by divine right. Where outsiders would have seen the all-powerful emperors disposing of a handful of dissidents accused as Christians, Justin depicted puppet-tyrants, enslaved to demons, contending against people allied with the one invincible and true God. Though they claimed to be exemplary citizens, some Christians covertly attacked the whole basis of Roman imperial power and preached instead, in the name of Jesus Christ, a radical message that was spreading rapidly throughout the cities of the empire.

Some Roman officials, dumbfounded by this Christian defiance, agreed with Marcus Aurelius's private assessment: what motivates the Christians is not courage but a perverse desire for notoriety. Other officials burst out angrily, as if suspecting that they were being manipulated by suicidal fanatics: "If you want to die, go kill yourselves, and do not bother us."[48] Pagans might well suspect their motives. If Christians believe that demons rule the world, if they thank God for their death sentences, why do they not kill themselves and be done with it? Why do they claim, on the contrary, to be good, even exemplary, citizens of a regime they profess to despise? Why does Justin, for all his defiance, insist that Christians, "more readily than any other people,"[49] pay their full share of all taxes, and that "we, more than any other people, are your helpers and allies in preserving peace"?[50]

Justin explains to the emperors that, in each of these cases, Christians intend to obey God, not the human government. As for suicide, he says:

> I will tell you why we do not do so, and yet why, when interrogated, we fearlessly confess. We have been taught that God did not make the world aimlessly, but for the sake of the human race. . . . If then we killed ourselves, we would be acting in opposition to the will of God. But when we are interrogated, we make no denial, because . . . we consider it impious not to speak the truth in all things, which we know pleases God.[51]

Christians pay their taxes, Justin continues, in obedience to Christ's own command ("Render unto Caesar . . . ").[52] As for their civic behavior, Christians serve One who demands complete righteousness, whose judgment no secret act or thought escapes.[53] God commands his people, too, to render obedience—although strictly limited and secularized obedience—to the human authorities. Justin and his fellow Christians had inherited the capacity to make this distinction from the experience of Jews living for centuries under foreign imperialism. Irenaeus borrows a rabbinic image to interpret Paul's saying that the "powers that be are ordained of God":

> Earthly rule has been appointed by God for the benefit of nations, so that, under the fear of human rule, men may not devour one another like fishes, but, by means of the establishment of laws, may restrain an excess of wickedness among the nations.[54]

Finally, Justin and his Christian contemporaries, having found themselves, like the Jews, often the target of public violence, had come to appreciate the government's role in preserving public order. So Athenagoras informs the emperors Marcus Aurelius and Commodus that Christians, like the Jews,

> pray for your government, that you may . . . receive the kingdom, son from father, and that your empire may receive increase and additions, and all people become subject to your rule, since . . . this is for our advantage, too, that we may lead peaceful and tranquil lives.[55]

Yet Justin, Irenaeus, and Athenagoras, each writing in full awareness of the imminent dangers of persecution, acknowledge that, if some human rulers may serve the purposes of God, others serve those of Satan. Athenagoras explains that

> because the demonic movements and functions proceeding from Satan . . . sometimes move men in one way and sometimes in another, as individuals and as nations, separately and collectively, some have thought that this universe is constituted without any definite order.[56]

Christians believe, nevertheless, that even at their worst, demonically inspired rulers, "in spite of their disobedience, cannot transgress the order prescribed for them." God retains ultimate power over his universe and holds in his hands the final vindication of his servants and the coming destruction of his enemies. Meanwhile, like Socrates, who, freed from demonic deception, "tried to deliver people from the demons,"[57] Christians maintain the truth of their freedom by repudiating pagan worship. So, Justin says, "you consecrate the images of your emperors when they die, and you call them gods; but we do not honor such deities as human beings have made and placed in shrines."⁵⁸

Justin admitted that he wrote in fear of his life, hoping desperately to change government policy, to convince the Roman authorities that Christians did not intend to be subversive; he himself, like the great majority of Christians, preferred to live quietly, and Christians did so wherever possible. In many cities Christian life continued uninterrupted, often for generations; yet many more than were persecuted must have nevertheless shared Justin's apprehension. What sounded like arrogant defiance was the response of people forced against their will to make the terrible choice between pagan sacrifice and death—between denying Christ or bearing witness to their faith in him to the end of their lives: the term *martyr*, in Greek, means "witness."

Some Roman officials, for their part, may have realized that such Christian attacks upon the Roman gods—and thus upon the emperors—could undermine the state's absolute claim upon its citizens and subjects; and that these inflammatory views, accompanied by passionate religious fervor, could catch fire among the disaffected and the restless, especially among subject nations and slaves. Thus Rome showed no toleration for these dangerous Christians.

One day Justin himself, as he had anticipated and feared, stood in court, arrested and charged with being a Christian. His judge, Rusticus, urban prefect of Rome, was Marcus Aurelius's personal friend and longtime advisor, who had inspired the young emperor, Marcus says, "with the idea of a state based upon equality and freedom of speech, and of a monarchy which values above all the liberty of the subject."⁵⁹ Justin probably knew that his judge's very name evoked the political philosophy with which Justin himself identified; for Rusticus proudly claimed to be descended from a famous Stoic philosopher who had defied the tyranny of the self-styled "lord and god," the emperor Domitian, and had paid for his courage with his execution.

Yet Rusticus acknowledged no affinity with Justin—much less the affinity Justin dared claim between himself and Socrates—and saw in this itinerant philosopher only a stubborn dissident who refused to obey Rusticus's simple command: "Obey the gods and submit to the emperors."⁶⁰ Both men—the judge and the accused— took for granted the implied connection between religious sacrifice and political submission. But Rusticus saw both as the minimum obligations of any citizen, while Justin and his companions saw such acts as betrayal of Christ, their true King.

After his interrogation, Rusticus repeated his demand: "Let us come to the point at issue—a necessary and urgent matter. Agree together to offer sacrifice to the gods."

Justin said, "No one of sound mind turns from piety to sacrilege."

The prefect said, "If you do not obey, you will be punished without mercy."

Justin and his companions replied, "Do what you will: we are Christians, and will not sacrifice to idols."

The prefect Rusticus then passed judgment, saying, "Those who have refused to sacrifice to the gods and yield to the emperor's edict are to be taken away to be beaten and beheaded, in accordance with the laws."[61]

Later generations of readers, whose perceptions were shaped by long-established Christian ideas that Justin and the other martyrs were simply following their religious convictions and were not offering a political challenge, have often missed seeing how genuinely radical Justin's stand actually was—as Rusticus, clearly, did not. Justin himself had argued that the state's policy of executing Christians was based upon a mistake. Christians were, in reality, the best of citizens, who willingly obeyed the laws and paid their full taxes.[62] This much was true; yet Justin also knew that Christians, himself included, refused to do the one thing that the magistrates actually *did* command them to do—to make token sacrifices to the gods or to the emperor's *genius.*

For Rusticus, Justin's refusal to perform such a routine token of loyalty belied the claims of these Christians to good citizenship. For most Romans, political and social obligations *were* religious obligations—the center of all that they held sacred. Only the Jews, of all the nations under Roman rule, had won the right to separate their political obligations from religious ones, to obey Roman law as subjects of the emperor but to worship their own God. The Roman historian Tacitus, a member of the senatorial aristocracy, wrote in his *Histories:* "Among the Jews, all things are profane that we hold sacred; on the other hand, they regard as permissible what seems to us immoral. . . . Proselytes to Jewry adopt the same practices, and the very first lesson they learn is to despise the gods, and shed all feelings of patriotism."[63] The Romans considered the Jews "atheists"—people who refused to worship the gods—but they were, so to speak, *licensed* atheists. Even Tacitus admitted that "whatever their origin, [the Jews'] observances are sanctioned by their antiquity,"[64] and the Romans respected tradition.

Christians, however, had no such excuse. Having broken with their fellow Jews to follow what Tacitus called a new and "deadly superstition,"[65] and having refused worship to the pagan gods, they set out, in effect, to secularize—and so radically to diminish—the power of social and political obligations. Thirty years after Justin and his companions were beaten and beheaded, the rebellious North African convert Tertullian, who had chosen baptism after he saw Christians die in the arena, boasted to his Roman rulers that executions only accelerated Christian conversion: "The more we are mown down by you, the more we multiply: the blood of Christians is seed!"[66]

Certain Christians, like followers of the Cynic philosopher Diogenes, dared denounce all the values of their society—all its political and religious "currency"—as counterfeit. They attacked the pretensions of the emperors as demonic lies and sought to expose their bronze and gilded images as a set of empty masks, or, worse, as masks for the human lust for power, inspired by evil spirits.

Cynical pagans might actually have agreed; the bolder among them dared even to say so, at least in private. Yet only a handful of proud philosophers and senators were willing to risk their lives to defy imperial power. But the boldest Christians not only defied pagan society to the death but also set out to create in its place a new social order—what Tertullian called "the Christian society"—based upon a new religious ideology and a new vision of human nature. The emperors rule by force and violence; but among the Christians, Tertullian said, "everything is voluntary." Instead of extracting taxes to pay for the emperors' luxuries, building projects, and wars, Christians voluntarily contributed

> to support the destitute, and to pay for their burial expenses; to supply the needs of boys and girls lacking money and power, and of old people confined to the home. . . . we do not hesitate to share our earthly goods with one another.[67]

People in need, especially old people, abandoned children, and widows, welcomed Christian generosity and flocked to the movement, where, Tertullian boasted, "we hold everything in common but our spouses," exactly reversing the practice in outside society, where, he said sardonically, most people voluntarily share nothing else![68]

As the religious basis of this new society, Christians were to look to one another and to themselves—not to pagan images, and certainly not to the imperial cult—to find "God manifest on earth." Clement, a neo-Platonist, urged Christians to turn away from "statues sculpted in human form . . . mere copies of bodies,"[69] to look within, to find there, within the moral consciousness of the human mind, an invisible image of the one invisible God. Since God created everyone "in his image," Clement added,

> both slave and free must equally philosophize, whether male or female in sex . . . for the individual whose life is framed as ours is may philosophize without education, whether barbarian, Greek, slave, whether an old man, or a boy, or a woman. For moral self-restraint is common to all human beings who have chosen it. And we admit that the same nature exists in every race, and the same virtue.[70]

Marcus Aurelius himself, a Stoic philosopher, might have agreed with this statement, at least in principle. But discussing such well-worn philosophic questions as universal human brotherhood in conversation with one's peers at the baths or at the dinner table was one thing. To allow people who openly despised the gods and flouted imperial authority to preach such things in public was something else. For public consumption, Marcus Aurelius no doubt preferred the official propaganda concerning imperial power to any form of moral egalitarianism, whether Stoic or Christian. For the Christian message could prove powerfully explosive in a society that ranked each person within a social hierarchy according to class, family, wealth, education, sex, and status—above all, the status that distinguished free persons from slaves. Within the capital city of Rome, three quarters of the population either were slaves—persons legally classified as property—or were descended from slaves. Besides being subjected to their owners' abuses, fits of violence, and sexual desires, slaves were denied such elementary rights as legitimate marriage, let alone legal recourse for their grievances. Clement attacked the widespread Roman custom of exposing abandoned infants on garbage dumps, or raising them for sale: "I pity the children owned by slave dealers, who are dressed up for shame,"[71] says Clement, and trained in sexual specialties, to be sold to gratify their owner's sexual tastes. Justin, in his *Defense of the Christians,* complained that "not only the females, but also the males" were commonly raised "like herds of oxen, goats, or sheep," as a profitable crop of child prostitutes. "And you," Justin accused the emperors, "receive profit from these, and duty and taxes from those whom you ought to exterminate from your realm!"[72] Many Christians were themselves slave owners and took slavery for granted as unthinkingly as their pagan neighbors. But others went among the hovels of the poor and into slave quarters, offering help and money and preaching to the poor, the illiterate, slaves, women, and foreigners—the good news that class, education, sex, and status made no difference, that every human being is essentially equal to any other "before God," including the emperor himself, for all humankind was created in the image of the one God.

The great majority of Christians of the first few centuries did not advocate—and probably did not imagine—that such moral equality could be implemented in society. Most assumed, no doubt, that they could realize such moral equality only in the coming Kingdom of God. Yet even such limited claims to moral equality aroused anger among educated and thoughtful pagans, as the African Christian Minucius Felix, writing a dialogue between pagans and Christians, articulates through his pagan character:

> "Everyone must be outraged—or, rather grieved—that certain people, uneducated, illiterate, and ignorant, dare to claim certainty concerning nature itself, and the divine being."[73]

But Minucius's Christian character challenged "my [pagan] brother, who expressed rage, grief, and indignation that illiterate, poor, and unskilled people" dared discuss subjects that baffled their betters:

> "Let him know that all people are begotten alike, with a capacity and ability for reasoning and emotion, without preference to age, sex, or social status. Nor do they gain wisdom by fortune, but have it implanted in them by nature . . . for intelligence is not given to wealth, nor is it acquired by study but is begotten with the very formation of the mind."[74]

Clement, too, scolded those "who have not recognized the autonomy of the human soul, which cannot be treated as a slave." And though he knew that such words might incite rebellion, he encouraged such behavior: "We [Christians] know that children, women, and slaves have often, against their fathers' or masters' or husbands' will, reached the highest pitch of excellence."[75] What Clement meant by that "highest pitch of excellence" was doing what Perpetua had done—rejecting allegiance to one's family, nation, and to the gods, in order to declare one's allegiance to God alone, anticipating the "glory" of public execution as a martyr. Minucius Felix, answering pagans who charged that Christians refused to offer sacrifices out of foolish and superstitious fear, declares that "our refusal is not an admission of fear, but an assertion of our true *liberty*!"[76]

Such defiant Christians as Justin and Perpetua understood liberty very differently than did their Roman masters. Marcus Aurelius and Rusticus, standing at the apex of Roman society, proudly claimed to rule in a way that "honors above everything else the liberty of the subject." To Marcus and his friends "liberty" meant living under the rule of a "good emperor"—that is, an emperor whom the Senate, consisting of wealthy and powerful men, approved. From his own point of view, Marcus and his colleagues admirably provided for such liberty; and men who have identified with their reign, from Plutarch through Gibbon, have agreed. In Gibbon's words:

> If a man were called to fix the period in the history of the world during which the condition of the human race was most happy and prosperous, he could, without hesitation, name that which elapsed from the death of Domitian to the accession of Commodus (i.e., the reigns of the emperors Nerva, Trajan, Hadrian, Antoninus Pius, and Marcus Aurelius). *The vast extent of the Roman Empire was governed by absolute power,* under the guidance of virtue and wisdom. *The forms of the civil administration were carefully preserved by Nerva, Trajan, Hadrian, and the Antonines, who delighted in the image of liberty* . . . the labors of these monarchs were overpaid by the immense reward that inseparably waited on their success; by the honest pride of virtue, and by the exquisite delight of beholding the general happiness of which they were the authors.[77]

Yet there were many—often at the opposite end of the social and political scale—who dissented. As the classicist Mason Hammond points out, it was under the reign of these "good emperors," famous for their caution and humanity, that the policy of persecuting Christians first became widespread.[78] Simultaneously the Roman provinces were racked with the revolt of the Jews under Trajan and Hadrian, and revolts of the Egyptians under Antoninus Pius and

Marcus Aurelius.[79] How many of those suffering the pressures of imperial power, the historian Naphtali Lewis asks, "would have recognized Gibbon's words as a description of the world in which they lived?"[80]

G. de Ste. Croix, in his massive Marxist history of social class in ancient times, indicts Christians for failing to criticize the dominant ideology of the Roman Empire. The Christians failed, he argues, because their ideas were molded by "irresistible social pressures"[81] (which he does not enumerate) and because of what he calls their "complete indifference, as Christians, to the institutions of the world in which they lived."[82] Yet Christian apologists certainly *did* attack not only the pagan gods and the imperial cult,[83] as we have seen, but also the traditional construction of the origins of the Roman Empire. They offered in its place a damning and, in effect, "demythologizing" view of Roman history. Tertullian, for example, challenges "the groundless assertion of those who maintain that, as a reward for their unique devotion to religion, the Romans have been raised to such heights of power as to become masters of the world."[84] Is "the progress of the empire," then, as Roman patriotic myth contends, "the reward the gods have paid to the Romans for their devotion"? On the contrary, says Tertullian, "if I am not mistaken, kingdoms and empires are acquired by wars, and expanded by victories. Moreover, you cannot have wars and victories without taking—and often destroying—cities."[85] In their wars of conquest, he continues, the Romans have destroyed and despoiled temples indiscriminately with houses and palaces. The Romans succeeded, he concludes, by subordinating their purported piety to their obsession for conquest.

Minucius Felix, too, challenged those who said the Romans "deserved their power" because of their consummate piety; he argued instead that the empire originated from a defensive pact formed by criminals and murderers: "Did not [the Romans] in their origin, when gathered together and fortified by crime, grow by the terror of their own ferocity?" First they started wars, drove their neighbors from their lands, and destroyed nearby cities through military force. Capturing, raping, and enslaving their victims, they increased their power: "The Romans were not so great because they were religious, but because they were sacrilegious with impunity."[86]

It was from this perspective on imperial power that Christians took their very different view of liberty from that of their Roman masters. They sided with a tradition of dissident philosophers who mocked the senatorial aristocracy's version of liberty as being, in effect, slavery. True liberty, such dissidents argued, involves freedom of speech—that is, the freedom to stand up to unjust rulers.[87] Conservative senators, of course, regarded this philosophic version of liberty as mere license—an invitation to anarchy. So long as they remained a persecuted, illegal minority, Christians insisted that only Christian baptism—certainly not the Roman government—conveyed liberty. For baptism liberated the convert simultaneously from sin, from enslavement to the pagan gods, and from the power of their human agents, who could only execute—and thus set free—Christian martyrs. Minucius Felix drew a rhetorical and vivid picture of a Christian who underwent torture for his faith, but maintained his liberty:

> "How beautiful is the spectacle to God when a Christian does battle with pain, when he is drawn up against threats, and punishment, and torture; when, mocking the noise of death, he treads underfoot the horror of the executioner; when *he raises up his liberty against kings and princes,* and yields to God alone . . . when, triumphant and victorious, he tramples upon the very man who has passed sentence upon him!"[88]

Out of such agony as Perpetua, Justin, and others endured, and that of Jewish martyrs before them,[89] was eventually born a new vision of the basis of social and political order—an order no longer founded upon the divine claims of the ruler or the state, but upon qualities that Christians believed were inherent within every man, and, some dared insist, within every woman as well, through our common creation "in God's image." The Christians of Justin's time, as we have seen, would not have imagined their vision as the basis for a political agenda. Yet sixteen hundred years later, in a totally different social and political context, American revolutionaries would invoke the same creation story against the British king's claim to divine right, declaring:

> We hold these truths to be self-evident; that all men are created equal, that they are endowed by their Creator with certain unalienable Rights . . .

In Justin's world—and some might argue even in our own—such alleged "truths" were anything but self-evident. Aristotle had deduced from observation what seemed to him far more obvious: that human beings are essentially unequal, some born to rule, and others to be slaves. But the Christian movement popularized the Hebrew creation story that implicitly asserted the intrinsic value of every human being; and throughout the Roman Empire, despite the Christians' criminal status and the consequent dangers that threatened them, the movement flourished. Tertullian even made the unprecedented claim that every human being has a right to religious liberty:

> It should be considered absurd for one person to compel another to honor the gods, when he should voluntarily, and in the awareness of his own need, seek their favor *in the liberty which is his right.* [90]

In centuries to come, others would infuse into the creation story even bolder moral visions and insist, for example, that human creation "in the image of God" not only conveys "unalienable rights" but also extends to people of every race, to slaves, to women, and, some would argue, to defective infants, or even to the unborn.

The legacy of such convictions would remain, for centuries and even millennia to come, an untried dream. When Perpetua and Justin, along with their Christian contemporaries, acted out their vision of liberty by refusing to sacrifice to the gods and the emperors, they marked themselves as targets for arrest, torture, and execution. So long as Christians remained members of a suspect society, subject to death, the boldest among them maintained that, since demons controlled the government and inspired its agents, the believer could gain freedom at their hands only in death.

# (III)

# GNOSTIC
# IMPROVISATIONS
# ON GENESIS

A S CHRISTIANITY SPREAD throughout the empire and took root, its leaders began to develop various strategies of community organization. They developed, too, ways of discriminating between those they accepted as orthodox ("straight-thinking") Christians and those they rejected as deviants, including, among the latter, many known as "gnostic" Christians.[1] Since to profess Christianity was still suspect and potentially dangerous throughout the Roman Empire, many Christian churches owed their coherence and their survival to the astuteness and courage of their leaders, the bishops. When Ignatius, bishop of Antioch in Syria, was arrested (c. 110 C.E.) and sent by ship to Rome for trial and execution, chained, as he said, to "ten leopards, I mean a band of soldiers,"[2] he spent his final journey writing letters to the churches surrounding his home church in Antioch and to the Christians in Rome, his final destination. Ignatius urged these and all other Christians to stand together under persecution and to maintain unanimous loyalty to the clergy, which he envisioned as a threefold hierarchy of bishop, priests, and deacons who ruled each church "in God's place,"[3] and who maintained communication among Christians scattered throughout the world.[4]

Such crises as a bishop's arrest and execution emphasized how much the threatened Christian groups needed strong leaders; Ignatius knew that he was appealing to a still emerging and fragile institutional system. What concerned Ignatius especially was that this system had not yet won the allegiance of all who counted themselves among the believers. Nor was there as yet, among Christian groups scattered throughout the Roman world, a single central organization. Christians in different provinces—and even in neighboring communities—demonstrated great diversity, from the wandering ascetics of Asia Minor[5] to the settled "house churches" that were becoming established in Asian and Greek cities.[6] Converts from Judaism, for example, whether they lived in Judea or Greece, Asia or Egypt, tended to borrow the structure of the synagogues, where a leader presided over a group of "elders," or in the Greek, *presbyteroi,* later translated as "priests." Other converts, originally Gentiles, developed a different administrative system adapted from large households, consisting of a group of servants, called in Greek *diakones,* which became the English term "deacons," headed by an "overseer," called in Greek *episcopos,* our word for "bishop." Within the next three centuries these bishops came to assume responsibility for specific areas, or dioceses, a pattern modeled on the organization of the Roman army.

But persecution, which, however intense, remained sporadic, was not the only reason that the majority of Christians came to accept an increasingly institutionalized structure to oversee each group internally and instruct and discipline its members. By the second century many Christians wanted to incorporate Jesus' moral fervor into everyday life by turning his Sermon on the Mount into a set of rules, an ethical system that set Christians apart from their pagan environment, and sometimes placed them in direct opposition to it; this ethical imperative became still another reason for the increasingly institutionalized church.

What distinguished Christians from everyone else, according to both pagan and Christian contemporaries, was their moral rigor, which impressed even pagans hostile to the movement. The famous Galen, for example, personal physician to the emperor Marcus Aurelius and the imperial family, admired Christian courage and "abstinence from the use of the sexual organs."[7] When the Christian philosopher Justin wrote to the same emperors to defend his fellow Christians, he boasted that they were people who had completely changed their attitudes and behavior in matters of sex, money, and racial relations:

> We, who used to take pleasure in immorality, now embrace chastity alone; we, who valued above everything else the acquisition

of wealth and possessions, now bring what we have into common ownership, and share with those in need; we, who hated and destroyed one another, refusing to live with those of a different race, now live intimately with them.[8]

The practices Justin praised—sexual self-restraint, sharing one's goods with the destitute, and living with people of all races—appealed especially, as we have seen, to those people most vulnerable to sexual abuse, financial exploitation, poverty, and racial hatred— that is, to freedmen, noncitizens, and slaves, to the despised and rejected within the Roman world. Despite the suspicion of certain Roman officials toward Christians, the movement, strengthened by its developing institutional structures, grew.

But as the churches became more institutionalized, some Christians resisted that process. For while certain bishops, including, for example, Irenaeus of Lyons, attempted to formulate community morals and to enforce discipline by teaching, penalizing, or expelling those who, for whatever reason, dissented, some, no doubt, resented these intrusions upon their behavior. Others, although they accepted the ethical basis of Christian teaching, regarded conformity, whether in doctrine or discipline, as something that only beginners needed to take seriously. Some ardent Christians wanted to recover the sense of spiritual transformation that they found in Jesus' message. For these Christians conversion meant more than accepting baptism and following a new set of moral rules derived from Jesus' teaching. Becoming a Christian meant discovering one's spiritual nature— discovering, as one teacher put it,

> who we are, and what we have become; where we were . . . whither we are hastening; from what we are being released; what birth is, and what is rebirth.[9]

Many Christians striving for a higher level of spiritual consciousness had no quarrel with what the bishops taught; they agreed that moral guidance concerning good works and sexual restraint was not only welcome but essential, for most people. But some Christians objected to being told what to think and how to behave. Although they agreed that the first step toward becoming a Christian was to accept the faith and receive baptism from the bishop, these Christians wanted to go further. They yearned to become spiritually "mature,"[10] to go beyond such elementary instruction toward higher levels of understanding. And this higher awareness they called *gnosis,* which means "knowledge," or "insight."[11] To achieve gnosis, these Christians said, they no longer needed the bishop or the clergy.

When Irenaeus, bishop at Lyons (c. 180 C.E.), discovered among his own congregation a large group of such Christians who sought to exempt themselves from his authority and set out to know God directly through gnosis, or immediate experience, he recognized—and even grudgingly respected—their spiritual purpose.[12] As bishop, however, he soon came into conflict with their determination to follow Christ in their own way. He decided that they were divisive and arrogant upstarts who threatened to undermine church unity and discipline, for they "disturb the faith of many by alluring them under a pretense of superior knowledge."[13] Above all, as we shall see, Irenaeus was concerned that gnostic teaching threatened the message of freedom that he and many others considered central to the gospel. Irenaeus read some of the writings of these gnostic Christians and engaged in conversation with several of them. He then composed a five-volume polemic against them, which he called "The Refutation and Overthrow of Falsely So-Called Knowledge (*Gnosis*)." The term "gnostics," now often used descriptively for such dissident spiritual seekers, may have been their own term, or it may have originated as a derisive name for those Christians whom Irenaeus regarded as self-appointed "know-it-alls."[14]

These so-called gnostics, then, did not share a single ideology or belong to a specific group; not all, in fact, were Christians. Those who did identify themselves as Christians included a wide variety of people who chose to follow their faith in their own way. Many gnostic Christians were members of Christian congregations, including both lay people and members of the clergy, who wanted no more than to supplement the teaching and worship common to all Christians with deeper insights derived from their own spiritual experience. Many gnostics also followed certain spiritual teachers who promised to initiate them into deeper mysteries of the faith.

Irenaeus directed his polemic primarily at the group of gnostic Christians whom members of his own congregation found most attractive and powerful—a group the bishop considered especially dangerous and divisive. These were followers of a spiritual master called Valentinus, who some forty years before Irenaeus wrote, and while Justin was still teaching in Rome, had joined the Christian group there as a newcomer (c. 140–160 C.E.). Before coming to Rome, Valentinus had already established himself among Christians of the Egyptian city of Alexandria as a poet, visionary, and spiritual teacher; and in Rome, where his abilities were widely recognized, he was considered a likely candidate for bishop. Even Tertullian, who would bitterly denounce Valentinus's followers a generation later, admitted that their teacher had been "a capable man, both in intelligence and eloquence."[15]

Valentinus urged Christians to go beyond the elementary steps of faith, baptism, and moral reform to spiritual illumination. His followers claimed, moreover, to have received from him access to secret teachings of Paul, the "deeper mysteries" that Paul reserved from his public teaching and taught only to a few chosen disciples in secret.[16] Other gnostics claimed to know the secret teaching of Jesus himself—teaching only hinted at, they said, in the New Testament gospels but revealed more fully in such secret writings as the *Gospel of Thomas,* the *Gospel of Mary Magdalene,* and the *Dialogue of the Savior.*[17]

Such writings, suppressed and lost for nearly sixteen hundred years, remained, until recently, virtually unknown. But in December of 1945, two years before the Dead Sea Scrolls were discovered in desert caves in Israel, copies of these very writings and many others were discovered unexpectedly in the Egyptian desert near the town of Nag Hammadi in Upper Egypt. This extraordinary find disclosed, in fact, more than fifty texts that date back to the first centuries of the Christian Era, including a collection of early Christian "gospels" and other writings attributed to Jesus and his disciples. While the original language of these texts was Greek (the language of the New Testament), the copies discovered in Egypt had been translated from Greek into Coptic, the common language of Egypt in the third and fourth centuries. Whether these writings—or which of them—contain authentic teaching of Jesus and his disciples we do not know, any more than we know with certainty which sayings or teachings in the New Testament are authentic. What the discovery certainly *does* offer, however, is extraordinary insights into the early Christian movement. For the first time, we can read firsthand works later condemned and destroyed by the bishops as heretical. Now for the first time the "heretics" can speak to us in their own words. For church leaders of the second century, including Ignatius, Justin, Irenaeus, Tertullian, and Clement, had attacked the gnostic Christians, condemned their teachings, and attempted to drive them out of the churches.

A century and a half later, when the emperor Constantine abruptly changed Roman policy from one of persecuting Christians to protecting and favoring them with massive gifts of money, tax exemptions, and enormous prestige, the bishops, now in political favor, sometimes used these new resources to promote unanimity; thus in 381, the Christian emperor Theodosius made "heresy" a crime against the state.

The texts discovered in a jar near Nag Hammadi show us more clearly than we had ever known that some of these so-called gnostic Christians sought divine illumination through a process of spiritual self-discovery.[18] The Christian bishops who called themselves orthodox might no doubt claim that they, too, sought spiritual illumination; but their methods differed considerably. Justin the philosopher followed a common Christian tradition when he called the ritual of baptism itself "illumination" and explained that "since at our birth we were born without our knowledge or choice, by our parents' union, and were raised with bad habits and false education," so converts had been born first as "children of necessity and ignorance." But Christians, through baptism, were born again as "children of choice and knowledge."[19] Justin sought to increase his own understanding of the faith—and that of his students—through moral action and philosophic discourse. Followers of Valentinus, on the other hand, tended to regard baptism as only the elementary initiation ritual, and one that, for many people, lacked real spiritual content.[20] Instead of following a philosophic path, like Justin, Valentinus looked within himself to dreams and visions to deepen his gnosis. He traced his own spiritual process, in fact, to a vision in which a newborn infant appeared to him and said, "I am the Logos."[21] Like Justin, Valentinus sought spiritual illumination in the Scriptures; but where Justin wrestled with their moral, philosophical, and historical dimensions, Valentinus claimed to explicate their "deeper meaning" through secret traditions known only to initiates like himself.[22] My first two books, written before *The Gnostic Gospels*, attempt to show how Valentinian Christians interpreted the New Testament Gospel of John and the letters of Paul.[23]

When gnostic and orthodox Christians disagreed, each reached back to the Scriptures that they revered in common, and each claimed the Scriptures' support. But gnostic and orthodox Christians read the same Scriptures in radically different ways; to borrow the words of the nineteenth-century poet William Blake, "Both read the Bible day and night; but you read black where I read white!"

The majority of orthodox Christians in the first and second centuries, like most Jews and Christians ever since, read the Scriptures as Justin did, primarily as practical guides to moral living. They read the Genesis story, in particular, as *history with a moral:* that is, they regarded Adam and Eve as actual historical persons, the venerable ancestors of our race; and from the story of their disobedience, orthodox interpreters drew practical lessons in moral behavior. Tertullian, for example, took Genesis 3 as an opportunity to warn his "sisters in Christ" that even the best of them were, in effect, Eve's co-conspirators:

> You are the devil's gateway. . . . you are she who persuaded him whom the devil did not dare attack. . . . *Do you not know that every one of you is an Eve? The sentence of God on your sex lives on in this age; the guilt, of necessity, lives on too.* [24]

In other contexts, Tertullian can derive from the story different moral lessons: for example, to warn against gluttony, because "eating led to Adam's fall,"[25] or to urge believers to marry only once, since God made for Adam "only one wife."[26] Orthodox Christians who disagree with one another over the interpretation of Genesis disagree primarily on the question of *which* moral to draw from it: for example, where Clement sees God's blessing on marriage and procreation in Paradise,[27] the fourth-century Christian ascetic Jerome will insist, as we shall see, that Adam and Eve were originally meant to be virgins, and were joined in marriage only after they sinned and were expelled in disgrace "from the Paradise of virginity."[28]

Gnostic Christians, on the other hand, castigated the orthodox for making the mistake of reading the Scriptures—and especially Genesis—literally, and thereby missing its "deeper meaning." Read literally, they said, the story of creation made no sense. Are we to believe that Adam and Eve actually heard God's footsteps rustling in the garden of Eden, as the text suggests, when it says that Adam and Eve hid themselves, for "they heard the sound of the Lord God walking in the garden in the cool of the day" (Genesis 3:8)? Or did God lie when he warned Adam and Eve, "You shall not eat of the fruit of the tree of the knowledge of good and evil, for on the day you eat of it you shall surely die" (Genesis 2:17), though they went on to live for hundreds of years? To whom was God speaking when he said, "Let *us* make man in *our* image" (Genesis 1:26)? And why did God try to keep from Adam and Eve the knowledge that he admits could make them "like one of us" (Genesis 3:22)?

Certain gnostic Christians suggested that such absurdities show that the story was never meant to be taken literally but should be understood as spiritual allegory—not so much *history with a moral* as *myth with meaning.* These gnostics took each line of the Scriptures as an enigma, a riddle pointing to deeper meaning. Read this way, the text became a shimmering surface of symbols, inviting the spiritually adventurous to explore its hidden depths, to draw upon their own inner experience—what artists call the creative imagination—to interpret the story. Irenaeus describes various gnostic interpretations of the creation story and then complains that "while they claim such things as these concerning the creation, every one of them generates something new every day, according to his ability; for, among them, no one is considered mature [or "initiated"] who does not develop some enormous fictions."[29] Consequently, gnostic Christians neither sought nor found any consensus concerning what the story meant but regarded Genesis 1–3 rather like a fugal melody upon which they continually improvised new variations, all of which, Bishop Irenaeus said, were "full of blasphemy."[30]

Gnostic Christians did not invent this technique of allegorical interpretation; on the contrary, pagan and Jewish teachers had used such methods for many generations to interpret venerated but puzzlingly archaic texts. Certain Stoic philosophers, for example, had suggested that the Homeric poems, the *Iliad* and the *Odyssey,* which formed the basis of Greek education, should not be read simply *literally* as accounts of ancient battles or of the gods' conflicts and amours. Such allegorists claimed that whoever looked beyond their obvious meaning and read them symbolically could find hidden in them the deeper truths of natural philosophy. Certain Jewish teachers, too, prominently including Jesus' contemporary the wealthy and educated Philo of Alexandria, applied allegorical exegesis to the Scriptures to discover the deeper meaning that they believed lay "beneath the surface."

Philo interprets the Genesis creation accounts in various ways. Sometimes he reads it as history with a moral, and he warns people against disobeying God, and warns men, in particular, against women, whose creation from Adam's side ended the first man's lofty and solitary communion with God and was, for Philo, "the beginning of all evils." But Philo also can interpret the story allegorically, as myth with meaning—that is, as a story containing profound truths hidden in symbols. In his ingenious *Allegorical Interpretation,* Philo takes Adam and Eve as representing two elements within human nature: he says that Adam represents the *mind* (*nous*), the nobler, masculine, and rational element, which is "made in God's image";[31] and Eve represents the body or *sensation (aisthesis)*, the lower, feminine element, source of all passion.[32] (The scholar Richard Baer shows, too, that Philo's view of men and women follows a similar—and predictable—pattern.[33])

Gnostic interpreters, equally fascinated with the story of Adam and Eve, found in the Garden of Eden a wild flowering of interpretations. Yet many of these gnostic interpretations, however diverse they appear, share a common—and entirely *unorthodox*—premise. For orthodox interpreters, both Jewish and Christian, tend to emphasize the distinction between the infinite God and his finite creatures —a distinction expressed, for example, by the twentieth-century Jewish theologian Martin Buber's description of God as "wholly other," which means, above all, other than human. Even the mystics of Jewish and Christian tradition who seek to find their identity in God often are careful to acknowledge the abyss that separates them from their divine Source. When the Dominican monk Meister Eckhart (c. 1260–1328 C.E.), for example, failed to do so and preached instead that "our whole perfection and blessing depends upon our stepping across the estate of creaturehood, and on getting at last to the Cause that has no cause"[34]—that is, attaining "God [who] lies hidden in the soul's core"[35]—his boldness so outraged the archbishop of Cologne that he succeeded in obtaining a papal bull condemning Eckhart's writings as heresy. And when the Jewish theologian Martin Buber sought to explore the sources of religious experience, he characterized the Jewish devotee's relationship to God as "I *and* Thou"; but no orthodox Jew, any more than an orthodox Christian, could say, with the Hindu devotee, "I *am* Thou."[36]

But gnostic interpreters share with the Hindu and with Eckhart that very conviction—that the divine being is hidden deep within human nature, as well as outside it, and, although often unperceived, is a spiritual potential latent in the human psyche. According to Ptolemy, a follower of Valentinus, the story of Adam and Eve shows that humanity "fell" into ordinary consciousness and lost contact with its divine origin.[37] Another follower of Valentinus, the author of the *Gospel of Philip,* says that human beings fell into the error of projecting divinity onto beings external to themselves, and so created religion:

> In the beginning, God created humanity. But now humanity creates God. This is the way it is in the world—human beings

invent gods and worship their creation. It would be more fitting for the gods to worship human beings![38]

Some gnostics adopted a pattern of interpretation similar to Philo's but changed the content. Instead of characterizing human psychodynamics, as Philo had, in terms of an interaction between *mind* and *sensation,* gnostics pictured it in terms of the interaction of *soul* and *spirit*—that is, between the *psyche* (ordinary consciousness, understood to include both mind and sensation) and the *spirit,* the potential for a higher, spiritual consciousness. Many gnostics read the story of Adam and Eve, consequently, as an account of what takes place within a person who is engaged in the process of spiritual self-discovery. The gnostic text called *Interpretation of the Soul,* for example, tells how the soul, represented as Eve, became alienated from her spiritual nature, and so long as she denied that spiritual nature and distanced herself from it, she fell into self-destruction and suffering. But when she became willing to be reconciled and reunited with her spiritual nature, she once again became whole; the gnostic author explains that this process of spiritual self-integration is the hidden meaning of the marriage of Adam and Eve: "This marriage has brought them back together again, and the soul has been joined to her true love, her real master,"[39] that is, to her spiritual self. Many other gnostic texts reverse the symbolism; the majority of the known gnostic texts depict Adam (not Eve) as representing the psyche, while Eve represents the higher principle, the spiritual self. Gnostic authors loved to tell, with many variations, the story of Eve, that elusive spiritual intelligence: how she first emerged within Adam and awakened him, the soul, to awareness of its spiritual nature; how she encountered resistance, was misunderstood, attacked, and mistaken for what she was not; and how she finally joined with Adam "in marriage," so to speak, and so came to live in harmonious union with the soul.[40] According to the gnostic text called *Reality of the Rulers,* when Adam first recognized Eve, he saw in her not a mere marital partner but a spiritual power:

> And when he saw her, he said, "It is you who have given me life: you shall be called Mother of the Living [Eve]; for it is she who is my Mother. It is she who is the Physician, and the Woman, and She Who Has Given Birth."[41]

The *Reality of the Rulers* went so far as to say that when Adam was warned by the creator to disregard her voice, he lost contact with the spirit, until she reappeared to him in the form of the serpent:

Then the Female Spiritual Principle came [in] the Snake, the Instructor; and it taught [them], saying, "What did he [say to] you [pl.]? Was it, 'From every tree in the Garden shall you [sing.] eat; yet—from [the tree] of recognizing evil and good do not eat'?"

The carnal Woman said, "Not only did he say 'Do not eat,' but even 'Do not touch it; for the day you [pl.] eat from it, with death you [pl.] are going to die.' "

And the Snake, the Instructor, said, "With death you [pl.] shall not die; for it was out of jealousy that he said this to you [pl.]. Rather your [pl.] eyes shall open and you [pl.] shall come to be like gods, recognizing evil and good." And the Female Instructing Principle was taken away from the Snake, and she left it behind merely a thing of the earth.[42]

An extraordinary gnostic poem called *Thunder: Perfect Mind* depicts the spirit, manifested variously as Wisdom and as Eve, speaking as follows:

> I am the first and the last.
> I am the honored one and the scorned one.
> I am the whore and the holy one.
> I am the wife and the virgin.
> I am the bride and the bridegroom,
>     and it is my husband who begot me.
> I am knowledge and ignorance. . . .
> I am foolish and I am wise. . . .
> I am the one whom they call life [Eve]
>     and you have called Death. . . . [43]

The *Secret Book of John* suggests that Adam's experience as he awakened to Eve's presence prefigures that of the gnostic who, sunk into a state of oblivion, suddenly awakens to the presence of the spirit hidden deep within. The *Secret Book* concludes as Eve, the "perfect primal intelligence," calls out to Adam—to the psyche (and so, in effect, to you and me, the readers)—to wake up, recognize her, and so receive spiritual illumination:

> I entered into the midst of their prison, which is the prison of the body. And I said, "Whoever hears, let him arise from the deep sleep." And he wept and shed bitter tears. Bitter tears he wiped from himself, and he said, "Who is it who calls my name, and whence has this hope come to me while I am in the chains of this prison?" And I said, "I am the intelligence [*pronoia*] of the pure

life; I am the thinking of the virginal spirit. . . . Arise and remember . . . and follow your root, which is I . . . and beware of the deep sleep."[44]

Gnostic Christians who projected such "bizarre inventions" onto Genesis ignored matters of practical morality—or so Bishop Irenaeus charged, and at first glance one must agree. For while their contemporary Christians were drawing moral injunctions from Genesis, certain gnostic Christians seemed to be merely improvising myths on the story of Paradise. Some gnostics dared go further: instead of blaming the human desire for knowledge as the root of all sin, they did the opposite and sought redemption through gnosis. And whereas the orthodox often blamed Eve for the fall and pointed to women's submission as appropriate punishment, gnostics often depicted Eve—or the feminine spiritual power she represented—as the source of spiritual awakening.[45]

Yet many gnostic Christians struggled with the same urgent ethical questions that preoccupied their orthodox contemporaries: Should Christians avoid marriage or embrace it? Are Christians, like Jews, commanded to "be fruitful and multiply"? What kind of relationship is possible, or desirable, between Christian men and women?

When gnostic Christians asked themselves these questions, however, they often approached them differently than did their orthodox contemporaries. Instead of formulating a set of community rules, some gnostic Christians sought instead to discover and articulate—precisely through the "bizarre inventions" of gnostic myth—the internal sources of desire and action. What fascinated them was psychodynamics, or, as they might have put it, pneumato-psychodynamics: the interaction between the *pneuma,* the spiritual element of our nature, and the *psyche,* that is, the emotional and mental impulses. The Valentinian author of the *Gospel of Philip,* speaking in mythic language, said, for example, that death began when "the woman separated . . . from the man"[46]—that is, when Eve (the spirit) became separated from Adam (the psyche). Only when one's psyche, or ordinary consciousness, becomes integrated with one's spiritual nature—when Adam, reunited with Eve, "becomes complete again"[47]—can one achieve internal harmony and wholeness. According to this Valentinian author, only the person who has "remarried" the psyche with the spirit becomes capable of withstanding physical and emotional impulses that, unchecked, could drive him or her toward self-destruction and evil. Irenaeus was wrong, then, to suggest that gnostic Christians ignored moral issues. But they sometimes engaged them in a way that encouraged each person to explore his or her own internal experience, believing that each one could discover the spirit within. Commenting on their method, Irenaeus said sarcastically that "they imagine that, by means of their obscure interpretations, each of them has discovered a god of his own!"[48] But what especially bothered Irenaeus was that gnostic Christians engaged moral issues in ways that made them seem indifferent—or worse, insubordinate—to the community ethics that the bishops sought to impose upon all believers alike.

Meanwhile certain radical gnostics, far from criticizing the bishops for being too severe, criticized them instead for being too lenient. One such gnostic Christian, the author of the *Testimony of Truth*, sided with the ascetics and railed against both orthodox and gnostics alike who endorsed marriage and procreation and who worshiped the God who had created such impurities. This radical teacher dared to tell the story of Paradise from the serpent's point of view, and depicted the serpent as a teacher of divine wisdom who desperately tried to get Adam and Eve to open their eyes to their creator's true—and despicable—nature:

> For the serpent was *wiser* than any of the animals that were in Paradise. . . . But the creator cursed the serpent, and called him devil. And he said, "Behold, Adam has become like one of us, knowing evil and good."[49]

Then he said, "Let us cast him out of Paradise lest he take from the tree of life and live forever" (Genesis 3:22). Who is this God, who calls evil "good" and good "evil"?

> What kind of God is this? First, he envied Adam that he should eat from the tree of knowledge. . . . And secondly he said, "Adam, where are you?" And God does not have foreknowledge, since he did not know this from the beginning. And afterwards, he said, "Let us cast him [out] of this place lest he eat of the tree of life and live forever." Surely he has shown himself to be a malicious envier. And what kind of God is this? Great is the blindness of those who read, and they did not know it.[50]

What church leader would not have bridled at a critic who turned the Genesis account upside down, and who blasted all Christians who married or conducted ordinary business for being ignorant, false, and foolish? The same gnostic author attacked the martyrs themselves as "empty martyrs, who witness only to themselves,"[51] and castigated their leaders as "blind guides,"[52] who were at best immature and at worst liars.

Church leaders like Irenaeus who confronted the followers of Valentinus must have found them almost as maddening as the more radical gnostics, but for different reasons. Valentinian Christians agreed with the bishop that practicing good works and sexual restraint was good for those they called "the many" but claimed these were optional for spiritual Christians like themselves.[53] Irenaeus complained that these gnostic positions were hard to pin down; they were as wildly inconsistent as their interpretations of the Scriptures. Irenaeus admitted that some Valentinians lived exemplary lives as celibates, but others, he said, only pretended piety to cover their secret licentiousness.[54] On the other hand, Clement of Alexandria praised the Valentinians he knew in Egypt because they, unlike most other "heretics," *approved* of marriage.[55]

Where *did* the Valentinian gnostics stand, then, on the questions that divided their Christian contemporaries—whether, for example, Christians should marry or remain celibate? One certainly would have expected to find a clear answer in their writings; for marriage (or, as the *Gospel of Philip* calls it, "the mystery of marriage") figured as a primary theme of their whole theology. Valentinian rituals apparently culminated in the sacrament they called the "bridechamber."[56] Yet astonishingly, in spite of all this, their writings on such practical questions as their attitude toward marriage remain so ambiguous that various scholars have convincingly argued opposite cases. The prominent Dutch scholar Gilles Quispel insists that the Valentinians virtually *required* marriage of gnostic Christians, and that they celebrated marriage—between gnostics, at any rate—as a sacrament, embodying the divine harmonies of masculine and feminine energies in the divine being.[57] The younger American scholar Michael Williams argues, on the contrary, that Valentinian Christians, like medieval Catholic mystics, used sexual imagery only to contrast actual marriage, which they considered to be "polluted," with heavenly marriage to Christ.[58]

The remarkable collection of sayings we know as the *Gospel of Philip* may offer us clues to sort out such contradictions, for its author challenged the way that most people set up moral questions in the first place. Christians then, as now, ordinarily assumed that certain acts are good and others bad; but they furiously debated *which* acts—marriage or celibacy, for example—belong to which category. The gnostic author of the *Gospel of Philip* rejects this whole way of thinking. As this author sees it, no act in itself—and specifically neither celibacy nor marriage—is necessarily good or bad. Instead the moral significance of any act depends upon the situation, intentions, and level of consciousness of the participants. This author characterizes such terms as "good" and "bad," like other pairs of opposites, as merely mental categories that necessarily imply one another:

> Light and darkness, life and death, right and left, are brothers of one another. They are inseparable. Because of this, the "good" are not good, nor the "evil" evil, nor is "life" life, nor is "death" death.[59]

For "the names given to things in the world are very deceptive,"[60] especially when one mistakes the names for reality. The author traces this deception directly back to the Garden of Eden, where Adam and Eve first sought to gain knowledge through such deceptive categories, by partaking of the *"tree of the knowledge of good and evil."* Then the law, based on the same categories, continued the same process of deception:

> The law was the tree. . . . For when [the law] said, "Eat this, do not eat that," it became the beginning of death.[61]

Leaders of the church who confronted such Valentinians among their congregations must have recognized themselves—and their "simpleminded" moralism—as the target of such criticisms; but they were not the only targets, for these gnostic Christians would have been equally critical of the advocates of asceticism. The *Gospel of Philip* suggests that those who say that celibacy is good err as much as those who pronounce marriage good—and those who call either bad err equally. It may be no accident, then, that not one of the extant Valentinian texts unequivocally endorses marriage over celibacy, or the opposite. The author of *Philip* implies instead that what each person should do depends upon each person's intention and level of consciousness. The same author compares the gnostic teacher to a householder who is responsible for the care of children, slaves, cattle, dogs, and pigs:

> [being] a sensible person, he knew what each one should eat. . . . Compare the disciple of God; if he is a sensible man, he understands what discipleship is all about. . . . He will not be

misled by the physical appearance of anyone, but will look at the condition of each one's soul, and so speak to each one.[62]

Yet the author of *Philip* warns that gnostic Christians are not to think of themselves as exempt from sin:

> Those who think that sinning does not apply to them are called "free" by the world. Knowledge of the truth makes such people arrogant. . . . It even gives them a sense of superiority over everyone else.[63]

The author goes on to quote and interpret Paul's letter to the Corinthians, saying,

> "Love builds up" [1 Corinthians 8:1b] . . . in fact, one who is really free through knowledge is a servant for the sake of love to those who have not yet been able to attain to the freedom of *gnosis.*[64]

But how was the gnostic Christian to deal with the actual experience of evil—and, in particular, evil found within himself or herself? Orthodox Christians often attempted to prescribe rules for the whole community, but the author of *Philip* suggests that one can deal with evil only in oneself:

> As for ourselves, *let each one of us dig down after the root of evil which is within one, and let one pluck it out of one's heart from the root. It will be plucked out,* if we recognize it. But if we are ignorant of it, it takes root in us and produces its fruit in our heart; it masters us. . . . it is powerful because we have not recognized it.[65]

The author advises, then, that each person practice self-examination and look for such potential sources of evil as envy, lust, anger, in his or her own intentions, words, and acts. What transforms one spiritually, according to the *Gospel of Philip,* is continual self-awareness and acknowledging the evil within oneself wherever one finds it.[66] This suggests that Valentinian Christians indeed may have rejected the bishops' commands, ignored community regulations, and followed their inner guidance, insisting that moral acts are essentially private matters that every person, or at least every mature person, must deal with independently.

Such independence, as we have seen, threatened church unity and discipline. Bishop Irenaeus charged that Valentinian Christians were concerned only for their own spiritual advantage, indifferent to the church as an institution. He accused them of "having no respect for others" (does he mean for the bishops in particular?) and for "thinking that they are better than any one else."[67]

But what bothered Irenaeus even more than the gnostics' rejection of moral absolutism or their violation of church discipline was that gnostic readings of Genesis threatened the message of freedom that had made Christianity so powerfully compelling to so many converts. This debate over Genesis revealed a major disagreement among second-century Christians, a disagreement whose outcome would shape church doctrine ever after.

As we have seen, the majority of Christian converts of the first four centuries regarded the proclamation of moral freedom, grounded in Genesis 1–3, as effectively synonymous with "the gospel." As Justin interpreted Jesus' message, it celebrated not only Christian freedom from domination by sexual passion, and from such passions as greed and hatred, but also from external domination by the Roman state. Clement of Alexandria praised Christian freedom to choose even death rather than yield to the oppressive weight of Roman social custom. Bishop Methodius, writing years later in Asia Minor, envisioned the whole of human history, ever since Eden, as a progressive evolution of human freedom, which culminates in the greatest freedom of all—the life of voluntary renunciation.[68] Gregory of Nyssa spoke for the whole tradition when he said, "The soul directly reveals its royal and excellent quality in that . . . it is governed and ruled autonomously by its own will."[69]

Most orthodox Christians agreed with many of their Jewish contemporaries that Adam's fatal misuse of this freedom was so momentous that his transgression brought pain, labor, and death into an originally perfect world. Yet Justin, Irenaeus, Tertullian, and Clement also agreed that Adam's transgression did not encroach upon our own individual freedom: even now, they said, every person is free to choose good or evil, just as Adam was.

These same church leaders unanimously denounced the gnostics for denying what the orthodox considered to be humanity's essential, God-given attribute, free will. For Irenaeus, the story of Adam and Eve proclaimed "the ancient law of human liberty."[70] Most other Christians also agreed with their Jewish contemporaries that the point of the creation story was that God bestowed upon every person the gift of moral freedom. Certain Christians, from Paul through Augustine, may have noted what this implied socially: that slavery is not a natural condition, as Aristotle had taught, but an artificial and sinful human invention.[71] (Yet neither Paul nor Augustine advocated abolishing slavery; instead, both, like the Stoic philosophers, urged slaves to use their moral freedom to overcome the hardships of servitude.)[72] For Clement of Alexandria, moral freedom is our glory; that we are made in the image of God really means that we have what he calls *autexousia,* a term often translated as "free will," but, more accurately, "the power to constitute one's own being."[73]

But gnostic Christians qualified—and some denied—this optimistic message of freedom. Certain radical gnostics ridiculed the orthodox claim that human beings have free will or, for that matter, any power to constitute their own destiny. The *Reality of the Rulers* depicted Adam, prototype of humanity, as a kind of victim, morally and physically crippled from the start. Betrayed and deceived by the forces of evil, created as a by-product of their desires and jealousies, Adam was helplessly caught within a battle of spiritual forces and could only hope that the powers above would defeat his tormentors and release their human prisoner from his cosmic confinement.

Valentinus and his followers did not go so far as to deny that human beings have free will; but they believed its role to be far more limited than orthodox Christians imagined. Human beings—or some of them, at least—may have moral freedom, they said, but human free will—even Adam's—was never so great as to bring suffering upon humanity, or to allow us to evade it altogether.[74] On the contrary, suffering is built into the structure of the universe itself. Followers of Valentinus expressed this conviction in a *precreation* myth that hinted that something else besides human sin—events far more primordial and powerful—already had cast a shadow of suffering over human existence. This was the story of Wisdom, whose "fall" occurred long before Adam's and long before he was created. As Ptolemy's disciples told the story, before the beginning of time there existed in the primal aeon only the primordial Source of all being, what they called the abyss, the depth, or primal origin, progenitor of all that was to come into being. After existing for immeasurable ages in a state of profound rest, this Source wanted other beings to know and love him; and so he brought forth from himself "the beginning of all things"[75] and projected this into his only companion, the primordial Silence, like sperm into a womb. The Silence conceived, so to speak, and brought forth a pair of emanations of divine being, the primordial Mind together with his counterpart, Truth—the first masculine, the second feminine, according to the gender of their Greek names. This pair, structured as a dynamic relationship between masculine and feminine energies, then brought forth a second pair, Logos and Life; and they, in turn, brought forth Humanity and the Church. Each pair of complementary divine energies brought forth others until the divine being reached its "fullness." Last of all, the youngest of these pairs consisted of What-has-been-willed together with his feminine counterpart, Wisdom (Sophia). In this way the Valentinians expressed their conviction that it is wisdom to live in harmony with "what [the Father] has willed."

But Wisdom belied her name and acted foolishly. Because she longed to know the Father, she rejected her place in the scheme of things, severed her relationship with What-has-been-willed, and plunged herself into a desperate search to understand the nature of her divine Source. As Irenaeus told her story,

> when she could not achieve her purpose, both because of the enormous depth and the incomprehensible nature of the Father, she stretched herself forward, and was in danger of being absorbed into His sweetness and dissolved into His absolute essence, until she encountered the Power that sustains and preserves all things, called "the Limit" . . . the power by whom, they say, she was restored and supported. Then, having with great difficulty been brought back to herself, she became convinced that the Father is incomprehensible.[76]

Then the Father, wanting to spare others from suffering as Wisdom had, sent a sixteenth pair of masculine and feminine energies, Christ and the Holy Spirit, to reveal to the other aeons that although none but the primal Mind could possibly comprehend God, all other beings, too, come from him, "in whom we live and move and have our being," and are to rejoice and celebrate together in this paradoxical knowledge.

When Wisdom was restored to her place within the divine being, she left her sufferings behind her. Followers of Ptolemy said that these sufferings—the fear, confusion, grief, and ignorance she suffered in her search for God—had to be excluded from the divine being. Yet Wisdom joined herself with Christ to recover the residual spiritual energy left in these experiences. Together, she and Christ set out to transform those sufferings: they turned her fear into water, her grief into air, her confusion into earth, and her ignorance into fire. Then they used these elements of suffering to create the present universe.[77]

The orthodox insisted that Adam and Eve inherited a perfect

world and brought upon it, through their misuse of free will, all the harms known to humankind. But the Valentinians believed that human beings, though they undoubtedly received a measure of freedom to make moral choices, are not free—nor ever were—to avoid suffering, from which the very universe itself was made. The orthodox church offered "good news" of human power and freedom; but the Valentinians, more like Buddhists, saw acceptance of suffering as the first prerequisite for spiritual understanding.

We may infer from the sophistication of many of their writings that Valentinian Christians tended to be people of education and privilege. If so, they may have been able to take their personal freedom for granted, as many people in the Roman Empire could not. And we may also infer that they knew from experience the limits of human freedom. For their myths suggest that even those who are gifted with freedom—moral and intellectual, of course, as well as social or political—must remain acutely aware of the limits of freedom and of the ways in which even the freest of human beings remain dependent upon what is beyond human power. The gnostics' vision was a dark one, pervaded by suffering; yet it was, nevertheless, a religious vision, in which ultimately everything depended upon what they called the will of the Father, that mysterious Source, the "abyss,"[78] who, according to the *Gospel of Truth*, "discovered ['his own'] in himself, and they discovered him in themselves, the incomprehensible, inconceivable one, the Father, the perfect one, the one who made the all."[79]

But orthodox Christians of the second and third centuries, from Justin and Irenaeus through Tertullian, Clement, and the brilliant teacher Origen, stood unanimously against the gnostics in proclaiming the Christian gospel as a message of freedom—moral freedom, freedom of the will, expressed in Adam's original freedom to choose a life free of pain and suffering. In the name of that moral freedom, Justin and Origen, among many others, chose to endure torture and death. Still others, in the name of that freedom, renounced all that the majority of their contemporaries believed made life worthwhile—home, family, wealth, and public reputation. So long as Christianity remained a persecuted movement, the majority of Christian preachers proclaimed the plain and powerful message of freedom that appealed to so many people within the Roman world— perhaps especially to those who had never experienced freedom in their everyday lives.

Finally, in the name of that freedom, as the Valentinians must have noted with irony, the orthodox suppressed gnostic teaching, and rejected their subtle reflections on the scope and limits of human choice. For as the churches, scattered throughout the world, became increasingly institutionalized, their leaders attempted to strengthen them against the pressures of persecution by joining them into a common doctrine and discipline. Irenaeus boasted that each group, however vulnerable on its own, belonged to a movement that was *universal,* or, in the Greek term, "catholic."[80] To the bishops, non-conformists and dissidents, even when they seemed to be sincere Christians intent on striking out on their own spiritual paths, were dangerous to the movement. The bishops may have been right; as Tertullian said, gnostic Christians agreed only to disagree. While certain groups demanded celibacy of all members, others may have encouraged people to decide these matters privately. Furthermore, some gnostics ridiculed those who died as martyrs, while others advocated martyrdom; a third group, like the Valentinians, urged people to accept martyrdom only if their sole alternative was to deny their faith in Christ. Equally divisive were the gnostic Christians who revered Eve, or the divine spirit they took her to represent, and accorded to their women members respect and participation increasingly denied to women in the institutionalized churches of the second and third centuries.[81]

Above all, their opponents charged that these dissident Christians challenged what the majority regarded as the fundamental theme of the Christian gospel: that human beings, created by God and endowed with moral freedom, received in baptism the power to live transformed lives, the power to overcome evil and death. Let us turn next to see how some of the boldest of these orthodox Christians actually put the "angelic life" into practice.

# (IV)

# THE "PARADISE OF VIRGINITY" REGAINED

OR MANY CHRISTIANS of the first four centuries and ever since, the greatest freedom demanded the greatest renunciation— above all, celibacy. This identification of freedom with celibacy involved a paradox, then as now, for celibacy (to say nothing of fasting and other forms of renunciation) is an extreme form of self-restraint. Yet as Christians saw it, celibacy involved rejection of "the world" of ordinary society and its multitudinous entanglements and was thereby a way to gain control over one's own life.

Advocates of renunciation insisted that the solitary Christian could achieve freedom unknown even to the emperor; and Marcus Aurelius, that most reflective of emperors, might well have agreed. As a young man, he longed for the freedom to devote himself to philosophic study and contemplation, but he reluctantly assumed the burdens of his imperial destiny. He accepted a marriage, arranged by his family, in which nine of the twelve or thirteen children his wife bore him died in infancy or childhood; he assumed the major responsibility for political decisions and for judging legal cases and precedents; and he served as commander in chief of the armies through decades of war and rebellions that racked the empire from Egypt and Africa to the provinces of Gaul and Germany. At times when other men might expect a few hours of leisure, Marcus's imperial presence was required at the theater or sports arena, where his subjects ridiculed him for surreptitiously bringing documents to read during the performances. Although Marcus well understood the irony that made the "master of the world" the slave of all his constituents, he consciously strove to suppress any temptation to ignore his obligations, which he regarded as his sacred duty. As he wrote in his private journal:

> In what I do, I am to do it with reference to the service of mankind; in what befalls me, I am to accept it with reference to the gods. . . . My own nature is a rational and civic [or "political," Greek, πολιτικήν] one; I have a city, and I have a country; as Marcus I have Rome, and as a human being I have the universe; and, consequently, what benefits these communities is the only good for me.[1]

Marcus admonished himself:

> When it is hard to shake off sleep, remind yourself that to be going about the duties you owe society is to be obeying the laws of human nature and your own constitution. . . . As a unit yourself, you help to complete the social whole; similarly, therefore, your every action should help to complete the life of society.[2]

More than two hundred years later the Christian convert Augustine, then a brilliantly successful young orator, was walking through the streets of Milan one night, dreading the speech he had to give the following day in praise of the emperor. In the midst of these anxieties he noticed a drunken beggar. Why, Augustine asked himself, did this beggar seem so happy, when he himself was so miserable? Augustine later described his overwhelming relief when at last he gave up his career, his ambition, the woman who had lived with him and borne him a son, as well as his impending marriage to a wealthy heiress, for the freedom of celibacy and renunciation. His pagan contemporaries regarded such renunciation not only as social suicide but as the worst impiety and dishonor. But Augustine came to believe that it meant no more than "dying to the world"—destroying the false self, constructed according to worldly custom and tradition, in order to "raise his own life above the world."[3]

Ascetically inclined Christians even projected their idealized celibacy back into Paradise, as we shall see, and turned the story of the first marriage into a story of two virgins whose sin and consequent sexual awakening ended in their expulsion from the "Paradise of virginity" into marriage and all its attendant sufferings, from labor pains to social domination and death.[4]

The renowned teacher and bishop Gregory of Nyssa (c. 331–

395 C.E.) declared, "Marriage, then, is the last stage of our separation from the life that was led in Paradise; marriage therefore . . . is the first thing to be left behind; it is the first station, as it were, for our departure to Christ."[5]

Even today, an adolescent who takes time to think before plunging into ordinary adult society—into marriage, and the double obligations of family and career—may hesitate, for such obligations usually cost nothing less than one's life, the expense of virtually all one's energy attempting to fulfill obligations to family and society, especially if one also wants to be recognized and celebrated within one's community. It is in this sense that Christian renunciation, of which celibacy is the paradigm, offered freedom—freedom, in particular, from entanglement in Roman society.

In classical Greek and Roman society, a young man or woman who hesitated or refused to marry the person chosen by his or her family would be considered insubordinate or possibly even insane. Many parents expected their daughters to marry at about the age of puberty or soon after; in aristocratic circles, advantageous marriages sometimes were arranged when the children were as young as six or seven. Through marriage, as the historian Peter Brown says, "a girl was conscripted as a fully productive member by her society, as was her spouse."[6] Young men were expected to marry between the ages of seventeen and twenty-five and then to place themselves at the service of their communities, according to their family tradition and station.

Most Roman citizens would probably have agreed with Aristotle that "a human being is a political animal" ($\pi o \lambda \iota \tau \iota \kappa \acute{\eta} \nu \ \zeta \acute{\omega} \omega \nu$), that the measure of one's worth was what one contributed to the "common good" or to the business of the state ($\pi o \lambda \acute{\iota} \tau \epsilon \upsilon \mu \alpha$), as defined by men of influence and power. Thus was social and political recognition bestowed. Anyone who chose to withdraw and to go a solitary way risked extreme ostracism: in Greek, the term "idiot" literally referred to a person concerned solely with personal or private matters ($\acute{\iota} \delta \iota o \varsigma$, "one's own") instead of the public and social life of the larger community.

Jesus' message attacked such assumptions. "What profit is it for a man if he gains the whole world, but loses his own soul?" Jesus asks in Matthew.[7] Jesus himself, as we have seen, belonged to the tradition of Jewish people who for many centuries had lived as groups of outsiders, often noncitizens, within the pagan empires of the Persians, Babylonians, Egyptians, Greeks, and Romans. These outsiders apparently rejected the view that human value depends upon one's contribution to the state and originated instead the idea that developed much later in the West as the "absolute value of the individual." The idea that each individual has intrinsic, God-given value and is of infinite worth quite apart from any social contribution—an idea most pagans would have rejected as absurd—persists today as the ethical basis of western law and politics. Our secularized western idea of democratic society owes much to that early Christian vision of a new society—a society no longer formed by the natural bonds of family, tribe, or nation but by the voluntary choice of its members.[8] From the classical point of view, however, those Christians who "renounced the world"—who rejected family, tribe, and nation—effectively declared themselves "idiots."

Even apart from renunciation of the world, the strict ethical attitudes of Christians had enormously raised the stakes involved in sexual activity. The casual sexual behavior that many pagans took for granted—homosexual encounters among mentors and friends at the baths, or the sexual use of slaves and prostitutes—were rejected by most Christians, who simultaneously rejected homosexuality, contraception, abortion, and infanticide. For most Christians, therefore, sexual activity risked conception and so involved both partners, potentially, at least, in the economic and social obligations of family life. The example of Jesus and his followers encouraged them instead to take the subversive path *away* from such obligations—toward freedom.

A famous Egyptian Christian named Anthony chose such freedom, and generations of ascetically inclined Christians loved to tell his story. Anthony was the son of affluent Christian parents who lived in a small town in Egypt around the year 260. When Anthony was about eighteen, his parents died and left him responsible for a large household. He had to care for his young sister, supervise the slaves, and manage three hundred acres of fertile and beautiful farmland. Some six months after his parents' death, Anthony was pondering his future when in church one day he heard the words Jesus spoke to a rich young man: "Go, sell what you have, and give to the poor, and you shall have treasure in heaven; come and follow me."[9] Anthony's biographer tells us that he immediately left the church and gave to the villagers the property he had received as his inheritance, "so that he and his sister would not be encumbered with it."[10] He sold all their possessions, gave most of the money to the poor, and kept only a little in reserve to provide for his sister; soon afterward, he placed her in a home with some ascetic Christian women and left the village, "watching over himself and patiently disciplining himself."[11]

Instead of marrying and entering into the lifelong obligations of a wealthy landowner in his hometown, Anthony took Jesus' words as permission—indeed, as encouragement—to shrug off these onerous responsibilities. Intense, solitary, and self-involved, Anthony was not seeking an easy escape from difficulty. Instead, he abruptly abandoned a traditional and respectable life to make his own way to self-discovery—and the discovery of God. Anthony devoted himself to *ascesis*—which literally means "exercise"—in order to "attend to his soul,"[12] but first he had to battle a residual desire for human company and approval. His biographer tells us that at first the devil tormented Anthony with "memories of his property; anxiety for his sister; intimacy with his relatives; desire for money and for power; and the manifold enjoyment of food and the other pleasures of life," and finally with vivid sexual fantasies.[13]

What Anthony wanted to learn was what human life was or could be apart from ordinary social expectations. He did not reject all human society but sought out the society of an aristocracy quite different from the local Egyptian landholders—experts, or so he believed, in the practice of divine wisdom. Though he rejected family, marriage, and kinship, he willingly subjected himself to those whose self-mastery he admired, and sought to become one of them: "he noticed the courtesy of one; another's constancy in prayer; one's humility; another's kindness," and, above all, "their devotion to Christ, and their love for one another."[14]

Anthony was to become famous among Christians as a spiritual pioneer, one who set out to discover what happens beyond the boundaries of civilization when one ventures alone into the harsh desert. Anthony—and others like him—sought the shape of his own soul, hoping to accept the terrors and ecstasies of direct and unremitting encounters with himself and, having mastered himself, to discover his relationship to the Infinite God.

The number of those who chose such *ascesis*, or spiritual "exercise," was not large, compared with the number of believers who increasingly crowded the churches in the third century, but their role is significant; for these hermits lived out the ideal of which many other Christians only dreamed. The classical scholar Ramsay Mac-Mullen estimates that during the century following Constantine's conversion the number of Christians grew from about five million to thirty million,[15] while the monks in Egypt came to number about thirty thousand.[16] These ascetics were called what Mother Teresa in Calcutta still calls them, "athletes" for God, and were revered as many people today revere certain athletes, men and women who discipline themselves to achieve what their thousands of admirers only dream of doing. Anthony and other ascetics spoke of their struggle for self-control in athletic terms, as an attempt to control the body and mind and to maintain both in seemingly effortless mastery. Many Christians who engaged in their own limited ascetic practices on certain days, and many more who may never have made the effort to control their diet and to strengthen themselves as "athletes" did, nevertheless, admire those who achieved such discipline.

Gregory of Nyssa, a married Christian from a wealthy family in Asia Minor, wrote with passionate regret that he wished he had dared "raise his own life above the world,"[17] to live for himself and for God alone, despite the expectations of family and friends and the pressures of social and political obligations. For, as he wrote, no doubt from his own experience,

> he whose life is contained in himself either escapes [sufferings] altogether, or can bear them easily, having a collected mind which is not distracted from itself; while he who shares himself with wife and child often has not a moment to give even to regretting his own condition, because anxiety for those he loves fills his heart.[18]

Gregory also understood how people suffer through their natural desire for children:

> There is pain always, whether children are born, or can never be expected; whether they live or die. One person has many children, but not enough means to support them; another feels the lack of an heir to the great fortune he has worked for. . . . one man loses by death a beloved son; another has a reprobate son alive; both equally pitiable, although one mourns over the death, the other over the life, of his son. Nor will I do more than mention how sadly and disastrously family jealousies and arguments, arising from real or imagined causes, end.[19]

Gregory describes how people pursue wealth, distinctions, public office, and power over others, making themselves "slaves of futility," all chasing illusions. But one who chooses to liberate himself from the chains of ordinary life "in a sense exiles himself entirely from human life by abstaining from marriage."[20] As a man bound by his multiple obligations, Gregory writes longingly of the freedom to be antisocial, to choose, as more valuable than anything else, his own, single life before God. Many people then—and many now, no doubt—may have considered the desire for the ascetic life to be selfish. But Gregory saw in that life the potential for becoming what God originally intended human beings to be: beings made "in God's image," radiant with his love and light; "the work and the excellence [of monks] is to contemplate the Father of all purity, and to beautify the lineaments of their own characters from the Source of all beauty."[21]

Gregory adds, "Let no one think that, in saying this, we deprecate marriage. We are well aware that it is not a stranger to God's blessing"; but, he continues, urging people to marry is entirely unnecessary, since "the common instincts of humanity plead sufficiently on its behalf," while virginity "thwarts these natural impulses."[22] Thus Christians repudiated what Marcus Aurelius regarded as the highest virtue, for, as we have seen, Marcus saw his religious destiny given in his familial, social, and political situation, and in the duties his imperial role placed upon him. Stoic philosophy encouraged him to embrace and even to love his fate, submit to its demands, and patiently endure its frustrations, whereas Christians sought the opposite—to free themselves from the bonds of tradition and custom, from what pious pagans called destiny.

An anonymous Christian, probably a near contemporary of the emperor Marcus, wrote a fictionalized biography of Clement, an aristocratic Roman convert who denied that destiny ruled his life, who rejected his family's demands and expectations, and who repudiated paganism, along with his own Greek education, to devote himself to God's truth alone. But like everyone else who had chosen that path, Clement found that the obstacles—the physical and emotional instincts that clamored for gratification—were within himself. Only those who dared deny these interior as well as exterior demands could claim chastity as their way to freedom.

For Clement, the "good news" of Christianity meant autonomy: that a Christian could actually defy destiny by mastering bodily impulses. Forces conjured by such names as Aphrodite and Eros, who overpowered their multiple human lovers, must now yield themselves, like beasts before a lion tamer, to the rational will. As Clement saw it, ascetic Christians were no longer at the mercy of uncontrollable forces—neither the powers of destiny, or fate, that Stoics revered, nor the passions that arose from within. Christian conversion promised an enormous gain in self-control for those "athletes" of asceticism.[23]

Clement knew, of course, that self-control was the practical gospel of Platonic and Stoic philosophers. But Plato considered self-control the rarest of all accomplishments, attained by Socrates alone, whereas Christians announced that this virtue was within reach of every convert, although not every convert could achieve perfect celibacy. The Christian teacher Origen called the teaching of pagan philosophers fine meals prepared for sophisticated palates, but "we [Christians] cook for the masses." Yet while Christian teachers popularized such philosophic attitudes, they also threw out much of what these philosophers taught.

Methodius, a celibate Asian Christian who served Christian churches in Asia and Greece as bishop and died a martyr (c. 260), wrote a famous polemic against the "great lie" of Greek philosophy and education—namely, the conviction that destiny, fate, and necessity are actual, external forces in the universe that control human affairs, and that sexual desire, like destiny, is beyond human control.

Methodius's polemic was a deliberate parody of Plato's *Symposium,* in which Plato praised the power of Eros—sexual desire—as one of the great cosmic forces. As Methodius saw it, Plato's *Symposium* epitomized false philosophic education. Where Plato showed in his *Symposium* a group of men fighting hangovers from the night before by praising the glories of erotic—and especially homoerotic—love, Methodius presents his *anti*-erotic *Symposium of the Ten Virgins* through the dramatis personae of ten women ascetics who compete with one another in praising virginity! Thecla, that famous ascetic, is the star debater, whose speech in praise of virginity wins the laurel crown.

The first speaker in Methodius's dialogue, Marcella, describes the whole course of human history as a progression toward freedom. Although marriage and procreation were necessary "in the beginning" to multiply the human race, they now represent only a crude and archaic relic of human origins, a kind of dinosaur age preceding the evolution of the true human being, the celibate.[24]

But the second speaker, Theophila, objects to Marcella and articulates instead the viewpoint of the many Christians who favor marriage and procreation and claim for both God's blessings. In the beginning, Theophila says, the Creator made man and woman; but "at the present time . . . humanity must cooperate in forming the image of God, so long as the world exists . . . for it is said, 'Increase and multiply' (Genesis 1:28)."[25] Theophila chides those who reject marriage: "We must not be offended at the ordinance of the Creator from which, indeed, we ourselves have our existence."

When Theophila finishes, Thaelia replies: If Christians were meant to take Genesis literally, Paul would not have spoken of Adam's union with Eve as a "great mystery" which signifies "Christ and the Church" (Ephesians 5:32). Without accusing Theophila directly, she charges that

> people who are undisciplined because of the uncontrolled impulses of sensuality in them dare to force the Scriptures beyond their true meaning, and so twist the sayings "Increase and multiply" [Genesis 1:28] and "Therefore a man shall leave his father and mother" [Genesis 2:24] into a defense of their own incontinence. . . .

As Thaelia sees it, such Christians use these passages to gratify themselves sexually, while pretending that their concern is with procreation. She admits that Paul did not *require* celibacy, but says he certainly preferred it for any who were capable of achieving this "means of restoring humanity to Paradise."[26]

Finally Thecla is introduced by her sister in virginity Arete (whose name in Greek means "virtue") as one "who yields to none in universal philosophy, having been taught by Paul in evangelical and apostolical doctrines."[27] Thecla sides with Thaelia and goes on to denounce the great lie of philosophical education: "The greatest of all evils is to say that this life is governed by inevitable necessities of fate."[28] Thecla herself stands as living evidence against those who say that one must "accept one's destiny"—whether that destiny arises from one's anatomy, or from the familial and social circumstances of one's birth. In praising human freedom, Thecla declares that only those who live in chastity actually achieve mastery of themselves and of their destinies. She addresses her sisters as women warriors who "struggle and wrestle, according to our teacher Paul. For she who has overcome the devil, having undergone the seven great struggles of chastity, comes to possess seven crowns." Whoever wins this battle receives "a masculine . . . and voluntary mind, one free from necessity, in order to choose, like masters, the things which please us, not being enslaved to fate nor fortune."[29]

Arete judges that Thecla's is the best speech in praise of virginity and awards her the crown for her defense of virginity as freedom. Thecla then stands in the place of honor and leads the others in a hymn to welcome Christ, their heavenly bridegroom; her sisters respond, in chorus, "I keep myself pure for Thee, O Bridegroom; and holding a lighted torch, I go to meet thee."[30]

This fanciful dialogue of virgins nevertheless reflects the actual activities of Christian women dedicated to asceticism who gathered throughout Asia Minor, as this group did, in households and gardens provided by wealthy members, to devote themselves to spiritual disciplines and to prayer. Because such women often did reject what their pagan neighbors and relatives regarded as their destiny and their fortune, Methodius believed they exemplified what Christian life really meant—the realization of human freedom.

For women, as several women historians recently have demonstrated, celibacy sometimes offered immediate rewards on earth, as well as eventual rewards in heaven. We have seen how Thecla's own story celebrated a young woman's achievement of autonomy as a "holy woman," an ascetic, evangelist, and healer; during the third and fourth centuries, an increasing number of Christian women resolved to follow her example and become "new Theclas."[31]

One of these was Melania the Younger, heiress to an enormous fortune from her noble Roman family. According to her biographer, Melania "had from her earliest youth yearned for Christ, and longed for bodily chastity." Her parents, however, "very forcibly united her in marriage with her blessed husband, Pinian, who was from a consular family, when she was fourteen years old and her spouse was about seventeen."[32] Melania first pleaded with Pinian to live with her in celibate marriage and then offered to give him all her wealth and property if he would agree to "leave [her] body free." But Pinian insisted that they first have two children to ensure the family succession; after that, "both of us together shall renounce the world."[33] First they had a daughter, whom they vowed to virginity; then, a son, who died in infancy. It grieved Pinian to see Melania "exceedingly troubled, and . . . giving up on life,"[34] and he hastily promised her that they would spend the rest of their lives in chastity. Not long afterward, when their young daughter also died, Pinian and Melania, after six years of marriage, when she was twenty and he was twenty-four, put on the rough clothes of peasants, gave up their ordinary social obligations, and fulfilled Christ's commands. They offered hospitality to strangers, gave money to the poor and destitute, visited the prisons and the mines to inquire which prisoners were held there for debt, and provided money for their release.

It was rumored that Melania and Pinian were now ready to go

further—in Jesus' words, to "sell all that you have, and give to the poor" (Matthew 19:21). At this, the slaves on their Roman estate rebelled, for they did not want to be sold, probably separately, on the open slave market, but preferred to be sold together to Pinian's brother. Melania's biographer says that she and Pinian suspected the brother of inciting the uprising because "he wanted to take all their property for himself; and in fact all their relatives schemed for their possessions, wanting to make themselves richer from them."[35] Pinian's father, they suspected, intended to give their possessions to his other children.

Although Melania and Pinian wanted to "renounce the world," they were intensely concerned to protect their rights to dispose of their riches themselves for the religious purposes they chose. Melania went to Serena, mother-in-law of the emperor Honorius, to ask for protection against their relatives' greed. Soon afterward, the emperor Honorius decreed that their possessions should be sold by government agents, and that the proceeds should go to Melania and Pinian. Thus, the young couple left Rome for the Holy Land with great anticipation: "they looked forward to scattering on the earth what they believed could store up pure treasures in heaven."[36] When they traveled to Africa, Augustine and his fellow bishops persuaded them to found and endow monasteries there. Later they visited the monks in Egypt and Jerusalem, where Melania constructed a monastery for ninety women. She lived there austerely, giving shelter to former prostitutes, studying the Scriptures and the church fathers, and struggling to establish her monastic community. She chose another woman to direct the monastery while she herself tended to the physical needs of her sisters, especially those who were sick. When Pinian died, Melania settled on the Mount of Olives in a tiny cell, where she prayed and meditated. There she constructed a chapel, a shrine to the martyrs, and another monastery for men in honor of her late husband.

Melania and Pinian, like many others before and since, saw renunciation as a higher alternative to family obligations—obligations all the heavier because they were, in worldly terms, so privileged. As the historian Elizabeth Clark so ably has shown, "renouncing the world" sometimes brought wealthy and aristocratic women like Melania practical benefits often denied to them in secular society. They could retain control of their own wealth, travel freely throughout the world as "holy pilgrims," devote themselves to intellectual and spiritual pursuits, and found institutions which they could personally direct.[37]

Virtually all Christians agreed that ascetics, especially celibates, were closer to the kingdom than married people; for hadn't Jesus praised those who "made themselves eunuchs for the sake of the kingdom of heaven" (Matthew 19:12) and called them "equal to angels" (Luke 20:36); and hadn't Paul described the celibate's dedication to Christ as a kind of spiritual marriage (1 Corinthians 6:17)? Enthusiasm for the ascetic life had spread quickly in Syria and in Asia Minor, the source of such radical Christian literature as the *Acts of Paul and Thecla;* and also in Egypt, where stories of Anthony and others attracted thousands of young Christians eager to test their strength in the wild and solitary deserts.

But not everyone accepted asceticism as a superior virtue. In Rome, when Melania and Pinian "renounced the world" (c. 390), the ascetic movement was explosively controversial, especially in rich and aristocratic circles. Even Christian parents like Melania's father protested when their children succumbed to the preaching of such enthusiasts of asceticism as Jerome, then secretary to Damasus, bishop of Rome. In his youth Jerome had lived with the hermits in the Syrian desert; and even after he had returned to civilized life, he loved to think of himself as an expert on asceticism. Later, he looked back on his experiences living in a cave and recalled

> how often, when I was living in the desolate, lonely desert, parched by the burning sun, how often I imagined myself among the pleasures of Rome! I used to sit alone, because my heart was filled with bitterness; my limbs stuck inside an ugly sackcloth, my skin black as an Ethiopian's. . . . Day after day I cried and sighed, and when, against my will, I fell asleep, my bare bones clashed against the ground. I say nothing about my eating and drinking. Even when sick, solitaries drink only cold water, and a cooked meal is considered excessive. And yet he who, in fear of hell, had banished himself to this prison, found himself again and again surrounded by dancing girls! My face grew pale with hunger, yet in my cold body the passions of my inner being continued to glow. This human being was more dead than alive; only his burning lust continued to boil.[38]

After two years, Jerome left the desert for Antioch, and later he went to Constantinople and Rome. It was there that the former monk became papal secretary and later spokesman for Damasus, the first pope to live with the princely panoply of ceremonial that has characterized the Vatican in post-Constantinian times.

Yet as the Christian movement gained in numbers and influence during the third and fourth centuries and finally became not only legal but imperially patronized, the situation of Christian bishops changed radically. No longer targets of arrest, torture, and execution, now they received tax exemptions, donations in gold, great prestige, and, in some cases, even influence at the imperial court. Now that becoming a Christian was no longer the heroic choice it had been for Christians like Perpetua, some of the most intense believers in the age of Constantine longed for the ascetic life as proof of devotion, a kind of self-inflicted martyrdom. As we have seen, many regarded ascetic Christians as celebrities, living examples of "God's athletes."

Moving among the most powerful Christians in Rome, Jerome adopted the role of spiritual advisor and devoted himself especially to a circle of aristocratic women, including Paula, a widow of enormous wealth. To her daughter Eustochium, Jerome wrote one of his most famous letters, urging her to embrace Christ alone:

> Always allow the privacy of your own room to protect you: always let the Bridegroom play with you within. Do you pray? You speak to the Bridegroom. Do you read? He speaks to you. When sleep overtakes you, he will come from behind and put his hand through the hole of the door, and your heart shall be moved for him.[39]

Jerome encouraged Eustochium to acknowledge her superiority, as virgin, over all married women, including her own married sister, Blaesilla: "Learn from me a holy arrogance: know that you are better than they are!"[40]

But the twenty-year-old Blaesilla, some months after her wedding, suddenly found herself a widow and, in her grief, ripe for religious conversion. For thirty days she suffered a high fever, and yet she obeyed Jerome's program of radical austerity. She slept on the ground, refused food, and devoted herself to penitential prayer. Her friends and relatives, shocked by the change in her, criticized or ridiculed her extreme practices—and her teacher. When she wasted away and died two months later, many people were openly bitter. Jerome reproached Paula in these words:

> When you were carried fainting out of the funeral procession, whispers such as these were audible in the crowd: "Isn't this what

we often have said? She weeps for her daughter, killed by fasting. She wanted her to marry again so that she might have grandchildren. How long must we refrain from driving these detestable monks out of Rome? Why don't we stone them or throw them into the Tiber river? They have misled this wretched lady; it is clear that she is not a nun by choice."[41]

But Jerome's critics vehemently blamed him for Blaesilla's death. His reputation as spiritual director was badly shaken. Still worse, his patron, Pope Damasus, had died several weeks before. Jerome hastily left Rome for the Holy Land, where Blaesilla's mother and sister, still devoted to their mentor, later joined him.

About five years later, a friend traveling from Rome brought to Jerome's monastic cell in Bethlehem a copy of a writing that challenged the supremacy of asceticism over married life. Its author, Jovinian, himself a celibate Christian monk, argued that celibacy in itself is no holier than marriage and accused certain fanatical Christians of having invented—and then having attributed to Jesus and Paul—this "novel dogma against nature."[42]

Jerome saw Jovinian as a serious threat and set out "to crush with evangelical and apostolical vigor the Epicurus of Christianity."[43] Yet Jerome also knew that Jovinian had once shared his enthusiasm for the ascetic movement. Barefoot and unshaven, Jovinian had dressed in a rough coat and grimy tunic, refused to eat meat or drink wine, and strictly avoided any contact with women. But after some years of these austerities, Jovinian underwent a change of heart and questioned whether they were spiritually beneficial. Although he remained sexually abstinent, he soon challenged certain premises of Christian asceticism on religious, and specifically on scriptural, grounds. Jerome tells us that Jovinian began from the "primary commands of God" concerning procreation (Genesis 1:28) and marriage (Genesis 2:24), and then, lest anyone object that these occur only in the Old Testament, Jovinian

> answers that it has been confirmed by the Lord in the gospel; "What God has joined together, let no one put asunder," and he adds immediately, "Be fruitful and multiply, and fill the earth" (Matthew 19:6; Genesis 1:28).[44]

Thus Jovinian rejected the common belief that celibate persons are holier than those who marry and declared that "virgins, widows, and married women, who have once gone through Christian baptism, if they are equal in other respects, are of equal merit."[45] Furthermore, abstinence from food or meat or wine does not make a person holier than one who enjoys them with gratitude toward their Creator. Jovinian concluded that all Christians who remain faithful to their baptismal vows can expect the same heavenly reward: heaven is not arranged in first-class, second-class, and third-class compartments, according to the degree of renunciation one has practiced in this life.

Such proposals brought upon their author a storm of abuse. Led by three future saints of the church—Jerome, Ambrose, and their younger contemporary Augustine—Pope Siricius, bishop of Rome, condemned what he called Jovinian's *scriptura horrifica* and, to protect innocent believers from what he called this "dangerous heresy," excommunicated him.

Jovinian vigorously protested his excommunication and wrote commentaries to prove that the Scriptures were on his side. Besides referring to God's original blessing on procreation and marriage, Jovinian named all the biblical figures, from the patriarchs to the apostles, who married and had children, and he added that Jesus joined in celebrating the marriage at Cana, where he turned water into wine.

When he turned to Paul to defend marriage, Jovinian, like Clement, two centuries before, found in the deutero-Pauline letters the support he needed:

> listen to the words of Paul: "I desire, therefore, that younger widows marry and bear children" [1 Timothy 5:14], and "marriage is honorable unto all, and the marriage bed undefiled" [Hebrews 13:4].[46]

When Jovinian *did* refer to Paul's authentic letters, he instinctively followed selective techniques of exegesis that certain Protestants later perfected. He ignored those passages that express Paul's religious preferences for celibacy (including much of 1 Corinthians 7), and seized instead upon those in which Paul offered merely pragmatic reasons for sexual abstinence, such as the statement that "concerning virgins I have no command from the Lord, but I give my opinions. . . . I think that it is good, 'because of the present distress,' for a person to remain as he is" (1 Corinthians 7:25–26). "Here," Jerome said, "our opponent goes utterly wild with excitement: This is his strongest battering ram with which he shakes the walls of virginity."[47]

According to Jovinian, where Paul *did* advise celibacy, he recommended it only on practical grounds, not moral ones. Jovinian himself endorsed and lived by such advice. He maintained his own celibacy, but warned others who made the same choice, "Do not be proud; you and your married sisters are equally members of the same church."[48]

When Jerome read Jovinian's treatise, he said, he heard "the hissing of the old serpent; by counsel such as this, the dragon drove man from Paradise."[49] What bothered Jerome especially was that Jovinian, despite his excommunication, was supported by some of the leading Christians of Rome—the same Christians for whom Jerome, the champion of asceticism, was now *persona non grata*. Jerome acknowledged that even though everyone praised celibacy, not everyone took it seriously, even as a qualification for the priesthood:

> That married men are elected to the priesthood, I do not deny; the number of virgins is not so great as that of the priests that are needed. Does it follow that because all the strongest men are chosen for the army, weaker ones should not be taken as well? . . . How is it, then, you will say, that frequently, when priests are ordained, a virgin is passed over, and a married man taken? Perhaps because he lacks other qualities in keeping with virginity.[50]

Jerome adds that many factors flaw elections:

> Sometimes the judgment of the commoner people is at fault; . . . often it happens that married people, who form the larger portion of the people, in approving married candidates, in effect approve themselves; and it does not occur to them that the mere fact that they prefer a married person to a virgin proves their inferiority to virgins.

Jerome dared point out that even bishops

> choose from the ranks of the clergy not the best, but the cleverest, men . . . or, as though they were handing out positions in an earthly service, they give them to their kinsmen or relatives; or they listen to the dictates of money. And, worse than all, they promote the clergy who smear them with flattery.[51]

When Jerome set out to refute Jovinian, he went through many of the scriptural passages cited by Jovinian and claimed that they supported opposite conclusions. Jerome was famous—and still is—for his knowledge of the Scriptures, and he undoubtedly knew that Genesis 2 describes the institution of marriage *before* the fall; but he tendentiously switched the order of verses in order to make it appear that marriage *followed* sin, and so fell under God's curse:

> As for Adam and Eve, we must maintain that before the fall they were virgins in Paradise; but after they sinned, and were cast out of Paradise, they were immediately married. *Then* we have the passage, "For this cause a man shall leave his father and mother, and cleave to his wife, and they shall become one flesh."[52]

Jerome declares that Jesus himself remained "a virgin in the flesh and a monogamist in the spirit," faithful to his only bride, the church, and adds that "although I know that crowds of matrons will be furious at me, . . . I will say what the apostle [Paul] has taught me. . . . indeed in view of the purity of the body of Christ, all sexual intercourse is unclean."[53] In such passages Jerome expresses a loathing for the flesh, the revulsion of a man ashamed of his own past sexual conduct, as he himself admitted. Other advocates of celibacy, however, from Clement to such married Christians as Tertullian in his early years[54] and Gregory of Nyssa, express no such revulsion. Indeed, much of the evidence we have surveyed suggests that loathing for the flesh was not, as some have tried to argue, the basis for advocating celibacy, although, in cases like Jerome's, such responses no doubt intensified the inclination toward celibacy.

Then Jerome finally turns to Paul:

> I will therefore do battle with the whole army of enemies. In the front rank I will set up the apostle Paul, and, since he is the bravest of generals, I will arm him with his own weapons, that is, with his own statements.[55]

Jovinian had invoked the deutero-Pauline letters, but Jerome draws primarily from what scholars regard as Paul's genuine letters, and emphasizes 1 Corinthians 7, infusing Paul's words with vehement hyperbole:

> If "it is good for a man not to touch a woman," it is bad to touch one. . . . [Paul allows marriage only] "because of fornication," as if one were to say, "it is good to eat the finest wheat flower," and yet to prevent a starving man from devouring excrement, I may allow him to also eat barley. . . . the reason why he says "it is better to marry" is that it is worse to burn. . . . It is as though he said, "it is better to have one eye than to be totally blind; it is better to stand on one foot and support the body with a cane than to crawl upon broken legs."[56]

Finally, Jerome accused Jovinian of secret and uncontrollable lust, and simultaneously ridiculed his fellow monk for remaining irreproachably celibate: "to prove that virginity and marriage are equal, he himself should marry; or, if he does not marry, it is useless for him to bandy words with us, when his acts are on our side."[57] That many prominent Roman Christians welcomed Jovinian's teachings proved no more than that Jovinian was pandering to a popular audience of self-indulgent Christians by giving them "scriptural authority to console their incontinence." Jerome, foreshadowing the Puritanism of a later time, caricatured Jovinian as

> our modern Epicurus, wantoning in his garden with his favorites of both sexes. Whenever I see a dandy, or a man who is no stranger to a hairdresser, with his hair nicely done and his cheeks all aglow, he belongs to your herd, or, rather, grunts in concert with your swine. To our flock belong the sad, the pale, the poorly dressed. . . . You have in your army . . . the full-bellied, the well-dressed, the luxurious . . . who defend you tooth and nail. Aristocrats make way for you; the wealthy print kisses on your face.[58]

When Jerome's books *Against Jovinian* arrived in Rome, they set off an uproar. Even those who agreed that virginity surpassed marriage were embarrassed by Jerome's vehemence. Jerome's influential friend Pammachius tried to withdraw his books from consideration but failed, for they were too sensational to suppress. Jerome, writing to thank Pammachius for his efforts, admitted that he never imagined that

> those on my own side would lay traps for me. I praise virginity to the skies, not because I myself possess it, but because, not possessing it, I admire it all the more.

His quarrel with Jovinian concerned one basic issue:

> He puts marriage on a level with virginity, while I make it inferior; he declares that there is little or no difference between the two states; I claim that there is a great deal. Finally . . . he has dared to place marriage on an equal level with perpetual chastity.[59]

To many twentieth-century readers, Jovinian's argument may sound like mere common sense against Jerome's fanaticism. Yet such Christian leaders and future saints as Siricius, bishop of Rome, Ambrose, bishop of Milan, Jerome himself, and Augustine condemned

Jovinian and placed his name on their growing list of heretics. Most Christians—all but the most radical, who rejected marriage altogether—acknowledged that Christians who honorably fulfilled their marital vows thereby pleased God; even Paul urged those who could not refrain from marriage to marry "in the Lord." But to claim that marriage is as meritorious as repudiating marriage "for the sake of the kingdom of heaven" implied Christian sanction for traditional pagan values, as if honoring family and social obligations—the ancient pagan ethical ideal in Christian dress—were morally equivalent to renunciation. Those Christians who proclaimed freedom from social and political entanglements defied those who valued human life according to its social contribution, and in the process, as we have seen, envisioned a new society based on free and voluntary choice. The majority of Christians married but continued nonetheless to assert the primacy of renunciation. In their resistance to conventional definitions of human worth based upon social contribution, I suggest, we can see the source of the later western idea of the absolute value of the individual—the value of every human being, including the destitute, the sick, and the newborn—quite apart from any contribution, real or potential, to the "common good."[60]

Those who actually chose renunciation often found, no doubt, the freedom they sought: we have seen how women who "renounced the world"—whether wealthy and aristocratic, like Melania, or women without means, like Thecla—thereby claimed the opportunity to travel, to devote themselves to intellectual and spiritual pursuits, to found institutions, and to direct them.

Yet the men who wrote most of the literature in praise of virginity undoubtedly also found, in chastity and renunciation, the rewards of liberty they sought—freedom from the oppressive weight of imperial rule, of custom, tradition, "destiny," or fate, and from the internal tyranny of the passions. The appeal of that ascetic life is by no means confined to the past: the twentieth-century writer Thomas Merton, who, following his conversion, entered a Cistercian monastery, no doubt was speaking of his own resolve as well as that of the early desert fathers when he said:

> What the fathers sought most of all was their own true self, in Christ. And in order to do this, they had to reject completely the false, formal self, fabricated under social compulsion "in the world."[61]

For the fourth-century theologian Augustine, who was to become the greatest teacher of the future Christian church, the climax of his conversion was his decision, inspired by the story of Anthony, to give up a Christian marriage that would have ensured him wealth and social status, along with a brilliantly promising career, to embrace the ascetic life. Augustine would eventually transform traditional Christian teaching on freedom, on sexuality, and on sin and redemption for all future generations of Christians. Where earlier generations of Jews and Christians had once found in Genesis 1–3 the affirmation of human freedom to choose good or evil, Augustine, living after the age of Constantine, found in the same text a story of human bondage. Yet as Augustine grew older, he argued that even the most saintly ascetic was not, in himself, capable of self-mastery; that all humankind was fallen; and that the human will was incorrigibly corrupt. This cataclysmic transformation in Christian thought from an ideology of moral freedom to one of universal corruption coincided, as we shall presently see, with the evolution of the Christian movement from a persecuted sect to the religion of the emperor himself.

# (V)

# THE POLITICS OF PARADISE

ARE HUMAN BEINGS CAPABLE OF governing themselves? Defiant Christians hounded as criminals by the Roman government emphatically answered *yes*. But in the fourth and fifth centuries, after the emperors themselves became patrons of Christianity, the majority of Christians gradually came to say *no*. Early Christian spokesmen, like Jews before them and the American colonists long after, had claimed to find in the biblical creation account divine sanction for declaring their independence from governments they considered corrupt and arbitrary. The Hebrew creation account of Genesis 1, unlike its Babylonian counterpart, claims that God gave the power of earthly rule to *adam*—not to the king or emperor but simply to "mankind" (and some even thought this might include women).[1] Most Christian apologists in the first three centuries would have agreed with Gregory of Nyssa, who followed rabbinic tradition by explaining that after God created the world "as a royal dwelling place for the future king,"[2] he made humanity "as a being fit to exercise royal rule" by creating it "the living image of the universal King."[3] Consequently, Gregory concludes, "the soul immediately shows its royal and exalted character, far removed as it is from the lowliness of private station, in that it owns no master, and is self-governed, ruled autocratically by its own will."[4] Besides dominion over the earth and animals, this gift of sovereignty conveys the quality of moral freedom:

> Preeminent among all is the fact that we are free from any necessity, and not in bondage to any power, but have decision in our own power as we please; for virtue is a voluntary thing, subject

to no dominion. Whatever is the result of compulsion and force cannot be virtue.[5]

Many Christian converts of the first three centuries—centuries in which civil authorities treated the church as a subversive sect—regarded the proclamation of αὐτεξουσία—the moral freedom to rule oneself—as virtually synonymous with "the gospel."

Yet with Augustine, in the late fourth and early fifth centuries, this message changed. The work of his later years, in which he radically broke with many of his predecessors, and even with his own earlier convictions, effectively transformed much of the teaching of the Christian faith. Instead of the freedom of the will and humanity's original royal dignity, Augustine emphasizes humanity's enslavement to sin. Humanity is sick, suffering, and helpless, irreparably damaged by the fall,[6] for that "original sin," Augustine insists, involved nothing else than Adam's prideful attempt to establish his own autonomous self-government.[7] Astonishingly, Augustine's radical views prevailed, eclipsing for future generations of western Christians the consensus of more than three centuries of Christian tradition.

As he matured, Augustine repudiated the Manichaean version of Christian doctrine he had embraced as an enthusiastic young seeker, a doctrine that categorically denied the goodness of creation and the freedom of the will. Augustine, the chastened convert, now claimed to accept Catholic orthodoxy, and affirmed both. But, as he grasped for ways to understand his own tumultuous experience, Augustine concluded that the qualities of that original state of creation no longer applied—at least not directly—to human experience in the present. Humanity, once given the unflawed glory of creation and the freedom of the will, actually enjoyed these only in those brief primordial moments in Paradise. Ever since the fall, they have been apprehended only in moments of inspired imagination, and even then but partially. For all practical purposes they are wholly lost.

Given the intense inner conflicts involving his passionate nature and the struggle to control sexual impulses he reveals in his *Confessions,* Augustine's decision to abandon his predecessors' emphasis on free will need not surprise us. Much more surprising, in fact, is the result. Why did the majority of Latin Christians, instead of repudiating Augustine's idiosyncratic views as marginal—or rejecting them as heretical—eventually embrace them? Why did his teaching on "original sin" become the center of western Christian tradition, displacing, or at least wholly recasting, all previous views of creation and free will?

The political and social situation of Christians in the early centuries had changed radically by Augustine's time. Traditional declarations of human freedom, forged by martyrs defying the emperor as anti-Christ incarnate, no longer fit the situation of Christians who now found themselves, under Constantine and his Christian successors, the emperor's "brothers and sisters in Christ." But Augustine's theory conformed to this new situation and interpreted the new arrangement of state, church, and believer in ways that, many agreed, made religious sense of the new political realities.

Both Augustine and his Christian opponents recognized the political dimensions of the controversy, yet none of them discussed government in what we would consider strictly political terms. Instead, since everyone agreed that the story of Adam and Eve offered a basic paradigm for ordering human society, argument over the role of government most often took the form of conflicting interpretations of that story. Let us consider, then, how Augustine and his predecessors—taking as their representative John Chrysostom—read, in opposite ways, the politics of Paradise.

Both John Chrysostom and Augustine, born around the year 354,[8] had grown up in an empire nominally Christian. During the forty years since Constantine's conversion to Christianity in 313, Christian emperors not only had reversed the orders of persecution but had poured magnanimous benefits upon the Christian churches. John was a young priest in Antioch when a public riot against the emperor's taxation policies had broken out, and angry crowds had smashed the statues of the emperor and his family. Rumors of the emperor's rage and his planned retribution preceded his return to Antioch. Yet John, so famous for his riveting speeches that he was later nicknamed *chrysostom,* "golden mouth," in this time of public crisis boldly declared to the crowds that the right of government belongs not to the emperor alone but to the human race as a whole: "In the beginning, God honored our race with sovereignty." For, John asked rhetorically, what else does it mean that God made us "in his image"? "The image of government [νῆς ἀρχῆς] is what is meant; and as there is no one in the heavens superior to God, so there is no one on earth superior to humankind."[9]

John's listeners, concerned with the immediate political crisis, might have wondered at first what he meant in specific political terms. Would the priest go on to say that the emperor embodied *in himself* the sovereignty God bestowed upon Adam? Did the emperor now represent God's rule to the rest of humankind, as some Christians previously had argued? John answered no to such questions. Instead he agreed with Gregory of Nyssa, who declared that since "any particular man is limited . . . the entire plentitude of humanity was included" in God's good gift of his own royal image:

> For the image is not in part of our nature, *nor is the divine gift in any single person . . . but this power extends equally to the whole race;* and a sign of this is that the mind is implanted alike in all; for all have the power of understanding and reflecting. . . . *they equally bear within themselves the divine image.* [10]

John wrote:

> For of governments, some are natural [φυσικαί], and others artificial [χειροτονηταί]: natural, such as the rule of the lion over the quadrupeds, or the eagle over the birds; artificial, as of an emperor over us; for he does not reign over his fellow slaves by any natural authority. Therefore it happens that emperors often lose their sovereignty. [11]

As John saw it, imperial rule epitomizes the social consequences of sin. Like his persecuted Christian predecessors, John ridiculed imperial propaganda that claimed that the state rests upon concord, justice, and liberty. On the contrary, he said, the state relies upon force and compulsion, often using these to violate justice and to suppress liberty. But because the majority of humankind followed Adam's example in sinning, government, however corrupt, has become indispensable and, for this reason, even divinely endorsed:

> [God] himself has armed magistrates with power. . . . God provides for our safety through them. . . . If you were to abolish the public court system, you would abolish all order from our life. . . . If you deprive the city of its rulers, we would have to live a life less rational than that of the animals, biting and devouring one another. . . . For what crossbeams are in houses, rulers are in cities, and just as, if you were to take away the former, the walls, being separated, would fall in upon one another, so, if you were to deprive the world of magistrates and the fear that comes from them, houses, cities, and nations would fall upon one another in unrestrained confusion, there being no one to repress, or repel, or persuade them to be peaceful through the fear of punishment. [12]

John believes that because of human sin, fear and coercion have infected the whole structure of human relationships, from family to city and nation. Everywhere he sees the disastrous results: "Now we are subjected to one another by force and compulsion, and every day we are in conflict with one another."[13]

While granting that the imperial system preserves social order, he charges that it tolerates—or, worse, even enforces—injustice, immorality, and inequality. Roman laws, John says, are, "for the most part, corrupt, useless, and ridiculous." They expose to torture or execution the man who steals clothes or money, but they ignore worse crimes: "Who would be considered wiser, by most people, than the persons considered worthy to legislate for the cities and nations? But yet to these wise men sexual immorality is unworthy of punishment; at least, none of the pagan laws . . . bring men to trial for this reason."[14] Chrysostom explains specifically what kind of case he has in mind: "If a married man has intercourse with a female slave, it seems to be nothing to pagan laws, nor to people in general."[15] Most people, he admits, would laugh at anyone who tried to bring such a case to court, and the judge would dismiss it. The same is true for a married man involved with an unmarried woman or with a prostitute. Roman law protects only the man's rights in such cases, but, Chrysostom declares, "we are punished, though not by the Roman laws, yet by God."[16]

Roman laws, John continues, allow dealers to enslave children and to train them in sexual specialties for sale as prostitutes. And pagan tradition praises the legislators as "common benefactors of the city" for instituting public entertainment that features, in the theaters, prostitutes and prostituted children and, in the sports arena, contests between men and wild animals:

> Those places, too, being full of all senseless excitement, train the people to acquire a merciless and savage and inhuman kind of temperament, and give them practice in seeing people torn in pieces, and blood flowing, and the viciousness of wild beasts upsetting everything. Now all these our wise lawgivers introduced from the beginning—so many plagues—and our cities applaud and admire them.[17]

So much for the masses; but what about the few who, chastened by the example of Adam's sin, and recovered from sin through baptism, exercise appropriate restraint over themselves? Such persons, Chrysostom declares, remain exempt from the punishment that falls upon the corrupt majority—exempt, in fact, from the constraints of human government as a whole: "For those who live in a state of piety require no correction on the part of the magistrates, for 'the law was not made for a righteous man.' But the more numerous, if they had no fear of these hanging over them, would fill the cities with innumerable evils."[18]

The tyranny of external government sharply contrasts with the liberty enjoyed by those capable of autonomous self-rule—above all, by those who, through Christian baptism, have recovered the capacity for self-government.[19] Chrysostom, like the apologists, identifies the former with the Roman Empire and the latter with the emerging new society that constitutes the Christian church: "There, everything is done through fear and constraint; here, through free choice and liberty."[20] The use of force, the driving energy of imperial society, is utterly alien to church government:

> Christians, more than all people, are not allowed to correct by force the faults of those who sin. Secular judges, indeed, when they have captured wrongdoers under the law, demonstrate that their authority is great by preventing them, even against their own will, from following their own desires; but in our case the wrongdoer most be corrected not by force, but by persuasion.[21]

What prevents church leaders from exercising the same authority as imperial magistrates, he explains, has nothing to do with lack of power, much less inferior status. On the contrary, he says, a priest's authority far *surpasses* the emperor's. What restrains a priest from attempting to use such authority, however, is religious principle:

> For neither has the authority of this kind to restrain sinners been given to us by law, *nor, if it had been given, should we have any place to exercise our power,* since God rewards those who abstain from evil out of their own choice, and not out of necessity. . . . If a person wanders away from the right path, great effort, perseverance, and patience are required; for he cannot be dragged back by force, nor restrained by fear, but must be led back by persuasion to the truth from which he originally swerved.[22]

The Christian leader, refraining not only from the use of force but even from the subtler pressures of fear and coercion, must evoke each member's voluntary participation. Failing that, he must respect, however misguided he considers it to be, each member's freedom of choice and action:

We do not have "authority over your faith," beloved, nor do we command these things as your lords and masters. We are appointed for the teaching of the word, not for power, nor for absolute authority. We hold the place of counsellors to advise you. The counsellor speaks his own opinions, not forcing his listener, but *leaving him full master of his own choice in what is said.* He is blameworthy only in this respect, if he fails to say the things that present themselves.[23]

Church government, unlike Roman government, remains wholly voluntary and, although hierarchically structured, is essentially egalitarian, reflecting, in effect, the original harmony of Paradise.

Yet Chrysostom remains uncomfortably aware that the actual churches he knows in Antioch and Constantinople fall far short of such celestial harmony. Having inherited his vision of the church from such heroic predecessors as Justin, Athenagoras, Clement, and Origen, Chrysostom, measuring the church of his own day against theirs, alternatively grieves and lashes out in anger:

Plagues, teeming with untold mischiefs, have come upon the churches. The primary offices have become marketable. Hence innumerable evils are arising, and there is no one to redress, no one to reprove them. Indeed, the disorder has taken on a kind of method and consistency of its own.[24]

Excessive wealth, enormous power, and luxury, Chrysostom charges, are destroying the integrity of the churches. Clerics, infected by the disease of "lust for authority," are fighting for candidates on the basis of family prominence, wealth, or partisanship. Others support the candidacy of their friends, relatives, or flatterers, "but no one will look to the man who is really qualified." They ignore, Chrysostom says, the only valid qualification, "excellence of character."[25] Pagans rightly ridicule the whole business: " 'Do you see,' they say, 'how all matters among the Christians are full of vainglory? And there is ambition among them, and hypocrisy. Strip them,' they say, 'of their numbers, and they are nothing.' "[26]

Could the vision forged by the embattled Christians of earlier times, who saw the church as an island of purity in an ocean of corruption, fit the circumstances of a state religion, a church that had come into imperial favor, wealth, and power? Chrysostom saw his church as still contending against powerful rivals.[27] He did not consider the possibility that his vision of the church, sanctioned by nearly four centuries of tradition, might no longer fit the situation of his fellow Christians at the beginning of the fifth century. Now that the world had invaded the church and the church the world, new questions had arisen: How, for example, were Christians to envision the new role of a Christian emperor and the legitimacy of his rule, not only over unruly pagans, but over Christians themselves (notably including the increasing flood of nominal converts)? And how were Christians to account for the unsettling new prominence of the churches, in which becoming a bishop now guaranteed a man tax exemptions, vastly increased income, social power, and possibly even influence at court?

The traditional Christian answers to the question of power no longer applied by the later fourth century, when not only Constantine but several others, including Theodosius the Great, had ruled as Christian emperors. Augustine's opposite interpretation of the politics of Paradise—and, in particular, his insistence that the whole human race, including the redeemed, remains wholly incapable of self-government—offered Christians radically new ways to interpret this unprecedented situation.

Whereas Chrysostom proclaims human freedom, Augustine reads from the same Genesis story the opposite—human bondage. As for αὐτεξουσία, the power to rule oneself, Augustine cannot acknowledge it as a reality, or even a genuine good, in his own experience, let alone for all humanity. And Augustine begins his reflections on government, characteristically, with introspection.

Recalling in the *Confessions* his own experience, Augustine instinctively identifies the question of self-government with rational control over sexual impulses. Describing his struggle to be chaste, Augustine recalls how, "in the sixteenth year of the age of my flesh . . . the madness of raging lust exercised its supreme dominion over me."[28] Augustine was powerless, a captive and victim. Through sexual desire, he says, "my invisible enemy trod me down and seduced me."[29] Of his sexual involvements he admits, "I drew my shackles along with me, terrified to have them knocked off."[30] Acknowledging that his friend was "amazed at my enslavement," Augustine reflects that "what made me a slave to it was the habit [*consuetudo*] of satisfying an insatiable lust."[31]

Had Augustine confessed as much to a spiritual advisor such as John Chrysostom, he would have been urged to undo the chains that bound him to bad habits and to recover and strengthen, like unused muscles, his own neglected capacity for moral choice. But Augustine in his *Confessions* came directly to challenge such assumptions. Free will is only an illusion—an illusion that Augustine himself once shared: "As for continence, I imagined it to be in the liberty of our own power, which I, for my part, felt I did not have."[32] As he grew older, Augustine changed his mind. Instead of indicting his own lack of faith in the power of free will, Augustine came to lash out at those who falsely assume that they *do* possess such power: "What man is there, who, being aware of his own weakness, dares so much as to attribute his chastity and innocence to his own virtue?"[33] The aging Augustine then takes his own experience as paradigmatic for all human experience—indeed, for Adam's: "Being a captive," he says, "I feigned a show of counterfeit liberty,"[34] as, he says, Adam had done, bringing upon himself and his progeny an avalanche of sin and punishment.

No wonder, then, that the Manichaean theory of human origins, which had "explained" the sense of helplessness he experienced, had at first attracted Augustine. He identified, too, with the way the Manichaeans interpreted the tendency to sin not simply as human weakness but (as the rabbis had taught of the "evil impulse," *yetser hara'*) as an internal energy actively resisting God's will. When he abandoned Manichaean theology, Augustine admitted he was at a loss to understand the Christian teaching on free will. Later he would claim, of course, that in denying the power of the will he was only repeating what Paul had said long before ("I do not do what I will, but I do the very thing I hate. . . . I can will what is right, but I cannot do it"; see Romans 7:15–25). Many Christians ever since—including that famous Augustinian monk Martin Luther—would find Augustine's interpretation of Paul's words persuasive. Yet such recent scholarly studies as the work of Peter Gorday confirm an impression that Augustine effectively *invented* this interpretation of Paul's words, by daring to apply them to the baptized Christian.[35] Augustine's Christian predecessors, including John Chrysostom and Origen, had assumed that Paul's statements about the will's incapacity applied only to those who lacked the grace of Christian baptism. Augustine himself acknowledged this and worked hard, he says, to understand the Catholic teaching (in his words) "that free will is the cause of our doing evil. . . . But I was not able to understand it clearly." Once he began to recognize the power of his own will, he says, "I knew that I had a will . . . and when I did either will or nill anything, I was more sure of it, that I and no other did will or nill; and here was the cause of my sin, as I came to perceive."[36] Yet far from relinquishing entirely the role of victim, Augustine says, "But what I did *against* my will, that I seemed to suffer rather than do. That I considered not to be my fault, but my punishment."[37]

Through the agonizing process of his conversion Augustine claims to have discovered that he was bound by conflict within his own will:

> I was bound, not with another man's chains, but with my own iron will. The enemy held my will, and, indeed, made a chain of it for me, and constrained me. Because of a perverse will, desire was made; and when I was enslaved to desire [*libido*] it became habit; and habit not restrained became necessity. By which links . . . a very hard bondage had me enthralled.[38]

Augustine came to see his own will, then, divided and consequently impotent: "Myself I willed it, and myself I nilled it: it was I myself. I neither willed entirely, nor nilled entirely. Therefore I was in conflict with myself, and . . . was distracted by my own self."[39] How did he account for such conflict? Augustine insists that, since he suffered much of this "against my own will, . . . I was not, therefore, the cause of it, but the 'sin that dwells in me': from the punishment of that *more voluntary sin, because I was a son of Adam.*"[40]

In his earlier writings, as Edward Cranz points out, Augustine expresses views on human freedom and self-government that virtually echo those of his predecessors, such as Chrysostom.[41] But in the fourteenth chapter of *The City of God* Augustine seems intent on proving that, even if Adam once had free will, he himself had never received it. Even in his account of Adam's case Augustine betrays his own ambivalence or, indeed, outright hostility toward the possibility of human freedom. What earlier apologists had celebrated as God's greatest gift to humankind—free will, liberty, autonomy, self-government—Augustine characterizes in surprisingly negative terms. Adam had received freedom as his birthright, but nonetheless, as Augustine tells it, the first man "conceived a desire for freedom,"[42] and his desire became, in Augustine's eyes, the root of sin, betraying nothing less than contempt for God. The desire to master one's will, far from expressing what Origen, Clement, and Chrysostom consider the true nature of rational beings, becomes for Augustine the great and fatal temptation: "The fruit of the tree of knowledge of good and evil is personal control over one's own will" *(proprium voluntatis arbitrium).*[43] Augustine cannot resist reading that desire for self-government as total, obstinate perversity: "The soul, then, delighting in its own freedom *to do wickedness,* and scorning to serve God

. . . willfully deserted its higher master."[44] Seduced by this desire for autonomy, Adam entered into a "life of cruel and wretched slavery instead of the freedom for which he had conceived a desire."[45]

Uncomfortably aware of a contradiction in his argument, Augustine explains that obedience, not autonomy, should have been Adam's true glory, "since man has been naturally so created that it is advantageous for him to be submissive, but disastrous for him to follow his own will, and not the will of his creator."[46] Admitting that "it does, indeed, seem something of a paradox,"[47] Augustine resorts to paradoxical language to describe how God "sought to impress upon this creature, for whom free slavery [*libera servitus*] was expedient, that he was the Lord."[48] Augustine insists, however, that whatever the constraints upon Adam's freedom, the first man was more free than any of his progeny, for only the story of Adam's misuse of free will can account for the contradictions he discovered within himself, his own will caught in perpetual conflict, "much of which I suffered against my own will, rather than did by my will."[49]

Augustine knows that most of his Christian contemporaries would find this claim incredible, if not heretical. John Chrysostom, indeed, warns the fainthearted not to blame Adam for their own transgressions. Answering one who asks, "What am I to do? Must I die because of him?," he replies, "It is not because of him; for you yourself have not remained without sin. Even though it is not the same sin, you have, at any rate, committed others."[50] That Adam's sin brought suffering and death upon humankind most Christians, like their Jewish predecessors and contemporaries, would have taken for granted. But most Jews and Christians would also have agreed that Adam left each of his offspring free to make his or her own choice of good or evil. The whole point of the story of Adam, most Christians assumed, was to warn everyone who heard it not to misuse that divinely given capacity for free choice.

But Augustine, intending to prove the opposite point, laboriously attempts to show that Adam, far from being the single individual Chrysostom envisioned, was instead a corporate personality. Pointing out that Adam's genesis from earth differs essentially from that of any of his progeny born through childbirth, Augustine declares:

> The entire human race that was to pass through woman into offspring was contained in the first man when that married couple received the divine sentence condemning them to punishment,

and *humanity produced what humanity became, not what it was when created, but when, having sinned, it was punished.* [51]

The punishment itself, Augustine continues, "effected in their original nature a change for the worse." Augustine derived the nature of that change from an idiosyncratic interpretation of Romans 5:12.

The Greek text reads, "Through one man [or "because of one man," δι' ἑνὸς ἀνθρώπου] sin entered the world, and through sin, death; and thus death came upon all men, *in that* [ἐφ' ᾧ] all sinned." John Chrysostom, like most Christians, took this to mean that Adam's sin brought death into the world, and death came upon all because "*all* sinned." But Augustine read the passage in Latin, and so either ignored or was unaware of the connotations of the Greek original; thus he misread the last phrase as referring to Adam. Augustine insisted that it meant that "death came upon all men, *in whom* all sinned"—that the sin of that "one man," Adam, brought upon humanity not only universal death, but also universal, and inevitable, sin. Augustine uses the passage to deny that human beings have free moral choice, which Jews and Christians had traditionally regarded as the birthright of humanity made "in God's image." Augustine declares, on the contrary, that the whole human race inherited from Adam a nature irreversibly damaged by sin. "For we all were in that one man, since all of us were that one man who fell into sin through the woman who was made from him." [52]

How can one imagine that millions of individuals not yet born were "in Adam" or, in any sense, "were" Adam? Anticipating objections that would reduce his argument to absurdity, Augustine declares triumphantly that, although "we did not yet have individually created and apportioned forms in which to live as individuals," what did exist already was the "nature of the semen from which we were to be propagated." [53] That semen itself, Augustine argues, already "shackled by the bond of death," transmits the damage incurred by sin. [54] Hence, Augustine concludes, every human being ever conceived through semen already is born contaminated with sin. Through this astonishing argument, [55] Augustine intends to prove that every human being is in bondage not only from birth but indeed from the moment of conception. And since he takes Adam as a corporate personality, Augustine applies his account of Adam's experience, disrupted by the first sin, to every one of his offspring (except, of course, to Christ, conceived, Augustine ingeniously argued, without semen).

When he describes the onset of original sin in Adam, Augustine chooses political language—and specifically the language of sexual politics.[56] He describes his experience of passion in political metaphors—as "rebellion" against the mind's governance. For in the beginning, when there was only one man in the world, Adam discovered within himself the first government—the rule of the rational soul, the "better part of a human being," over the body, the "inferior part." Augustine, influenced, no doubt, by his study of Platonic philosophy, characterizes their respective roles in political terms: the soul by divine right is to subjugate every member of its "lower servant," the body, to the ruling power of its will. Within Adam as within Eve both soul and body originally obeyed the authority of rational will: "Although they bore an animal body, yet they felt in it no disobedience moving against themselves. . . . Each received the body as a servant . . . and the body obeyed God . . . in an appropriate servitude, without resistance."[57]

But the primal couple soon experienced within themselves not only the first government on earth but also the first revolution. Adam's assertion of his own autonomy was, Augustine insists, tantamount to rebellion against God's rule. Augustine appreciates the aptness with which the punishment for this uprising fits the crime: "The punishment for disobedience was nothing other than disobedience. For human misery consists in nothing other than man's disobedience to himself."[58] Augustine stresses, however, that the penalty for sin involves more than bodily impulses rebelling against the mind. Instead, the "flesh" that wars against the "law of the mind" includes, he says, the "whole of one's natural being."[59] The commonest experiences of frustration—mental agitation, bodily pain, aging, suffering, and death—continually prove to us our incapacity to implement the rule of our will, for who would undergo any of these, Augustine asks, if our nature "in every way and every part obeyed our will?"[60]

But what epitomizes our rebellion against God, above all, is the "rebellion in the flesh"—a spontaneous uprising, so to speak, in the "disobedient members":

> After Adam and Eve disobeyed . . . they felt for the first time a
> movement of disobedience in their flesh, as punishment in kind
> for their own disobedience to God. . . . The soul, which had taken
> a perverse delight in its own liberty and disdained to serve God,
> was now deprived of its original mastery over the body.[61]

Specifically, Augustine concludes, "the sexual desire [*libido*] of our disobedient members arose in those first human beings as a result of the sin of disobedience . . . and because a shameless movement [*impudens motus*] resisted the rule of their will, they covered their shameful members."[62] At first, the Adam and Eve whom God had created enjoyed mental mastery over the procreative process: the sexual members, like the other parts of the body, enacted the work of procreation by a deliberate act of will, "like a handshake." Ever since Eden, however, spontaneous sexual desire is, Augustine contends, the clearest evidence of the effect of original sin: this, above all, manifests passion's triumph. What impresses Augustine most is that such arousal functions independently of the will's rightful rule: "Because of this, these members are rightly called *pudenda* [parts of shame] because they excite themselves just as they like, in opposition to the mind which is their master, as if they were their own masters."[63] Sexual excitement differs from other forms of passion, Augustine contends, since in the case of anger and the rest, it is not the impulse that moves any part of the body but the will, which remains in control and consents to the movement. An angry man makes a decision whether or not to strike; but a sexually aroused man may find that erection occurs with alarming autonomy. Augustine considers this irrefutable evidence that lust *(libido),* having wrested the sexual organs from the control of the will, now has "brought them so completely under its rule that they are incapable of acting if this one emotion [*libido*] is lacking."[64] So disjoined is will from desire that even a man who wills to be sexually aroused may find that *libido* deserts him.

> At times, the urge intrudes uninvited; at other times, it deserts the panting lover, and, although desire blazes in the mind, the body is frigid. In this strange way, desire refuses service, not only to the will to procreate, but also to the desire for wantonness; and though for the most part, it solidly opposes the mind's command, at other times it is divided against itself, and, having aroused the mind, it fails to arouse the body.[65]

The experience of arousal apart from any action taken, Augustine insists, itself is sin: "Such disobedience of the flesh as this, which lies in the very excitement, even when it is not allowed to take effect, did not exist in the first man and woman."[66] Augustine admits, however, that

> the trouble with the hypothesis of a passionless procreation controlled by the will, as I am here suggesting it, is that it has never

been verified in experience, not even in the experience of those who could have proved that it was possible. In fact, they sinned too soon, and brought upon themselves exile from Eden.[67]

But Augustine believes that each person *can* verify from experience the radical leap to which his own inner turmoil impelled him—the leap that identifies sexual desire itself as evidence of, and penalty for, original sin. That each of us experiences desire spontaneously *apart* from will means, Augustine assumes, that we experience it *against* our will. Hence, he continues, sexual desire naturally involves shame: "A man by his very nature is ashamed of sexual desire."[68] What proves the truth of such assertions, Augustine believes, is the universal practice of covering the genitals and of shielding the act of intercourse from public view.[69]

One might, of course, ask the obvious question: Is it not possible to experience desire *in accordance with the will* (as, for example, when engaging in intercourse for the purpose of procreation)? Chrysostom would say yes; but Augustine's very definition of sexual desire excludes that possibility. Having entered into human experience through an act of rebellion against the will, desire can never cooperate with will to form, so to speak, a coalition government. For Augustine, "lust is an usurper, defying the power of the will, and tyrannizing the human sexual organs."[70]

Augustine believes that by defining spontaneous sexual desire as the proof and penalty of original sin he has succeeded in implicating the whole human race, except, of course, for Christ. Christ alone of all humankind, Augustine explains, was born without *libido*—being born, he believes, without the intervention of semen that transmits its effects. But the rest of humankind issues from a procreative process that, ever since Adam, has sprung wildly out of control, marring the whole of human nature.

What, then, can remedy human misery? How can anyone achieve internal balance, much less establish social and political harmony between man and woman, man and man? Augustine's whole theology of the fall depends upon his radical claim that no human power can effect such restoration. Knowing, however, that many philosophically minded people (including philosophically educated Christians from Justin Martyr through Chrysostom) stand against him and would invoke against his argument the evidence of all who successfully practice self-control—pagan philosophers and Christian ascetics alike—Augustine seizes the offensive. There are, he admits, a few people who restrain their passions through self-control, leading temperate, just, and holy lives. But while others honor such people for their achievement, Augustine accuses them, in effect, of neurosis: "This is by no means a healthy state due to nature [*sanitas ex natura*], but an illness due to guilt [*languor ex culpa*]."[71] For not only the "common mass of men, but even the most godly and righteous," he insists, are ravaged by sin and dominated by passion. The Stoic attempt to achieve *apatheia*—mastery of passion—he dismisses as leading its practitioners into arrogance and isolation from the rest of humanity, "not tranquility."[72] Thus ridiculing such efforts to reassert the power of the will, Augustine concludes that the "rebellion in our members, . . . that proof and penalty of man's rebellion against God," is not only universal but also ineradicable. Part of our nature stands in permanent revolt against the "law of the mind"—even among the philosophers, even among the baptized and the saints. And since, he insists, everyone, even the most advanced ascetic, confronts the same continual insurrection within, Augustine concludes that humankind has wholly lost its original capacity for self-government.

Augustine draws so drastic a picture of the effects of Adam's sin that he embraces human government, even when tyrannical, as the indispensable defense against the forces sin has unleashed in human nature. His analysis of internal conflict, indeed, leads directly into his view of social conflict in general. The war within us drives us into war with one another—and no one, pagan or Christian, remains exempt. So, he explains, "while a good man is progressing to perfection, one part of him can be at war with another of his parts; hence, two good men can be at war with one another."

In the beginning, Augustine agrees with Chrysostom, politics began at home:

> The union of male and female is the seed-bed, so to speak, from which the city must grow. . . . Since, then, a man's home [*hominis domus*] ought to be the beginning or elementary constituent of the city, and every beginning serves some end of its own, and every part serves the integrity of the whole of which it is a part, it follows clearly enough that domestic peace serves civic peace, that is, that the ordered agreement of command and obedience among those who live together in a household serves the ordered agreement of command and obedience among citizens.[73]

Recognizing that Adam and Eve originally were created to live together in a harmonious order of authority and obedience, superiority and subordination, like soul and body, "we must conclude," says Augustine, "that a husband is meant to rule over his wife as the spirit rules the flesh." But once each member of the primal couple had experienced that first internal revolt in which the bodily passions arose against the soul, they experienced analogous disruption in their relationship with one another. Although originally created equal with man in regard to her rational soul, woman's formation from Adam's rib established her as the "weaker part of the human couple."[74] Being closely connected with bodily passion, woman, although created to be man's helper, became his temptress and led him into disaster.[75] The Genesis account describes the result: God himself reinforced the husband's authority over his wife, placing divine sanction upon the social, legal, and economic machinery of male domination.

Apart from the relationship between the sexes, however, Augustine again agrees with Chrysostom that "God did not want a rational being, made in his image, to have dominion over any except irrational creatures; not man over men, but man over the beasts."[76] Unlike man's dominion over woman, man's dominion over other men violates their original equality; hence, "such a condition as slavery could only have arisen as a result of sin."[77] Augustine diverges sharply from Chrysostom, however, when he traces how sin, transmitted from the primal parents through sexual reproduction, infected their offspring, so that now "everyone, arising as he does from a condemned stock, is from the first necessarily evil and carnal through Adam."[78] So Cain, when another form of carnal desire, envy, overcame his rational judgment, murdered his brother, exemplifying the lust for power that now dominates and distorts the whole structure of human relationships.

Those who share Augustine's vision of the disastrous results of sin must, he believes, accept as well the rule of one man over others—master over slave, ruler over subjects—as the inescapable necessity of our universal fallen nature:

> Such, as men are now, is the order of peace. Some are in subjection to others and, while humility helps those who serve, pride harms those in power. But as men once were, when their nature was as God created it, no man was a slave either to man or to sin. However, *slavery is now penal in character, and planned by that law which commands the preservation of the natural order and forbids its disturbance.*[79]

Human nature, Augustine explains, instinctively desires social harmony: "By the very laws of his nature man is, so to speak, forced into social relationships and peace [*societatem pacemque*] with other men, so far as possible."[80] Yet sin distorts this universal impulse, turning it instead into the enforced order that constitutes "earthly peace."

Certain scholars have emphasized—quite rightly—how carefully Augustine qualifies his affirmation of secular government. The Dutch scholar Henrik Berkhof, writing during the Second World War, takes Augustine as representing what he calls the "theocratic" view, which subordinates the interests of the state to those of the church. Wilhelm Kamlah, writing in Germany after the war, declares that Augustine's theory deprives the state of any claim to ultimate religious value, regarding it, in effect, as a "necessary evil."[81] R. Markus points out that as Augustine matured, he decisively rejected the classical belief—earlier shared even by Christians who were enamored of the "Christian empire"—that the state and its power served humanity's ultimate good. Augustine expresses no illusions, certainly, about the rulers' motives for enforcing peace. Even a solitary criminal, he says, "demands peace in his own home, and, if need be, gets it by sheer brutality. He knows that the price of peace is to have everyone subject to some one head—in this case, to himself."[82] Should such a man gain power over a larger society, Augustine continues, he would rule through the same brutal impulse:

> Thus it is that all men want peace in their own society, and they all want it on their own terms. When they go to war, what they want is to make, if they can, their enemies their own, and to impose on them the victor's will, and call it a peace. . . . Sinful man hates the equality of all men under God, and, as though he were God, loves to impose his own sovereignty upon his fellow men.[83]

Such pragmatic and negative assessments of the function of government are not, of course, original with Augustine. As we have seen, Justin Martyr, addressing the emperors Antoninus Pius, Marcus Aurelius, and Lucius Verus two and a half centuries earlier, had borrowed an image from philosophical tradition[84] to say that those who rule by brute force "have just as much power as robbers in a desert."[85] Marcus Aurelius used the same image in his own *Meditations*[86]—as, indeed, does Augustine in another famous passage:

"Without justice, what then are kingdoms but great robberies? For what are robberies themselves but little kingdoms?"[87] No more original is Augustine's insistence that political authority is not natural to man but a result of his sinful condition.[88] Justin's younger colleague Irenaeus had described how

> God imposed upon humankind the fear of men since they did not acknowledge the fear of God, so that, being subject to human authority and kept under restraints by their laws, they might attain to some degree of justice. . . . Earthly rule, therefore, has been appointed by God, and not by the devil, for the benefit of nations . . . so that, under fear of human rule, people may not devour one another like fishes.[89]

Irenaeus was drawing in turn upon much older tradition—using, in fact, a rabbinic image to interpret Paul's warning to Christians about the positive uses of governmental coercion (Romans 13:1–6).

Yet Augustine's predecessors Justin and Irenaeus had affirmed the necessity of coercive government only for "those outside." Both, like Chrysostom, clearly discriminate between the coercive government necessary for outsiders and the internal rule of the church. Baptized Christians, Justin and Irenaeus agree, essentially have recovered from the damage inflicted by sin. Baptism transforms converts from their former state as "children of necessity and ignorance . . . to become children of choice and knowledge," washed clean of sin, illuminated, and, Justin says, "by our deeds, too, found to be good citizens and keepers of the commandments."[90]

Augustine agreed with his predecessors in delineating two distinct modes of relationship—one motivated by impulses of domination and submission, the other by mutually affirming love. But what sets Augustine's mature position apart from that of his predecessors is his refusal simply to identify the first with the state and the second with the church. As he redefines them, the "city of man" and the "city of God" cut across both categories. Even baptized Christians are not exempt from either the war of conflicting impulses or the need for external government.

Augustine insists, on the contrary, that all government remains only a superstructure imposed upon the internal rebellion that sin has instigated within everyone, pagan and Christian alike. Consequently he believes the situation of the baptized Christian is far more complex than Chrysostom imagined. The Christian, like the unbeliever, has to contend against the enemy within that holds power over his will; hence he, too, needs the help of external discipline. So even in his domestic life, Augustine says, although the Christian longs for heaven,

> where there will be no further need for giving orders to other human beings, . . . meanwhile, in case anyone in the household breaks its peace by disobedience, he is disciplined by words or whipping or other kinds of punishment lawful and licit in human society, and for his own good, to readjust to the peace he has abandoned.[91]

If Christians cannot even be trusted to govern themselves, how are they to approach church government? Later in his life Augustine came to endorse, for the church as well as the state, the whole arsenal of secular government that Chrysostom had repudiated—commands, threats, coercion, penalties, and even physical force. Whereas Chrysostom had defined his own role as that of advisor, not ruler, Augustine, like Ignatius of Antioch, sees the bishop as ruling "in God's place." One of Augustine's favorite images for church leaders, as for their model, Christ, is that of the physician, ministering to those who have been baptized but, like himself, are still sick, each one infected with the same ineradicable disease contracted through original sin.[92] Augustine tends, consequently, to discount the patients' opinions. It is the physician's responsibility not only to administer to sick and suffering humanity the life-giving medication of the sacraments, but also to carry out, when necessary, disciplinary procedures as a kind of surgery.

This vision of the church, advocated by others, such as Augustine's close friend and fellow bishop Alypius, corresponds in a sense to Augustine's own experience. In his *Confessions* he admits how desperately lost, sick, and helpless he felt, believing his will to be morally paralyzed, as he awaited the revelation of grace mediated through the church to penetrate him from without and effect his healing.[93] But other Christians surely would not have recognized their own experiences in his account. The British monk Pelagius, for one, sharply objected, criticizing Augustine's *Confessions* for popularizing a kind of pious self-indulgence. How, then, did Augustine's idiosyncratic views on the effects of original sin—and hence on the politics of the church and state—come to be accepted in the fifth and sixth centuries, first by the leadership of the Catholic church and then by the majority of its members? The question is, of course, wildly ambitious; but let us attempt to sketch out the beginning of an answer.

Let us consider first how the conflicting views of Chrysostom and Augustine might sound to their contemporaries. By the beginning of the fifth century Catholic Christians lived as subjects of an empire they could no longer consider alien, much less wholly evil. Having repudiated the patronage of the traditional gods some two generations earlier, the emperors now sometimes used military force to help stamp out pagan worship. Furthermore, the two sons of Theodosius the Great, reigning since his death in 395 as emperors of East and West, continued their father's policy of withdrawing patronage from Arian Christians and placing themselves wholly in alliance with the Catholic bishops and clergy. An earlier generation of Christian bishops, including Eusebius of Caesarea, deeply impressed by the events they had witnessed and convinced that they lived at a turning point in history, had hailed Constantine and his successors as God's chosen rulers. Augustine, like most of his fellow Christians, once had shared that conviction. But after two generations the Christian empire and its rulers, if no longer alien, remained in many respects all too human. By the beginning of the fifth century few who dealt with the government firsthand—certainly not Chrysostom and finally not Augustine either—would have identified it with God's reign on earth.[94]

The mature Augustine offers a theology of politics far more complex and compelling than any of its rivals. Chrysostom claimed that imperial rule is unnecessary for believers, but Augustine insists that God has placed everyone, whether pagan or priest, equally in subjection to external government. Yet Augustine's reasoning diverges sharply from the naïve endorsement of Constantine's court theologian, Eusebius. Augustine's dark vision of a human nature ravaged by original sin and overrun by lust for power rules out uncritical adulation and qualifies his endorsement of imperial rule.[95] That same dark vision impels him to reject Chrysostom's more optimistic premise that imperial power is necessary for pagans, but, in effect, superfluous in the lives of pious citizens. Augustine, on the contrary, places secular government at the center of human society, indispensable for the best as well as the worst among its members. For a Christian, civic obligations rank second, certainly, to one's obligation to God (or, as this usually meant in practice, to the church). Yet apart from direct conflict of interest, even the bishop must render appropriate obedience to secular authority.[96] Augustine acknowledges the emperor's rule, however limited (or even however brutal), to be, nevertheless, as permanent and ineradicable—in this world, at least—as the effects of original sin. More effectively than either Eusebius on the one hand or Chrysostom on the other, Augustine's theory enabled his contemporaries to come to terms both with the fact of Christian empire and with its intractably human nature.

For if the fifth-century state no longer looked so evil as it once had, the church, in turn, no longer looked so holy. Chrysostom, holding to his by now essentially sectarian theory, deplored what had happened to the church since imperial favor first shone upon Christians: first, the massive influx of nominal converts; and second, the way that a shower of imperial privileges had radically changed the dynamics—and raised the stakes—of ecclesiastical politics. But what Chrysostom could only denounce, Augustine could interpret. Challenging the traditional model of the church and the assumption on which it rested—free will—Augustine's theory of original sin could make theologically intelligible not only the state's imperfections but the church's imperfections as well.

Secondly, while changing the way Catholic Christians understood the psychological and religious meaning of freedom (*libertas*), Augustine's theory bore the potential for changing as well their understanding of, and relationship to, political liberty. Throughout the Roman republic men of wealth and power tended to agree that *libertas* meant living under the rule of a "good governor," that is, an emperor of whom the senate approved.[97]

We have seen, however, that certain Christians, among others, despised the patricians' version of *liberty*, regarding it as a euphemism for *slavery*—that is, for political subjugation induced by the totalitarian rule of the later Caesars. For some people, *liberty* meant freedom from superior authority and freedom from constraint—including, for example, freedom of speech.

We have seen, too, how Christians, so long as they remained a persecuted, illegal, and minority sect, sided with the latter position. We recall how Minucius Felix, writing c. 200 C.E., rhetorically described the Christian who, undergoing torture for his faith, maintains his *libertas*:

> "How beautiful is the spectacle to God when a Christian does battle with pain, when he is brought up against threats, and punishment, and torture; when, mocking the noise of death, he treads underfoot the horror of the executioner; when *he raises up his liberty against kings and princes,* and yields to God alone . . . when, triumphant and victorious, he tramples on the very one who has passed sentence upon him."[98]

Repudiating the charge that Christians were afraid for superstitious reasons to offer pagan sacrifice, Minucius Felix had declared that "it is not a confession of fear, but an assertion of our true liberty."[99] Tertullian, Minucius's contemporary, when he challenged imperial authority in the name of that "liberty which is [the individual's] right,"[100] had assumed that the term meant freedom from superior authority.[101]

Augustine, on the contrary, having denied that human beings possess any capacity whatever for free will, accepts a definition of liberty far more agreeable to the powerful and influential men with whom he himself wholeheartedly identifies. As Augustine tells it, it is the *serpent* who tempts Adam with the seductive lure of liberty. The forbidden fruit symbolizes, he explains, "personal control over one's own will."[102] Not, Augustine adds, "that it is evil in itself, but it is placed in the garden to teach him the primary virtue"—obedience. So, as we noted above, Augustine concludes that humanity never was really meant to be, in any sense, truly free. God allowed us to sin in order to prove to us from our own experience that "our true good is free slavery"[103]—slavery to God in the first place and, in the second, to his agent, the emperor. Idiosyncratic as it sounds, Augustine's paradox finds a parallel in the political rhetoric of his contemporaries. Claudian, pagan court poet and propagandist in the service of Stilicho and of Honorius, the Christian emperor of the West, challenges those who call the emperor's rule slavery (*servitium*): "Never is liberty more appreciated than under a good king!"[104] During the following centuries a similar view was incorporated into the imperial Catholic mass, which directs the priest to pray that, "the enemies of peace being overthrown, Roman liberty may serve Thee in security" (*secura tibi serviat Romana libertas*).[105]

Finally, anyone observing the contrast between the careers of the two bishops might well conclude that Augustine's version of the politics of Paradise proved effective in dealing with the politics of the fifth-century Roman Empire, whereas Chrysostom's version failed. Both Augustine, born in Tagaste, North Africa, in 354, and John Chrysostom, born in Antioch either the same year or a few years earlier,[106] grew up in a world ruled for more than a generation by Christian emperors—a succession interrupted only by Julian's abrupt two-year reversion to imperial patronage of paganism. But Augustine's responses to the new constellation of imperial power were very different from Chrysostom's.

Chrysostom lost his father at a young age, was raised with his sister by his Christian mother, was baptized at the age of eighteen, and became a monk. In one of his first publications, *Comparison Between a King and a Monk,* written at a time when the world, the imperial court, and the church were mingling in unprecedented ways, Chrysostom passionately defended sacred against secular power—a theme that would preoccupy him throughout his lifetime. Some twelve years later, as we noted earlier, after the people of Antioch had rioted and smashed the imperial statues in protest against the emperor, John Chrysostom addressed an audience waiting in terror of imperial reprisals, and dared proclaim, not, as Augustine might have, that even the Christian is subject to the emperor, but that the emperor himself needs the priest and is subject to the priest's superior authority: "He is himself a ruler, and a ruler of greater dignity than the other; for the sacred laws place under his hands even the royal head."[107] When the bishop intervened with the emperor to settle the crisis, John said that those events proved to unbelievers "that the Christians are the saviors of the city; that they are its guardians, its patrons, and its teachers. . . . Let all unbelievers learn that the fear of Christ is a bridle to every kind of authority."[108]

In 397 Chrysostom received an unexpected summons to Constantinople, the eastern capital of the empire. Hurrying there in secret, he was surprised to find himself appointed bishop of Constantinople, a position near the pinnacle of ecclesiastical power. By canon law of 391, the bishop of Constantinople ranked second only to the bishop of Rome; but often a man in that position, as chief spiritual advisor to the emperor, to the imperial family, and to the whole court, surpassed all others in actual influence. Eutropius, the brilliant and powerful eunuch who controlled much of court politics for the emperor Arcadius, his ineffectual young charge, had arranged for the appointment. Eutropius probably guessed that the pious and eloquent Chrysostom had neither the taste nor the talent for court politics. Eutropius was right; Chrysostom was so impolitic, so concerned with his responsibilities as moral advisor to the powerful, advocate for the destitute and oppressed, and austere guardian of clerical discipline, that within three years he had offended virtually everyone who had once welcomed his appointment. His acts of social conscience turned powerful people among the court and clergy against him. And his attempt to build a hospital for lepers directly outside the city walls set off a "war" of protest that ended with his expulsion from office.[109] One historian concludes that Chrysostom "proudly disdained the favor of the court, on which the high position of his episcopate alone rested, by his foolish idealism."[110] Another wonders whether he deserves to be revered as a saint and martyr or condemned "comme un idéaliste dépourvu de finesse diplomatique, un zélote sans tact, ou un fanatique incapable de nuances et victime de son emportement."[111] John's admirers attributed the bishop's actions to his deep religious convictions and to his uncompromising moral consciousness. Yet even they could see how those very qualities had led to accusations of "hardness and rudeness," and of arrogance intolerable in a man in his position, and so played into the hands of his enemies.

After six years in office Chrysostom learned that his enemies had prevailed over his former supporters: deposed from episcopal office, perhaps narrowly escaping death, he began under heavy guard the arduous journey into exile. Ill and alone, defended and consoled by a few loyal friends, he lived only three years longer. But Chrysostom's convictions never swerved: secular and spiritual powers are antithetical and mutually exclusive. From exile he wrote to his close woman friend and supporter, the deaconess Pentadia, words that no doubt express his reflections upon his own sufferings, as well as upon hers:

> I rejoice . . . and find the greatest consolation, in my solitude, in the fact that you have been so manly and steadfast, and that you have not allowed yourself to do wrong. . . . Be glad, therefore, and rejoice over your victory. For they have done everything they could against you. You, who knew only the church and your monastic cell, they have dragged out into the public eye, from there to the court, and from court to prison. They have brought false witnesses, have slandered, murdered, shed streams of blood . . . and left nothing undone to terrify you, and to obtain from you a lie. . . . But you have brought them all to shame.[112]

Now consider Augustine. Born into a nonpatrician family, Augustine tells us that his pagan father, Patricus, a man habitually unfaithful to Augustine's mother, not only failed to "root out the brambles of lust" from his son but expressed pleasure in his adolescent son's sexual appetite. (Perhaps Augustine had his hot-tempered father somehow in mind when he complained that "traditional education taught me that Jupiter punishes the wicked with his thunderbolts, and yet commits adultery himself!") His Christian mother, Monica, patiently endured her husband's infidelities, Augustine says, but "most earnestly implored me not to commit fornication." As a young man he would have been embarrassed to take such "woman-ish" advice; much later, looking back, he came to believe that God had spoken to him through his mother, and that "when I disregarded her, I disregarded [God]." Augustine sought a secular career with intense ambition and plunged into the life of the city—theatrical performances, dinner parties, rhetorical competition, many friend-ships. After various earlier sexual relationships he lived for years with a lower-class woman who engaged his passions and bore him a son, but then he abandoned her for the sake of a socially advan-tageous marriage his mother arranged for him. Yet once he had become a successful rhetor, Augustine found himself divided. Al-though attracted to philosophical and religious contemplation, he was unwilling to give up marriage and career. Then, at the age of thirty-two, spurred by stories of the desert solitaries, he renounced the world and was baptized. Three years later, having "given up all hope in this world," Augustine went to Hippo to set up the commu-nal monastic life he intended to enter. Later he protested to his congregation that he had had no intention whatever of seeking church office and expressed ambivalence about his successful ec-clesiastical career: "I was grabbed, I was made a priest . . . and, from there, I became your bishop."[113]

The church that Augustine chose to join, as Peter Brown points out, "was not the old church of Cyprian"—not, that is, the select community of the holy, willing to risk persecution and death or, lacking the opportunity for martyrdom, eager to leave the world;

> it was the new, expanding church of Ambrose, rising above the Roman world like "a moon waxing in its brightness." It was a confident, international body, established in the respect of Chris-tian emperors, sought out by noblemen and intellectuals, capable of bringing to the masses of the known civilized world the eso-teric truths of the philosophy of Plato, a church set no longer to defy society but to master it.[114]

As Augustine understood their task, having learned it from Am-brose, church leaders participate in the divinely ordained work of government: "You teach kings to rule for the benefit of their people; and it is you who warn the people to be subservient to their kings."[115] At the time of Augustine's baptism, the Catholic church was in the process of consolidating its identification with imperial rule. Armed with support from the emperor Honorius, the leaders of the western church, intent on preventing a rival group of Christians from returning to favor, committed themselves to the policy of implementing imperial authority and so, in the process, asserting and consolidating the primacy of Catholicism over all its Christian rivals.

Augustine's position as bishop of a provincial North African city can scarcely be compared with Chrysostom's far more prominent position three years later in the capital city of the eastern empire. Still, in accepting the episcopate, Augustine, too, became a public figure and ruler of a community. When his authority was challenged by the rival church of Donatists, Augustine came to appreciate—and manipulate—the advantages of his alliance with the repressive power of the state. His opponents were Christians who had refused to acknowledge the episcopacy of Caecilian, elected bishop of Carthage in 311, on the grounds that Caecilian had allowed Roman government authorities to confiscate and destroy his church's copies of the Scriptures during the Great Persecution of 303–304. Called Donatists after one of their leaders, Donatus of Casae Nigrae, these Christians identified with the "church of the martyrs." Donatist Christians denounced the "unholy alliance" between Catholic Christians and the Roman state. Echoing Chrysostom's principle, they insisted that the church must employ only spiritual sanctions and not force.

Yet Augustine abandoned the policy of toleration practiced by the previous bishop of Carthage and pursued the attack on the Donatists. Like Chrysostom, he praised the church's use of persuasion, not force; yet he himself, after beginning with polemics and propaganda, turned increasingly to force. First came laws denying civil rights to non-Catholic Christians; then the imposition of penalties, fines, eviction from public office; and finally, denial of free discussion, exile of Donatist bishops, and the use of physical coercion. According to Catholic historians, the Donatist cause became increasingly identified with active resistance to authority, including outbreaks of violence.[116] Despite his earlier misgivings, Augustine came to find military force "indispensable" in suppressing the Donatists and "wrote the only full justification, in the history of the early church, of the right of the state to suppress non-Catholics."[117] He came to realize, he explained, that fear and coercion, which Chrysostom had considered necessary only to govern outsiders, were necessary within the church as well; many Christians as well as pagans, he noted regretfully, respond only to fear.[118]

After Augustine had spent more than thirty years battling the Donatists, he was dismayed to confront Christians he called the Pelagians who, despite many differences, as we shall see in Chapter 6, shared with the Donatists both a sectarian view of the church and an insistence on free will. When his own party was outvoted in the Christian synods, Augustine unhesitatingly allied himself with imperial officials against the clergy who defended Pelagius. In 416 Innocent, bishop of Rome, received from African synods two condemnations of Pelagian ideas, together with a long personal letter from Augustine and his closest associates as well as an open letter from Augustine challenging Pelagius. The documents went beyond a condemnation of Pelagius and his followers. They went on to warn, in Peter Brown's words, that

> the ultimate consequence of [Pelagian] ideas . . . cut at the roots of episcopal authority. . . . The documents claimed that by appeasing the Pelagians the Catholic church would *lose the vast authority it had begun to wield as the only force that could "liberate" men from themselves.* [119]

Pelagius's supporters would make the counterclaim (and with reason) that they were following ancient tradition concerning the church and human nature—tradition most recently championed by John Chrysostom himself. But the declarations of the African synods, engineered primarily by Augustine and his associates, signaled a major turning point in the history of western Christianity. They offered to the bishop of Rome and to his imperial patrons a clear demonstration of the political efficacy of Augustine's doctrine of the fall. By insisting that humanity, ravaged by sin, now lies helplessly in need of outside intervention, Augustine's theory could not only validate secular power but justify as well the imposition of church authority—by force, if necessary—as essential for human salvation.

Augustine, having outlived by twenty-seven years his exiled and disgraced colleague, achieved, unlike John Chrysostom, a position of extraordinary power and influence in the Roman world, until his death on 28 August 430. Augustine's ideas certainly did not win immediate or universal acceptance. Throughout the following century, until the Council of Orange in 529, Augustine's views were ardently debated. Even in the centuries following that council, which endorsed Augustine's views, many theologians held—or were accused of holding—"semi-Pelagian" views. Yet far beyond his lifetime, even for a millennium and a half, the influence of Augustine's teaching throughout western Christendom has surpassed that of any other church father. There are many reasons for this, but I suggest, as primary among them, the following: It is Augustine's theology of the fall that made the uneasy alliance between the Catholic churches and imperial power palatable—not only justifiable but necessary—for the majority of Catholic Christians. Augustine's doctrine, of course, was not, either for him or for the majority of his followers, a matter of mere expedience. Serious believers concerned primarily with the deeper questions of theology, as well as those concerned with political advantage, could find in Augustine's theological legacy ways of making sense out of a situation in which church and state had become inextricably interdependent.

The eventual triumph of Augustine's theology required, however, the capitulation of all who held to the classical proclamation concerning human freedom, once so widely regarded as the heart of the Christian gospel. By the beginning of the fifth century those who still held to such archaic traditions—notably including those the Catholics called Donatists and Pelagians—came to be condemned as heretics. Augustine's theory of Adam's fall, once espoused in simpler forms only by marginal groups of Christians, now moved, together with the imperially supported Catholic church that proclaimed it, into the center of western history.

# (VI)

# THE NATURE
# OF NATURE

WE HAVE SEEN HOW Christian perspectives on freedom
and the power of the will changed as the situation of
Christians changed from that of persecuted sectarians to
that of the emperor's coreligionists. In this chapter I wish to point
out another element of Augustine's theology that accompanied this
enormous transformation: the holistic view of nature that came to
dominate Christian thought, and whose first principle is that human
beings wield—or once did, through Adam—great power over nature (an apparent paradox, given Augustine's conviction that human
beings, whose common ancestor had the power to transform nature,
now are powerless to evade the consequences of that transformation).

For millennia, Jews and Christians have attempted to explain the
mystery of human suffering as moral judgment—the price of Adam
and Eve's sin. The creation story of Genesis, addressing the question
Why do we suffer and why do we die?, makes the empirically absurd
claim that death does not constitute the natural end of all lives but
intruded upon our species solely because Adam and Eve made the
wrong choice. According to Genesis, God said to the woman,

> "I will greatly multiply your pain in childbearing; in pain you
> shall bring forth children, yet your desire shall be for your hus-
> band, and he shall rule over you." And to Adam he said, "Be-
> cause you have listened to the voice of your wife, and have eaten
> of the tree of which I commanded you, 'You shall not eat of it,'
> cursed is the ground because of you; in toil you shall eat of it all
> the days of your life; thorns and thistles it shall bring forth to you;
> . . . In the sweat of your face you shall eat bread till you return

to the ground, for out of it you were taken; you are dust, and to
dust you shall return."

(GENESIS 3:16–19)

Thus pain, oppression, labor, and death are punishments that we (or
our ultimate ancestors) *brought upon ourselves.* "In the beginning" the
willful choice of the first man and woman changed the nature of
nature itself, and all humankind thereafter suffered and died.

Perhaps part of the power of this archaic story, from which
Christians have inferred a moral system, lies in its blatant contradiction of everyday experience, its attribution of supernatural power to
certain human beings. What Adam's supernatural power once effected, Paul declares, only Christ's supernatural power can undo:
*"For as by a man came death, by a man has come also the resurrection of
the dead.* For as in Adam all die, so also in Christ shall all be made
alive" (1 Corinthians 15:21–22). The gospels claim that Jesus' mer-
est word could not only still a thunderstorm and heal diseases but call
the dead back to life. In the Sermon on the Mount Jesus himself
demanded that his followers control their own natures by taking
moral responsibility for their acts, and mastering such instinctual
responses as anger and sexual desire (Matthew 5:21–22, 27–28).

Zealous Christians of the first few centuries, as we have seen,
tested the extreme limits of human virtue (Latin *virtus,* literally
"strength") by demonstrating their power over their own sexuality.
Many early Christians also believed that they could triumph even
over death, not only in the future resurrection but here and now, if
they could break the power of natural impulses—above all, sexual
desire.[1] According to the Gospel of Luke Jesus himself had said:

> *"The children of this age marry, and are given in marriage; but those
> who are accounted worthy of the age to come and the resurrection from
> the dead neither marry nor are given in marriage, nor can they die any
> more; for they are equal to the angels in heaven, and, being children of
> God, are children of the resurrection."*
>
> (LUKE 20:34–36)

Inspired by such words, many Christians pursued that unnatural—or,
as they would say, supernatural—life.

Yet stories of heroic ascetics, including the story of Jerome's
protégée the young widow Blaesilla, who died in her attempted
asceticism, raised obvious questions among Christians, as well as
among their critics. What is the extent—and what are the limits—of
human choice? What can we control, and what is beyond us? Can we

actually govern sexual desire, suffering, and death, or do these conditions belong to the structure of nature? Are they "acts of God" and thus beyond our power—or is this power a matter of degree? Is death, in particular, *natural*? Or is it *unnatural,* an enemy, as Paul said (1 Corinthians 15:26), intruding on human life because of Adam's sin?

During the formative period of Christian tradition, as we have seen, many thoughtful Christians struggled to understand not only the nature of the universe but human nature in particular. During the fourth and fifth centuries, certain Christians—including Pelagius, a devout Catholic ascetic from Britain—influenced by Greek science and philosophy, argued in his later teaching that human desires and human will, in themselves, have no effect on natural events—that humanity neither brought death upon itself nor could it, by an act of will, overcome death: death was in the nature of things, despite the clear statement to the contrary in Genesis. But Pelagius's contemporary Augustine vehemently rejected this view of nature, and the majority of Christians for more than a thousand years thereafter followed his example.

During his later years, as we have seen, Augustine argued against those who agreed with John Chrysostom,[2] and then against followers of Pelagius, both of whom insisted that Christians, through their baptism, are free to make moral choices; that, although our will cannot affect the course of nature, it can—and must—effect our moral decisions. By 417, the city of Rome was so divided between the supporters and the opponents of Pelagius that partisans of both sides had actually rioted in the streets. Two years earlier, two councils of bishops in Palestine had declared Pelagius orthodox; but two opposing councils of African bishops, led by Augustine and his colleagues, condemned him and persuaded Pope Innocent, bishop of Rome, to take their side. When Innocent died, his successor, Pope Zosimus, at first declared Pelagius's teaching orthodox; but after receiving vehement protests from Augustine and other African bishops, he reversed himself and excommunicated Pelagius.[3]

By this time, too, Christian bishops had learned to use for their own purposes not only ecclesiastical censure but also imperial power.[4] During the battle against Pelagius and his advocates, many of them influential Romans,[5] Augustine and his colleagues openly courted the emperor's support. Augustine's friend and fellow African bishop Alypius brought eighty Numidian stallions as bribes to the imperial court and successfully lobbied there against Pelagius.

The result gratified Augustine: in April 418, not only did the pope excommunicate Pelagius, but the emperor Honorius condemned the newly declared heretic and ordered him fined, expelled from office, and exiled along with his intransigent supporters.

The exiled Pelagius died soon afterward; but the most energetic of his followers refused to yield. Julian of Eclanum, an articulate and intellectual young Italian bishop, took up Pelagius's views and extended them. Julian even dared challenge the powerful Augustine, the most famous theologian of his day, and engaged the aging bishop in a battle that obsessed Augustine during the last twelve years of his life.

Augustine, summoning all his eloquence and fury, argued for a view of nature utterly antithetical to scientific naturalism. It was human choice—Adam's sin—that brought mortality and sexual desire upon the human race and, in the process, deprived Adam's progeny of the freedom to choose not to sin. Augustine amplified his argument in the six volumes of his *Opus Imperfectum Contra Julianum* ("Unfinished Work Against Julian"). Although Augustine is perhaps the greatest teacher of the church, this last work of his has so far remained untranslated into English.

Augustine's views prevailed, but the question is why? Why did the eloquent, passionate, and politically able Augustine finally succeed, after more than a decade of struggle, in having Pelagius's powerful supporters and friends, many of whom were monks, priests, bishops, and lay Christian persons, condemned as heretics, exiled, and deposed? How did Augustine persuade the majority of Christians that sexual desire and death are essentially "unnatural" experiences, the result of human sin?[6]

Certainly neither Pelagius nor Augustine set out to be "scientific" in anything like our sense of the word; neither, I suspect, would have regarded the term as a compliment. Instead, both began their reflections upon the natural universe with a common religious perspective, beginning with Genesis 1–4, from which each drew very different conclusions.

Pelagius, who shared the common Christian conviction that nature was good, as God created it, and that humankind was morally free, made in God's image, was dismayed when he first read Augustine's *Confessions*. For years Pelagius had respected Augustine's work, especially *On Free Will*, the treatise praising human freedom that Augustine had written as a young man. But when Augustine wrote his *Confessions* in his mature years, he declared that he had overestimated the power of human freedom. Now, he said, he realized that human beings are not free, as Adam was, to resist sin. We have no power to choose not to sin, and we cannot even control our sexual impulses. What is worse, "fleshly desire"—*concupiscentia carnis*—involves far more than its surface manifestations, which are only a symptom of deeper impulses that baffle, confound, and defeat our best attempts to control them.[7] Yet since everyone is conceived, as Augustine argued, through sexual desire, and since sexual desire is transmitted to everyone through the very semen involved in conception, he concludes, as we have seen, that all humankind is tainted with sin "from the mother's womb."

Augustine's theory, as we have also seen, was a radical departure from previous Christian doctrine, and many Christians found it pernicious. Many traditional Christians believed that this theory of "original sin"—the idea that Adam's sin is directly transmitted to his progeny—repudiated the twin foundations of the Christian faith: the goodness of God's creation; and the freedom of the human will. Most Christians agreed, at any rate, that even if before baptism we are stained by sin—Adam's sin and our own—baptism cleanses the believer from *all* sin, so that, in the words of the Egyptian teacher Didymus the Blind, "now we are found once more such as we were when we were first made: sinless and masters of ourselves."[8] In their argument with Augustine, Pelagius and his followers could claim the support of the revered fathers of the church, from Justin, Irenaeus, Tertullian, and Clement of Alexandria in the second century through John Chrysostom in the fourth.

According to his biographer Georges de Plinval, Pelagius himself had once agreed with the majority of his Jewish and Christian contemporaries—and with Augustine himself, for that matter—that death came upon the human race to punish Adam's sin. Yet as Augustine developed his view into a theory of human depravity, Pelagius's followers came to argue the opposite.[9] Universal mortality cannot be the result of Adam's punishment, since God, being just, would not have punished anyone but Adam for what Adam alone had done; certainly he would not condemn the whole human race for one man's transgression. Mortality, therefore, must belong to the structure of nature: mortality, which human beings share with every other species, is not, nor ever was, within the power of any human being to choose or reject.

Julian of Eclanum, the son of one of Augustine's fellow bishops, and himself the bishop of a provincial town in southern Italy, saw the controversy between Pelagius and Augustine engage Christians from Rome to Africa.[10] Julian, who once shared the nearly universal admiration for Augustine's learning and teaching, became convinced that on the question of nature, the aging bishop was simply wrong. He charged, too, that Pelagius's opponents had engineered his condemnation through personal influence at court, bribery, and false accusations. He himself intended to defend Pelagius's views through the serious theological debate he believed they deserved. Thus Julian championed and extended the ideas earlier expressed by John Chrysostom and other Christian teachers in order to reduce to absurdity Augustine's idea of original sin.

Augustine's enormous error, Julian believed, was to regard the present state of nature as punishment. For Augustine went further than those Jews and Christians who agreed that Adam's sin brought death upon the human race: he insisted that Adam's sin *also* brought upon us universal moral corruption. Julian replied to this that "natural sin" does not exist":[11] no physically transmitted, hereditary condition infects human nature, much less nature in general. To understand the human condition, Julian says, we must begin by distinguishing what is *natural* from what is *voluntary.*[12] Which conditions belong to the structure of nature, and so to "acts of God" beyond our power, and which depend upon human choice? What is natural, and therefore beyond our will, and what is voluntary?

Such questions led both Julian and Augustine back to Genesis, and each claimed its authority. Julian insisted that neither death nor sexual desire troubled Adam and Eve in Paradise, for both death and desire were, "from the beginning," natural:

> God made bodies, distinguished the sexes, made genitalia, bestowed affection through which bodies would be joined, gave power to the semen, and operates in the secret nature of the semen—and God made nothing evil.[13]

What about death? Doesn't Genesis teach that death is punishment for sin? Certainly, Julian responds, but not *physical* death. He insists that the death one suffers as punishment for Adam's sin is different from the universal mortality natural to all living species. Although the Genesis account says that God warned Adam that "on the day" of his transgression, "you shall surely die," Adam did not die *physically.* Instead, Julian says, Adam began to die morally and spiritually from the day he chose to sin. Adam's progeny confronts the same choice that Adam faced. For God gives to every human being what he gave to Adam—the power to choose one's own moral destiny, the power to choose the spiritual way of life or spiritual self-destruction. As for original sin, "the *merit of one single person is not such that it could change the structure of the universe itself.*"14

But Augustine insists that through an act of will Adam and Eve *did* change the structure of the universe; that their single, willful act permanently corrupted human nature as well as nature in general. Augustine's position is paradoxical in that he attributes virtually unlimited power to the human will but confines that power to an irretrievable past—to a lost paradise. According to Augustine, human power alone reduced us to our present state, one in which we have wholly lost that power. In our present state of moral corruption, what we need *spiritually* is divine grace, and what we need *practically* is external authority and guidance from both church and state.

Augustine, in his debate with Julian, contrasts actual human experience with an imaginative reconstruction of our lost Paradise—human life as he believes it "ought to be," a condition in which women experience painless childbearing and enjoy marriage without oppression or coercion.15 But now Eve is under punishment, for God had said to her, "I will greatly multiply your pains in childbearing; in pain you shall bring forth children, yet your desire shall be for your husband, and he shall rule over you" (Genesis 3:16). As a result, Augustine says, women suffer the nausea, illness, and pains of pregnancy as well as the painful contractions of parturition that accompany normal labor. Many women experience the greater agonies of miscarriage, or "tortures inflicted by doctors, or the shock and loss of giving birth to an infant stillborn or moribund."16 According to Augustine, these sufferings are not *natural,* but prove that nature itself, as we now experience it, is diseased:

> *Nature, which the first human being harmed, is miserable.* . . . What passed to women was not the burden of Eve's fertility, but of her transgression. Now fertility operates under this burden, having fallen away from God's blessing.17

As woman's fertility brings involuntary suffering, so also does sexual desire: the blight of male domination has fallen upon the whole structure of sexual relationships.18 In their dealings with men, as in the pains they suffer with their children, women experience the consequences of the fall. Augustine catalogues these sufferings like a man who has felt and witnessed them: some babies, he says, are born blind, deaf, deformed, or without the use of their limbs; and others are born into such other forms of human suffering as demonic insanity or chronic and fatal disease. Even the fortunate ones, the children born normal and healthy, Augustine says, evince the terrifying vulnerability that pervades nature: every infant is born ignorant, wholly subject to passions and sensations, bereft of reason or articulate speech, entirely helpless.[19]

As Eve's sin brought suffering upon women, Adam's sin brought suffering upon men, according to Genesis 3:17–19:

> Cursed is the ground because of you; in toil you shall eat of it all the days of your life; thorns and thistles it shall bring forth to you; and you shall eat the plants of the field. In the sweat of your face you shall eat bread till you return to the ground, for out of it you were taken; you are dust, and to dust you shall return.

As God had first created it, the earth was free of thorns and thistles, bringing forth a marvelous abundance of food, according to Augustine. Then Adam sinned, and "all nature was changed for the worse";[20] thorns and thistles suddenly sprang up from the once fertile land. God had placed man in Eden "to till it and to cultivate it," and before he sinned, Adam worked "not only without laboring, but, indeed, with pleasure for the soul."[21] But now, Augustine says, every man experiences pain, frustration, and hardship in his labor, as every woman does in hers: the miseries of human nature now beset both sexes "from infancy to the grave."[22]

Worst of all is what awaits us at the end—"the last enemy, death." In the beginning, God granted "the power to live, not any necessity of dying."[23] Death was in no sense *natural* but arose only after Adam chose to sin, bringing upon himself and all his progeny this dreadful agony, along with "the innumerable forms of illness that bring people to death."[24] Adam's single arbitrary act of will rendered all subsequent acts of human will inoperative. Humankind, once harmonious, perfect, and free, now, through Adam's choice, is ravaged by mortality and desire, while all suffering, from crop failure, miscarriage, fever, and insanity to paralysis and cancer, is evidence of the moral and spiritual deterioration that Eve and Adam introduced. Ever since Augustine, the hereditary transmission of original sin has been the official doctrine of the Catholic church.

Augustine thus denies the existence of nature *per se*—of nature as natural scientists have taught us to perceive it—for he cannot think of the natural world except as a reflection of human desire and will. Where there is suffering, there must have been evil and guilt, for,

Augustine insists, God would not allow suffering where there was no prior fault. How, Augustine challenges Julian, could a just and all-powerful God allow infants to suffer

> the evils that nearly all infants suffer in this transitory life, if nothing calling for punishment were contracted from parents? Without a glance you bypass those evils which . . . all of us see them suffer. You say, "Human nature, at the beginning of life, is adorned with the gift of innocence." We agree, in regard to personal sins, but not about original sin. . . . You must explain why such great innocence is sometimes born blind or deaf. If nothing deserving punishment passes from parents to infants, who could bear to see the image of God sometimes born retarded, since this afflicts the soul itself? Consider the plain facts; consider why some infants suffer from a demon.[25]

In reply, Julian cites the New Testament Gospel of John, in which Jesus is asked whether a certain man was born blind because he had sinned or because his parents had sinned. Jesus answers, "Neither, but so that the glory of God might be revealed in him" (John 9:3), and proceeds to heal the man, restoring his sight. For Augustine, this story is irrelevant; what Jesus says about one man he healed cannot apply to people in general:

> These words cannot be applied to the innumerable infants born with such a wide variety of physical and mental handicaps. For many, indeed, are never healed, but die, disabled by their disabilities . . . even in infancy. Some infants retain the disabilities with which they were born, while others are afflicted with even more.[26]

Suffering *proves* that sin is transmitted from parents to children: "If there were no sin, then infants, bound by no evil, would suffer nothing harmful in body or soul under the great power of the just God."[27] To say that infants are innocent but suffer nonetheless, Augustine believes, is to abandon faith in divine justice. Augustine taunts Julian, "You see your whole heresy shipwrecked upon the misery of infants!"[28]

For Augustine, natural and moral evils collapse into one another. But Julian objects that "what is natural cannot be called evil," to which Augustine answers, "To say nothing of many other natural defects that afflict the body, we could regard natural deafness as an evil."[29] Such a perception of evil necessarily implicates everyone, for such infirmities as deafness are part of everyone's experience. What we now call *nature* we have come to know only in a state of chronic disease.

Julian predictably opposes this view and says that Augustine, like the Manichaeans, "defends natural evil . . . against the truth of the Catholic faith."[30] Christian faith, as Julian sees it, rests upon what he calls the five praises: the praise of creation; the praise of marriage; the praise of the law; the praise of the saints; the praise of the will. He rejects Augustine's equation of suffering with evil and guilt, and insists that nature is good—although, he admits, its "good" includes physical suffering.

Julian answers Augustine's reading of Genesis 3 point for point, claiming to have

> explained these things from the sound testimonies of the Scriptures, so that nothing remains of all Augustine's arguments and propositions that has not been refuted. . . . I proved that many things in his invention are false, many foolish, and many are sacrilegious.[31]

As for Augustine's claim that Eve's punishment has fallen upon all women, "This indeed is insane that the pains of parturition came into being because of sin."[32] Labor pains, which form part of "the condition of the sexes," have nothing to do with sin.[33] Innocent animals, including cattle, sheep, and cats, experience similar contractions to expel foetuses from the womb. If labor pains indicate sin, why do baptized women, released from sin, experience them as other women do? Furthermore, Julian continues, the severity of labor pains varies considerably. Arguing that extreme pain in childbirth cannot be regarded simply as a universal "given," Julian observes that

> certain barbarian women and nomads, accustomed to endure physical exertion, give birth in the course of their travels with such facility that, without stopping, they go out to gather food for their young, and continue on their way, transferring the burden of their womb to their shoulders; and, in general, village women do not require physicians for childbirth. . . . in fact, where luxury and softness increase, more women die in childbirth.[34]

But why does God say to Eve, "I will greatly multiply your pain in childbearing; in pain you shall bring forth children; yet your desire shall be for your husband, and he shall rule over you" (Genesis 3:16)? Julian insists that the passage means exactly what it says. The painful contractions that women, like animals, suffer are a natural part of the birth process *(naturaliter instituta).* 35 But the suffering involved in that natural process was increased and amplified in Eve's case to punish her disobedience. Man's rule over woman, Julian adds, forms part of the order of nature, "an institution of nature, not a punishment for sin."36 Both Julian and Chrysostom concede, however, that male domination, like labor pain, while originating in God's "good" creation, may become, through sin, both painful and oppressive.

What about the man? Julian recalls the language of Genesis 3:17–19, emphasizing the words that refer to Adam's *experience* of nature:

> Cursed is the ground *in your works;* in sorrow *you shall eat from it all the days of your life;* thorns and thistles it shall bring forth *for you,* and you shall eat the produce of the field, in the sweat of your face you shall eat bread, until you return to the earth, for you were taken from it; for you are earth, and you shall return to earth.

Although the passage gives no hint that thorns, thistles, and sweat already existed on earth before sin, Julian asks, did these, then, as Augustine claims, spring up only after Adam's transgression, to punish Adam and his progeny?

Even before sin, Julian points out, Adam's task was to cultivate the garden (Genesis 2:15), as Eve's work was to bear children (Genesis 1:28). As contractions already formed a natural part of a woman's labor, Julian says, so sweating, exertion, and physical pain formed part of the man's. "Sweat is a natural help in physical exertion,"37 not an innovation introduced to punish sin. Furthermore, Julian continues, just as in the case of women, the extent to which a man suffers in his work varies according to his physical condition, social position, and cultural situation. Not all men sweat in the fields; the rich do not labor, and not all who work sweat: "Some work with hard labor; others, with responsibilities." Some accomplish their work by thinking and writing, or engage in philosophy and learning; others choose, as their only "exercise" *(askesis)*, an ascetic vocation.

What actually changed, then, after sin? For Julian the Genesis passage does not indicate a universal and permanent change in nature, or even in human nature, nor does the passage intend to express objective fact. Would God curse and blight the innocent earth because of human sin? Are we to believe Augustine that thornbushes and thistles—species previously nonexistent—suddenly sprang up on earth to torment us? No, Julian argues; instead, the passage expresses the subjective experience of one who sins. Calling the earth " 'cursed in [Adam's] works' expresses the viewpoint of a person who is spiritually dying," the emptiness of one who, having "failed to cultivate his own possibilities," projects onto the world his own sense of loss. Such a person foolishly sees the earth itself—indeed, all of nature—as cursed and afflicted. Yet, Julian adds—perhaps referring to the pessimistic Augustine himself—"this lie cannot injure nature, nor the earth, in this curse, but only his own person, and his own will."

The person who is spiritually dying, then, experiences nature as resistant, hostile, the source of nearly intolerable frustrations and disasters. So Cain and Abel, who shared the same human nature but differed in their exercise of will, experienced nature in entirely different ways. Abel successfully cultivated the fields and praised God for his abundant harvest. He experienced no evil at the hands of nature herself, but only at his brother's hands: "That first death clearly showed that it was not a bad thing to die, for the righteous one was the first one to die." But when Cain, on the contrary, chose to sin, polluting the ground with his brother's blood, his own act set him into an antagonistic relationship with the earth, "as if by a curse from the earth, as it is written: 'cursed are you from the earth' " (Genesis 4:11).[38]

For Julian, such sufferings are more than merely a projection onto the world of one's own anger, grief, and terror. Cain's story suggests to Julian that sin actually has the power to transform the experience of the sinner. One who first chooses to sin, and then becomes enmeshed in sin, actually experiences life as unremitting misery. As Julian sees it, Augustine is just such a person: one whose view of "vitiated nature" reflects back to him his own obstinate sinfulness. Such a person would see bodily death, too, as Augustine characterizes it, as the final and worst affliction of all, as a kind of punishment. To this Augustine angrily replies, How *else* could anyone envision our "last enemy"?

Julian answers that the sentence concerning death ("until you return to the earth from which you came; for you are earth, and you shall return to earth") shows God's mercy, not his wrath: "Through the promise of an end to suffering he consoles humankind." Everyone, "through the natural senses," remains vulnerable to pain, but God promises that every suffering known to humankind "is moderated by the specific span of time, as though God were to say, 'Truly, you shall not suffer this forever,' but only 'until you return to earth.'"

> Our mortality is not the result of sin, but of nature! Why does Genesis not say, "because you sinned and transgressed my precepts"? This should have been said, if bodily dissolution were connected with a crime. But recall, what does it say? "because you are earth." Surely this is the reason why one returns to earth, "because you were taken out of it." If this, then, is the reason God gives, that one was from earth, I think it can be assumed that one cannot blame sin. Without doubt it is not because of sin, but because of our mortal nature . . . that the body dissolves back into the elements.[39]

That death forms a natural and necessary condition of human existence Christ himself confirms; for, Julian says, he teaches that God created and blessed human fertility, even before sin, to "replenish the earth" that was to be depleted by mortality.

Physical death merely offers us the necessary transition to eternal life, "so that in the corruptible bodies of the holy ones, eternal glory shall prevail, 'for this corruptible must put on incorruption, and this mortal must put on immortality'" (1 Corinthians 15:53). Julian continues to quote Saint Paul:

> "Death, where is your victory? Grave, where is your sting? The sting of death is sin . . ." That is, you, eternal death, who bear the sting of sin, wounding those who have abandoned justice, if you were not armed with this sting—that is, voluntary sin—you would not harm anyone![40]

Those who allow themselves to be wounded by sin and who live, consequently, in guilt, anger, terror, and despair, may experience, through their own fault, with unspeakable agony, the "sting of death." Yet, Julian adds,

> you see this sin and this sting shattered by people of faith, who resist sin through God, "who gives us the victory." Such persons pass from corruptible life on earth to eternal life with God.

Julian says that "God created fully innocent natures, capable of virtue according to their will,"[41] not only in Paradise, but now as well. Human nature—mortal, sexual, and vulnerable as it is—participates in the wholeness and goodness of the original creation.

Augustine, when he looks at nature, sees the opposite. For

Augustine, the truth of his own experience (and so, he believes, of everyone's) involves, above all, human helplessness. Three primary experiences—infancy, sexuality, and mortality—offer, he believes, irrefutable evidence of such helplessness. Julian, however, answers that "human nature in infants is whole and sound, and, in adults, capable of choosing [good or evil]."

But since Augustine believes that suffering comes from prior guilt, he rejects the moral innocence of infants and insists upon their helplessness, their incapacity to survive by themselves, much less to speak or reason. For Augustine finds the rage, weeping, and jealousy of which infants are capable proof of original sin, and he recalls his own infancy for confirmation. Augustine chides these "foolish new heretics," and especially their spokesman Julian ("O abominable and damnable voice!"), for saying that, even apart from sin, the natural human condition includes not only mortality but all its accompanying forms of disease and deformity. "Behold, then," Augustine mocks, "the Paradise of the Pelagians":

> Let us place there, then, men and women dedicated to chastity, struggling against sexual desire; pregnant women, nauseated, pale, unable to tolerate nourishment; others in labor, pouring forth immature foetuses in miscarriage; others, groaning and screaming in labor; and those that are born, all wailing, or laughing at one moment, then talking and babbling, later brought into school, that they might be taught to read, under the threat of whips, crying like girls because of an ingenious variety of punishments; and above all, innumerable diseases; incursions of demons, and attacks with various blows, some by which they are tormented, others by which they are consumed; and those, indeed, those who are healthy, are nurtured through difficult times of suffering through their parents' solicitude, for there are bereavements and mourning everywhere. . . .
>
> But the task is a long one, to relate how many evils abound in this life.[42]

In his later life, Augustine had only contempt for those who regarded sexual desire as a natural energy which every person may express or sublimate—who held that one's sexual impulses, in other words, are subject to one's will. For Augustine, these assumptions were facile and contrary to his own experience. What he believed instead was that we are helpless to control sexual desire; that "this diabolical excitement of the genitals"[43] arises in everyone, hideously out of control. Even in marriage he finds "boundless sloughs of lust and damnable craving."[44] If not for the restraints imposed by Christian marriage, "people would have intercourse indiscriminately, like dogs." Julian calls sexual desire "vital fire"; but Augustine admonishes us:

> Behold the "vital fire" *which does not obey the soul's decision, but, for the most part, rises up against the soul's desire* in disorderly and ugly movements.[45]

Julian believes that Augustine confuses sexual excess with desire itself; we must, he says, choose how we express that desire. Augustine replies in anger:

> Who can control this when its appetite is aroused? No one! In the very movement of this appetite, then, it has no "mode" that responds to the decisions of the will. . . . What married man *chooses* that the appetite be aroused, except when needed? What honest celibate *chooses* that the appetite *ever* be aroused? Yet what he wishes he cannot accomplish. . . . In the very movement of the appetite, *it has no mode corresponding to the decision of the will.*[46]

Bitterly, Augustine adds:

> You say, "In the married, it is exercised honestly; in the chaste, it is restrained by virtue." *Is this your experience of it?* . . . Indeed, since it is very pleasant, let the married effusively and impulsively seek each other whenever it titillates. . . . Let the union of bodies be legitimate wherever this, your *"natural good,"* spontaneously arises![47]

Julian was evidently restrained in sexual matters, and probably had little experience of the passions Augustine describes. Yet Augustine's question came from the heart, for the celibate Augustine was, by his own admission, insatiable, a man who never married and whose experience of sexual pleasure was illicit and guilt-provoking. Augustine assumes that frustrated desire is universal, infinite, and all-consuming. Julian, who had once—and probably briefly—been married to the daughter of a bishop, in a ceremony celebrated by a family friend as renewing the innocence of Adam and Eve, obviously wrote from a different kind of experience. For Julian, sexual desire is innocent, divinely blessed, and, once satisfied, entirely finite. Sexual desire, as Julian sees it, offers us the opportunity to exercise our capacity for moral choice.

Augustine concludes that not only are we helpless in infancy, and defenseless against sexual passion, but we are equally helpless in the face of death. We die; *therefore* we must be guilty of sin. For if we are not all sinners, then God is unjust to let us all die alike, even infants prematurely born, who have had no opportunity to sin.

If we are helpless before physical death, we are also helpless before spiritual death. This is a paradox; for spiritual death, Augustine says, comes from choosing evil; but even in our "free will" we are incapable of avoiding evil. *We choose evil involuntarily,* even "against our better judgment." Even when we want to do good, we cannot. "Is one driven, then," Julian asks, "by a captive will?" Yes, replies Augustine. "If a person is aware of the 'law of the [bodily] members,' and cries out with Paul, 'I cannot do what is good,' should you not say that the person is driven to evil by a captive will?"[48] So, Augustine concludes, physical death and spiritual death collapse into one: both rule over a lost humankind.

But according to Julian, here, too, Augustine confuses physiology with morality. Death is not a punishment for sin but a natural process, like sexual arousal and labor pains, natural, necessary, and universal for all living species. Such processes have nothing to do with human choice—and nothing to do with sin:

> Whatever is *natural* is shown not to be *voluntary*. If [death] is *natural*, it is not *voluntary*. If *voluntary*, it is not *natural*. These two, by definition, are opposites, like necessity and will. . . . The two cannot exist simultaneously; they cancel each other out.[49]

Although we are helpless before physical death, Julian says, *spiritual* death is a matter of choice. Here we are not mere animals but can exercise the free choice that God bestowed upon humankind in creation. Our free will engages us in the sphere of the *voluntary*— and the multiple possibilities available to individual choice: "Naturalia ergo necessaria sunt; possibilita autem voluntaria" ("Natural things, therefore, are necessary; possible things are voluntary").[50]

Although death is necessary and universal, each of us has the means—indeed, the responsibility—to choose the response we take to our mortal condition. Rather than resisting death as a mortal enemy, Julian says, the sinner may welcome death or even seek it as a relief from the sufferings induced by sin, while the saint may receive death as a spiritual victory. No one, saint or sinner, escapes suffering, which remains unavoidable in nature. Yet each of us holds in our hands our spiritual destiny, which depends upon the choices we make.

For more than twelve years Augustine and Julian debated, shouting back and forth their respective views, until Augustine died. After considerable controversy, the church of the fifth century accepted his view of the matter and rejected Julian's, having concluded that Augustine, the future saint, read Scripture more accurately than the heretic Julian. Recently, however, several scholars have pointed out that Augustine often interprets scriptural passages by ignoring fine points—or even grammar—in the texts. Augustine attempts to rest his case concerning original sin, for example, upon the evidence of one prepositional phrase in Romans 5:12, insisting that Paul said that death came upon all humanity because of Adam, *"in whom* all sinned." But Augustine misreads and mistranslates this phrase (which others translate "in that [i.e., because] all sinned") and then proceeds to defend his errors *ad infinitum,* presumably because his own version makes intuitive sense of his own experience.[51]

When Julian accused him of having invented this view of original sin, Augustine indignantly replied that he was only repeating what Paul had said before him. Had not the "great apostle" confessed that even he was incapable of doing what he willed?

> *I do not do what I will, but I do the very thing I hate. . . . So then it is no longer I that do it, but sin which dwells in me. For I know that nothing good dwells in me, that is, in my flesh. I can will what is good, but I cannot do it.*
>
> (ROMANS 7:15–18)

Augustine's argument has persuaded the majority of western Catholic and Protestant theologians to agree with him; and many western Christians have taken his interpretation of this passage for granted. But, as Peter Gorday has shown,[52] when we actually compare Augustine's interpretation with those of theologians as diverse as Origen, John Chrysostom, and Pelagius, we can see that Augustine found in Romans 7 what others had not seen there—a sexualized interpretation of sin and a revulsion from "the flesh" based on his own idiosyncratic belief that we contract the disease of sin through the process of conception. Other theologians assumed that Paul used these words to dramatize the situation of one who, still unbaptized and unredeemed, lacks hope; for Paul goes on to praise God for his own freedom, found in Christ:

> *Thanks be to God, through Jesus Christ our Lord. . . . For the law of the spirit of life in Christ Jesus has set me free.*
>
> (ROMANS 7:25; 8:2)

Augustine alone applied the despairing expressions of the previous passage to the baptized Christian; other readers assumed that the triumphant and joyful note of the rest of the chapter expressed Paul's experience of his life in Christ.

Julian often attends more carefully than Augustine to the wording and context, but he, too, reads his own experience—experience very different from Augustine's—into the biblical texts. The controversy between Augustine and Julian, as the German scholar Bruckner says, comes down to a clash between "two different worldviews." Bruckner happens to side with Augustine, claiming that "the strength of Augustine's view must be in his 'deeper experience of life'" (which depths Bruckner does not elaborate).[53] Augustine's argument may be arbitrary, but Bruckner contends that his *"deeper religious experience . . .* more adequately interprets the contents of the Holy Scriptures than the *superficial rationalism* of Julian."[54] The British scholar John Ferguson disagrees and sides instead with his fellow Briton Pelagius. What Bruckner takes as evidence of Augustine's "deeper religious experience" Ferguson sees as his stubborn refusal to acknowledge the data of ordinary experience:

> There is another side to our experience, of equal validity, and that is our knowledge of our own free will. It is there that Augustine lapses alike from logic and from common human experience.[55]

And so, after 1600 years, the argument goes on.

If Julian's argument looks simple—merely common sense—that simplicity is deceptive. In fact, it presupposes a Copernican revolution in religious perspective. That we suffer and die does not mean that we participate in guilt—neither Adam's guilt nor our own. That we suffer and die shows only that we are, by nature (and indeed, Julian would add, by divine intent), mortal beings, simply one living species among others. Arguing against the penal interpretation of death, Julian says, "If you say it is a matter of *will,* it does not belong to *nature;* if it is a matter of nature, it has nothing to do with *guilt.*"[56]

Like Copernicus's revolution, Julian's threatens to dislodge humanity, psychologically and spiritually, from the center of the universe, reducing it to one natural species among others. He rejects Augustine's primary assumption that Adam's sin transformed nature. To claim that a single human will ever possessed such power reflects a presumption of supernatural human importance. When Augustine claims that a single act of Adam's will "changed the structure of the universe itself," he denies that we confront in our mortality a natural order beyond human power.[57] For Augustine insists that we became susceptible to death solely through an act of will: "Death comes to us by *will,* not by *necessity.*"[58]

Why did Catholic Christianity adopt Augustine's paradoxical—some would say preposterous—views? Some historians suggest that such beliefs validate the church's authority, for if the human condition is a disease, Catholic Christianity, acting as the Good Physician, offers the spiritual medication and the discipline that alone can cure it. No doubt Augustine's views did serve the interests of the emerging imperial church and the Christian state, as I have tried to show in the preceding chapter.

For what Augustine says, in simplest terms, is this: human beings cannot be trusted to govern themselves, because our very nature—indeed, *all* of nature—has become corrupt as the result of Adam's sin. In the late fourth century and the fifth century, Christianity was no longer a suspect and persecuted movement; now it was the religion of emperors obligated to govern a vast and diffuse population. Under these circumstances, as we have seen, Augustine's theory of human depravity—and, correspondingly, the political means to control it—replaced the previous ideology of human freedom.

Yet the requirements of an authoritarian state alone cannot account for the durability of such teaching throughout the centuries. We can see, too, that such interpretations of suffering as the result of sin are by no means limited to Christianity, much less to Catholicism. Jewish tradition has interpreted personal tragedy similarly, attributing, for example, the sudden death of an infant to the demon Lilith, to whose malevolence the child's parents had made themselves susceptible either through the husband's infidelity or the wife's insubordination. Some rabbis of ancient times would explain, too, to a young widow that she herself caused her husband's sudden heart attack by neglecting ritual regulations concerning the timing of intercourse.[59] Religions far from both Judaism and Christianity often express similar assumptions. A Hopi child is bitten by a poisonous spider while playing near its hole. As the boy hovers between life and death, the medicine man learns that the boy's father has neglected to prepare ritual ornaments for Spider Woman, the tribe's protector, which, he proclaims, has brought on his son's illness.[60]

The British anthropologist Evans-Pritchard tells the story of a sorcery investigation that followed the death of several Azande tribespeople who were resting in the shade of a granary that suddenly collapsed, killing them. The Azande fully recognized what we would call "natural causes": that the wood had begun to rot and crumble, that the nails had given way, that the supports were weakened by weeks of rain. The question was not why the granary collapsed, but why it collapsed at the very moment when these particular people could be trapped and crushed beneath it.[61] The Azande expected to find—and claimed to find—the cause of this disaster in human evil. But Jesus of Nazareth, referring to a remarkably similar disaster, challenged a similar assumption among his fellow Jews by asking, "Those eighteen upon whom the tower in Siloam fell and killed them, do you think that they were worse than any of the people who lived in Jerusalem?" and answering, "I tell you, No . . ."[62] But Jesus' dissent was an anomaly. The overwhelming weight of traditional Jewish and Christian teaching—and perhaps a human tendency to accept personal blame for suffering—implies that suffering and death are the wages of sin.

If Augustinian theology, or that of the rabbis or shamans who have also attributed suffering to sin, served only as a means of social control, why would people accept such sophistry? Why do people *outside* religious communities often ask themselves, as if spontaneously, the same questions, and give similar answers, blaming themselves for events beyond their power as if they had caused—or deserved—their own suffering?

The "social control" explanations assume a manipulative religious elite that *invents* guilt in order to dupe a gullible majority into accepting an otherwise abhorrent discipline. But the human tendency to accept blame for misfortunes is as observable among today's agnostics as among the Hopi or the ancient Jews and Christians, independent of—even prior to—religious belief. For quite apart from political circumstances, many people need to find reasons for their sufferings. Had Augustine's theory not met such a need—were it not that people often *would rather feel guilty than helpless*—I suspect that the idea of original sin would not have survived the fifth century, much less become the basis of Christian doctrine for 1600 years. I am not speaking, now, of cases in which guilt may be appropriate—cases in which people have chosen to take certain risks, or to inflict pain upon themselves or others, with predictable results. Instead I am speaking of those cases in which guilt seems to be an inexplicable, irrational, inappropriate response to suffering. But why would anyone *choose* to feel guilty?

One may know perfectly well the statistical possibilities concerning natural disasters, freak accidents, and life-threatening diseases and regard these—theoretically, at least—as fully natural phenomena. But when such events suddenly threaten (or spare) one's own life, questions occur, so to speak, in the first person. Like the Azande, one asks not what *caused* the earthquake, fire, or disease (for this may be obvious enough) but "Why did this happen now, in this way, to this person?"

What are we to make, I wonder, of this peculiar preference for guilt? Augustine would, I suspect, take it as evidence that human nature itself is "diseased," or, in contemporary terms, neurotic. I would suggest, instead, that such guilt, however painful, offers reassurance that such events do not occur at random but follow specific laws of causation; and that their causes, or a significant part of them, lie in the moral sphere, and so within human control. Augustine, like the Hebrew author of Genesis 2–3, gives religious expression to the conviction that humankind does not suffer and die randomly, but for specific reasons. Asserting one's own guilt for suffering may also encourage one to make specific, perhaps long overdue, changes. Guilt invites the sufferer to review past choices, to amend behavior, redress negligence, and perhaps by such means improve his or her life.

Psychologically simple and compelling, Augustine's view accords with responses that, for many people, arise as if instinctively in the face of suffering: Why has this happened? And why me? Augustine's answer simultaneously acknowledges and denies human helplessness; in this paradox, I suspect, its power lies.

To the sufferer, Augustine says, in effect, "You *personally* are not to blame for what has come upon you; the blame goes back to our father, Adam, and our mother, Eve." Augustine assures the sufferer that pain is unnatural, death an enemy, alien intruders upon normal human existence, and thus he addresses the deep human longing to be free of pain. But he also assures us that suffering is neither without meaning nor without specific cause. Both the cause and the meaning of suffering, as he sees it, lie in the sphere of *moral choice,* not *nature.* If guilt is the price to be paid for the illusion of control over nature—if such control is, as Julian argued, in fact, an illusion—many people have seemed willing to pay it.

By contrast, Julian offers a much reduced sense of power over nature. Our human ancestors no longer are the mythical, semimagic beings celebrated in Jewish legend—for instance, Adam, the ball of whose foot shone more glorious than the sun, whose radiant presence filled the universe with light . . . whose body spanned the continents, and whose shining face filled the angels with envy and awe.[63]

The Protestant Christian painter and engraver Dürer depicted the awesome power of Adam and Eve, as tradition had taught him, in vivid form. While they stand ready to take the fateful bite of that forbidden fruit, a cat waits at their feet, poised to pounce upon the unsuspecting mouse. Her capacity for murderous violence—and that of all living creatures—is about to be unleashed by human sin.[64]

Julian denies that the human will has this power over nature: "All that a person has from nature . . . he has from necessity" . . . since everything in nature depends upon an "immutable order."[65] Free will is not impotent, as Augustine argues, but it enables us "either to *consent* to wrongdoing, or to *refrain* from it." Free will provides the possibility of moral action. Julian might agree with the gnostic or Buddhist precept that "all life is suffering," yet he does not take this as an indictment of human existence, as if ordinary life were an illusion or the result of a "fall," or a form of spiritual death. Instead, Julian stands upon the Jewish and Christian tradition that affirms the essential goodness of the created world: "What is natural cannot be qualified by evil."[66]

Yet if suffering is necessary and normal, misery is optional. Misery, which Augustine equates with suffering, involves, as Julian sees it, human choice: it involves specific—and specifically *sinful*—ways one chooses to deal with natural conditions. One person accepts a terminal disease with patience, faith, and love, taking it as the occasion for spiritual growth; another rages against God and nature and weeps with self-pity and terror, turning inevitable suffering into nearly intolerable misery. So, Julian explains, although every one of us will die, "death is not always an evil; since, to the martyrs, for instance, it is for the sake of glory."[67] Julian would agree with the Buddhist teacher who pointedly rejects the usual Christian view of death as, in Paul's words, the "last enemy." For those who are on the path to enlightenment, "death is not . . . an enemy to defeat, but a compassionate friend." But those who choose to indulge in anger, envy, pride, and the consuming fears that suffocate faith, Julian says, experience the physical vulnerabilities common to our species with their pain "greatly increased" through their own fault.

Augustine's holistic, antinaturalistic view of nature—one in which Adam's will directly affected natural events, and in which suffering occurs solely because of human fault—appeals, then, to the human need to imagine ourselves in control, even at the cost of guilt. Julian's alternative, although more consonant with a scientific view of nature, is not in itself scientific but religious—a view that rests upon the ancient affirmation that the world, as originally created, is good, and that each person bears responsibility for moral choice.

Augustine's theology resembles the moralizing views of suffering that arise in many cultures, but with a difference. For unlike all other views, the Augustinian theory of original sin claims that our moral capacity has been so fatally infected that human nature as we know it cannot be trusted. Consequently, Augustine does not urge people to remedy their situation, as the Hopi shaman might, nor, like a rabbi, does he call them to moral reform; for humanity's moral disease is not only universal but also, apart from divine grace, incurable. Throughout western history this extreme version of the doctrine of original sin, when taken as the basis for political structures, has tended to appeal to those who, for whatever reason, suspect human motives and the human capacity for self-government. The counterpoint to the idea of original sin expressed in the hope of humanity's capacity for moral transformation, whether articulated in utopian and romantic versions or in the sober prose of Thomas Jefferson, has appealed, conversely, to more optimistic temperaments.

Yet, as we have seen, Christians during the first centuries would not have imagined that their vision of a society characterized by liberty and justice could be the basis for a political agenda. Instead, most Christians, like many Jews, saw such freedom, and the elevation of the oppressed, as blessings to be anticipated in the Kingdom of God (as Luke says Jesus did). Among the Jews, the Essenes attempted to live out this egalitarian idea in their monastic community as a model of that coming kingdom; and certain Christians, too, like the author of the New Testament book of Acts, projected a similar ideal back onto the early Christian movement during the "golden age" of the apostolic church. Centuries, even millennia, would pass before such visions began to inform actual political aspirations and institutions; and only the most optimistic among us may still hope that such visions will one day achieve political reality.

Meanwhile, we have seen how Christian practices and perceptions concerning sexuality, politics, and human nature changed from the first century through the fourth; how after Jesus had called people to prepare for the coming Kingdom of God, and Paul proclaimed both its imminence and its radical demands, some intensely ascetic Christians in subsequent generations tried to put their teachings into radical practice, while others attempted to accommodate Christian teaching to existing social and political structures.

We have seen, too, that when state persecution pressed Christians to revere the emperors and the gods, the boldest among them, like Perpetua and her companions, defied government officials in the name of liberty and maintained their loyalty to Jesus, crucified for treason against Rome, as their "divine King," and others, like Justin, denounced the emperors and all their gods as the panoply of devils. These embattled Christians forged a vision of what Tertullian called the new "Christian society," which he boasted was marked by freedom from compulsion, voluntary contributions for the welfare of all members, mutual love, and common faith.

As the Christian movement grew, despite persecution, and increasingly developed its own internal organization, its leaders expelled nonconformists from their ranks, including gnostic Christians. They insisted that only orthodox Christians preached the true gospel of Christ—the message of moral freedom, given in creation and restored in baptism.

Some of the most intense Christians, who refused any compromise with "the world," sought to realize that liberty through the ascetic life, rejecting familial, social, and political obligations in order to recover the original glory of humankind, created in the "image and likeness of God." After the persecutions ended, asceticism offered a new path for uncompromising "witness"—a new form of self-chosen martyrdom.

Finally, we have seen how Christian views of freedom changed as Christianity, no longer a persecuted movement, became the religion of the emperors. Augustine not only read into the message of Jesus and Paul his own aversion to "the flesh," but also claimed to find in Genesis his theory of original sin. In his final battle against the Pelagians, Augustine succeeded in persuading many bishops and several Christian emperors to help drive out of the churches as "heretics" those who held to earlier traditions of Christian freedom. From the fifth century on, Augustine's pessimistic views of sexuality, politics, and human nature would become the dominant influence on western Christianity, both Catholic and Protestant, and color all western culture, Christian or not, ever since. Thus Adam, Eve, and the serpent—our ancestral story—would continue, often in some version of its Augustinian form, to affect our lives to the present day.

# EPILOGUE

W HAT, THEN, are you saying?" asked a friend of mine, himself a distinguished scholar of early Christianity. "Whose side are you on? Are you saying that the real Christianity is more like John Chrysostom and the Pelagians (God forbid) than like Augustine? Or are you just saying that they all made interesting and different, but all politically and motivationally mixed and a little bit crazy, responses to what they took to be the gospel?"

This question, coming from him, startled me, since he certainly knows from his own experience how historical investigation differs from religious inquiry. Yet his question reminded me that when I was a graduate student at Harvard and dissatisfied with the representatives of Christianity I saw around me, I wanted to find the "real Christianity"—and I assumed that I could find it by going back to the earliest Christians. Later I saw that my search was hardly unique: no doubt most people who have sought out the origins of Christianity have really been looking for the "real Christianity," assuming that when the Christian movement was new, it was also simpler and purer.

What I found was the opposite of what I'd expected, for my professors were exploring the complex history of the construction of the New Testament, and, most surprising of all, they were investigating gnostic gospels and other writings attributed to Jesus' disciples—ancient papyrus texts discovered near Nag Hammadi in Upper Egypt in 1945. Fascinated by these writings, I realized that instead of simplifying the search for the "real Christianity," these texts made it more baffling; they suggested that during the first two centuries the Christian movement may have been even more diversified than it is today. For today, virtually all Christians revere the same canon of Christian writings—the collection of twenty-six books we call the New Testament; most share a common creed; and most celebrate, in various ways, the same rituals (baptism and eucharist). But during the first and second centuries, Christians scattered throughout the world, from Rome to Asia, Africa, Egypt, and Gaul, read and revered quite different traditions, and various groups of Christians perceived Jesus and his message very differently.

In the present book, I set out to see how Christians have interpreted the creation accounts of Genesis. But what intrigued me especially was this question: since the representatives of Christian orthodoxy, from Justin through Irenaeus, Tertullian, Clement, and Origen, had denounced gnostic interpretations of Genesis in the name of moral freedom, how could the majority of Christians in the fifth century be persuaded to give up this primary theme of Christian doctrine—or, at least, to modify it radically—following Augustine's reinterpretation of Adam's sin? This book shows where the question led me.

What I did *not* find in the process of this research was what I had started out to find—a "golden age" of purer and simpler early Christianity. What I discovered instead is that the "real Christianity"—so far as historical investigation can disclose it—was not monolithic, or the province of one party or another, but included a variety of voices, and an extraordinary range of viewpoints, even among the saints (witness Augustine and Chrysostom!), as well as among those denounced as heretics, from Valentinus to Julian, and even, as we have seen, within the New Testament writings themselves. From a strictly historical point of view, then, there is no single "real Christianity."

Yet in saying this I recall how William James, writing his *Varieties of Religious Experience,* distinguishes between his psychological analysis of religious experience and the value judgments—positive or negative—that one can make about such experience; the same distinction applies to historical analysis. James distinguishes two modes of inquiry concerning anything:

> First, what is the nature of it? . . . what is its constitution, origin and history? And second, What is its importance, meaning, or significance now that it is once here? The answer to the one question is given in an *existential judgment* or proposition. The answer to the other is a *proposition of value* . . . what we may, if

we like, denominate a *spiritual judgment.* Neither judgment can be deduced immediately from the other.

As James points out:

> If our theory of revelation-value were to affirm that any book, to possess it, must have been composed automatically . . . or that it must exhibit no scientific and historic errors and express no local or personal passions, the Bible would probably fare ill at our hands. But if, on the other hand, our theory should allow that a book might well be a revelation in spite of errors and passions and deliberate human composition, if only it be a true record of the inner experience of great-souled persons wrestling with the crises of their fate, then the verdict would be much more favorable. You see that the existential facts by themselves are insufficient for determining the value . . . with the same conclusions of fact before them, some take one view, and some another, of the Bible's value as a revelation, according as their spiritual judgment as to the foundation of value differs.

The same proves true of the post-biblical history of Christianity. Some readers of this book, reflecting on the various ways that Christians interpreted Genesis throughout the first four hundred years of Christian history, may conclude that certain theologians—Augustine, or the Pelagians, for example—were opportunistic or mistaken; others will conclude the opposite.

For my own part, I came to realize that using historical means to explore the origins of Christianity most often does not solve religious questions but can offer new perspectives upon these questions. I had long been impressed, for example, with Augustine's perceptive and candid observations of his own experience in his *Confessions,* and with many of the psychological and theological insights he expresses in such works as the *City of God* and *On the Trinity.* Since graduate school I had taken for granted, too, the conventional orthodox view of Pelagius and his followers as superficial rationalists who stubbornly and inexplicably resisted the deeper truths of Augustinian theology. But after investigating Augustine's views in the Pelagian controversy and those of his opponents, I concluded, as this book shows, that even his admirers would do well to reassess and qualify Augustine's singular dominance in much of Western Christian history.

Finally, I came to see that more important, to me, than taking sides on such specific issues—especially since my own position has changed as my perspective and situation changed—is the recognition of a spiritual dimension in human experience. This recognition, after all, is what all participants in Christian tradition, however they disagree, share in common—and share, for that matter, with many people who are involved in Christian tradition only peripherally, or not at all.

# NOTES

## INTRODUCTION

1. C. Geertz, cited in D. Tracy, *The Anagogical Imagination: Christian Theology and the Culture of Pluralism* (New York, 1981), 7, n. 18.

2. For example, see R.M. Grant, *Early Christianity and Society* (San Francisco, 1977); G. de Ste. Croix, *The Class Struggle in the Ancient Greek World from the Archaic Age to the Arab Conquests* (New York, 1981); R. MacMullen, *Christianizing the Roman Empire (A.D. 100–400)* (New Haven, 1984); W. Meeks, *The First Urban Christians: The Social World of the Apostle Paul* (New Haven, 1983); P. Veyne, articles cited in Chapter 1, also "The Roman Empire," in *A History of Private Life* 1: *From Pagan Rome to Byzantium,* ed. P. Veyne (Cambridge, Mass./London, 1987), 9–233.

3. Tertullian, *Apology* 39.

4. P. Gorday, *Principles of Patristic Exegesis: Romans 9–11 in Origen, John Chrysostom and Augustine* (New York/Toronto, 1983).

## CHAPTER ONE

For a more technical and scholarly discussion of this material, see E. Pagels, "Adam and Eve, Christ and the Church: A Survey of Second-Century Controversies Concerning Marriage," in *The New Testament and Gnosis: Essays in Honor of R. McL. Wilson,* ed. A.H.B. Logan and A.J.M. Wedderburn (Edinburgh, 1983), 146–175.

1. For an excellent discussion of the Hellenistic period, see V. Tcherikover, *Hellenistic Civilization and the Jews* (Philadelphia, 1961); on the time of Jesus, see S. Safrai and M. Stern, *The Jewish People in the First Century* (Philadelphia, 1974, vol. 1, and 1976, vol. 2); M. Smith, "The Zealots and the Sicarii," *Harvard Theological Review* 64 (1971), 1–19; J. Gager, *Kingdom and Community: The Social World of Early Christianity* (New Jersey, 1975); A. Segal, "Society in the Time of Jesus," chap. 2 of *Rebecca's Children: Judaism and Christianity in the Roman World* (Cambridge, Mass., 1986).

2. Josephus, the Jewish historian born in 37 C.E., wrote a detailed and polemical history of the Herods and the Jewish war, in which he personally participated: see *The Jewish War*, trans. G.A. Williamson, in the Penguin series (Middlesex, England, 1959, reprinted 1972).

3. Josephus, *The Jewish War* 2,5,2; *Jewish Antiquities* 17,10; M. Hengel, *Crucifixion in the Ancient World and the Folly of the Message of the Cross*, trans. J. Bowden (Philadelphia, 1977), especially chaps. 4 and 7. I am grateful to my colleague Professor Thomas Boslooper for pointing out to me this reference.

4. A. Segal, *Rebecca's Children*, 39.

5. Josephus, *Antiquities* 18,136. According to Jewish custom Herod's marriage to his sister-in-law was of questionable legitimacy.

6. See accounts in Mark 1:4–7; Luke 3:1–20.

7. Josephus, *Antiquities* 20,107–112; cf. also *The Jewish War* 2,224. Josephus's figures, like those of other ancient historians, are not necessarily accurate.

8. Cf. A. Segal, "Jesus, the Jewish Revolutionary," chap. 3 in *Rebecca's Children*, 68–95.

9. J. Neusner, *From Politics to Piety: The Emergence of Pharisaic Judaism* (Englewood Cliffs, N.J., 1973); see also E. Rivkin, *A Hidden Revolution: The Pharisees' Search for the Kingdom Within* (Nashville, Tenn., 1978); M. Smith, "Palestinian Judaism in the First Century," in M. Davis, ed., *Israel: Its Role in Civilization* (New York, 1986); A. Segal, *Rebecca's Children*, chap. 5: "Origins of the Rabbinic Movement," 117–41.

10. M. Smith, "Palestinian Judaism in the First Century," in *Israel: Its Role in Civilization*, ed. M. Davis (New York, 1956); J. Neusner, *From Politics to Piety: The Emergence of Pharisaic Judaism*; Segal, "Origins of the Rabbinic Movement," in *Rebecca's Children*, 117–141.

11. As Peter Brown strikingly states in his forthcoming book, *The Body and Society: Men, Women, and Sexual Renunciation in Early Christianity*.

12. P. Veyne, "La Famille et l'amour sous le Haut-Empire romain," *Annales* 33,1 (1978), 35–63; "L'homosexualité à Rome," *Communications* 35 (1982), 26, summarized in "The Roman Empire," in *A History of Private Life* I: *From Pagan Rome to Byzantium*, ed. P. Veyne (Cambridge, Mass./London, 1987), 9–49 (section on marriage), and 51–69 (on slavery).

13. P. Veyne, "The Roman Empire," 217, in *A History of Private Life*.

14. Athenagoras, *Legatio pro Christianis* 11.

15. Justin, 1 *Apology* 14–16; 27–29; 2 *Apology*; Tertullian, *Apology* 3.

16. See R. MacMullen, *Christianizing the Roman Empire* (New Haven, 1984), for a different assessment of conversion, especially in Constantinian times.

17. L.M. Epstein, *Marriage Laws in the Bible and the Talmud* (Cambridge, Mass., 1942).

18. Josephus, *Life*, 75; 426–428. Whether Josephus actually was bigamous is not clear from the text.

19. Josephus, *Jewish Antiquities* 17,1,2; 15.

20. *Mishna Yebamot* 6,6.

21. The *Book of Jubilees* 3,8–14.

22. Ibid., 3,26–31.

23. *Mishna Gittin* 9,10.

24. As we shall see, the author of the Gospel of Matthew apparently modified this view; for discussion, pp. 22–23.

25. This passage has engendered much discussion: see, for example, the commentaries on 1 Corinthians by H. Conzelmann, *Der erste Brief an die Korinther* (Göttingen, 1969); R. Scroggs, "Paul and the Eschatological Woman," in *Journal of the American Academy of Religion* 40 (1972), 283–303, and the reply by E. Pagels, "Paul and Women: A Response to Recent Discussion," in *Journal of the American Academy of Religion* 42 (1974), 538–549.

26. G.B. Shaw, "The Monstrous Imposition upon Jesus," reprinted in W. Meeks, ed., *The Writings of Saint Paul* (New York, 1972), 296–302.

27. As Clement of Alexandria attests; *Stromata* 3,74.

28. *Acts of Paul and Thecla*, 7.

29. *Ibid.*, 6.

30. *Ibid.*, 8–9.

31. *Ibid.*, 20.

32. R. Söder, *Die apokryphen Apostelgeschichten und die romanhafte Literatur der Antike* (Stuttgart, 1932); L. Radermacher, *Hippolytus und Thecla: Studien zur Geschichte von Legende und Kultus* (Vienna, 1916); J.D. Kaestli, "Les Principales Orientations de la recherche sur les Actes apocryphes," in *Les Actes apocryphes des Apôtres*, ed. F. Boron (Geneva, 1981).

33. For discussion see D. MacDonald, *The Legend and the Apostle: The Battle for Paul in Story and Canon* (Philadelphia, 1983), 21,90–96.

34. "Mothers of the Church: Ascetic Women in the Late Patristic Age," in *Women of Spirit*, ed. R.R. Ruether and E. McLaughlin (New York, 1979), 74; see also her discussion "Virginal Feminism in the Fathers of the Church," in *Religion and Sexism*, ed. R.R. Ruether (New York, 1974), 150–183; and also the provocative monograph by S. Davies, *The Revolt of the Widows* (Carbondale, Ill., 1980).

35. *Acts of Thomas* 9,83–87.

36. *Ibid.*, 9,88.

37. See, for example, the *Acts of Andrew* 5–7, and discussion in E. Pagels, "Adam and Eve, Christ and the Church," 151–158; also G. Theissen, *The Sociology of Early Palestinian Christianity*, trans. J. Bowden (Philadelphia, 1978).

38. *Epistle to Diognetus* 5,6.

39. *Epistle of Barnabas* 10,1–12; 19,4.

40. Clement of Alexandria, *Stromata* 3,49.

41. The African Christian Tertullian (c. 200) declares that Christians are not "Indian Brahmins or gymnosophists, who live in forests, and exile themselves from ordinary human life." *Apology* 42.

42. For discussion, see H. Koester, *History and Literature of Early Christianity* (Berlin/New York, 1980), vol. 2, 97–146, 261–307; M. Dibelius and H. Conzelmann, *The Pastoral Epistles* (Philadelphia, 1972); D. MacDonald, *The Legend and the Apostle.*

43. Cf. W. Meeks, "Paul: The Domesticated Apostle," in *The Writings of Saint Paul* (New York, 1972).

44. For an excellent and detailed discussion, see D. MacDonald, "The Pastoral Epistles Against 'Old Wives' Tales,'" chap. 3 in *The Legend and the Apostle*, 54–77.

45. Recently, Elizabeth Fiorenza and other scholars have shown how the introduction of such traditional patriarchal attitudes profoundly affected the situation of Christian women, from ancient times to the present. See, for example, *In Memory of Her: A Feminist Theological Reconstruction of Christian Origins* (New York, 1983).

46. For a more detailed discussion of Clement's exegesis, see E. Pagels, "Adam and Eve, Christ and the Church," 153–155. For Clement's own words, see *Stromata*, vol. 3, published in a fine English translation by J. Oulton and H. Chadwick, in *Alexandrian Christianity*, vol. 2, 40–92, in *The Library of Christian Classics* (Philadelphia, 1954).

47. Clement, *Stromata* 3,49.

48. *Ibid.*, 3,49–50.

49. *Ibid.*, 3,53.

50. *Ibid.*, 3,51,85.

51. *Ibid.*, 3,84.

52. *Ibid.* 3,81–82; Irenaeus, *Libris Quinque Adversus Haereses* 3,28,8. Hereafter cited as AH.

53. Clement, *Stromata*, 3,102.

54. *Ibid.*

55. Clement, *Paidagogos* 2,83.

56. Irenaeus, AH 3,22,4.

57. Clement, *Stromata* 3,94; 103.

58. Irenaeus, AH 3,23,5.

59. Such views were by no means unique to Clement; certain Stoic philosophers had propounded similar views, which Clement here sets forth in Christian dress. For discussion see P. Veyne, "La Famille et l'amour sous le Haut-Empire romain," *Annales* 33,1 (1978), 35–63; R.L. Fox, "Living Like Angels," in *Pagans and Christians* (New York, 1987), 336–374.

60. Clement, *Stromata* 3,57–58.

61. Clement, *Paidagogos* 2,95.

62. *Ibid.*, 2,97f.

63. Clement, *Stromata* 6,100.

64. Clement, *Stromata* 7,12.

65. Clement, *Stromata* 7,64.

66. On Paul's ambivalence, see E. Pagels, "Paul and Women: A Response to Recent Discussion," cited in note 25 above.

# CHAPTER TWO

For a more technical and scholarly discussion of the material included in Chapter 2, see E. Pagels, "Christian Apologists and the 'Fall of the Angels': An Attack on Roman Imperial Power?" in *Harvard Theological Review* 78,3–4 (1985), 301–325.

1. Tertullian, *Apology* 1.

2. *Ibid.*, 2.

3. As one philosophically minded critic, Celsus, complained; Origen, *Contra Celsum* 3,44.

4. As several distinguished scholars recently have pointed out: see R.M. Grant, *Early Christianity and Society* (San Francisco, 1977); R. MacMullen, *Christianizing the Roman Empire* (New Haven/London, 1984); W. Meeks, *The Moral World of the First*

*Christians* (Philadelphia, 1986). For a fascinating study of Christian accommodation, see D. Balch, *Let Wives Be Submissive: The Domestic Code in I Peter* (California, 1981).

5. For pagan views of Christians, see the classic study by P. de Labriolle, *La Réaction païenne. Étude sur la polémique antichrétienne du Ier au IVe siècle,* 2nd ed. (Paris, 1948); R. MacMullen, *Paganism in the Roman Empire* (New Haven, 1981); R.L. Wilken, *The Christians as the Romans Saw Them* (New Haven, 1984). Recently the distinguished scholar R.M. Grant has gathered evidence of what he calls "Christian Devotion to the Monarchy," in *Early Christianity and Society,* 13–43.

6. *Passio Sanctarum Perpetuae et Felicitas* 3, trans. H. Musurillo, in *The Acts of the Christian Martyrs* (Oxford, 1972), 106–131. Hereafter cited as *Passio Perpetuae.*

7. For discussion, see W. Meeks, *The Moral World of the First Christians,* 22–28.

8. *Passio Perpetuae* 3.

9. *Passio Perpetua* 5.

10. *Ibid.,* 6.

11. *Ibid.,* 10.

12. *Ibid.,* 15.

13. *Ibid.,* 16.

14. *Ibid.,* 18.

15. *Ibid.,* 20.

16. *Ibid.,* 21.

17. *The Martyrs of Lyons,* 60, in *The Acts of the Christian Martyrs,* 81.

18. Justin, 2 *Apology* 12.

19. Justin, 1 *Apology* 25. Emphasis added.

20. Justin, *Dialogue with Trypho,* 2.

21. *Ibid.*

22. See G.E.M. de Ste. Croix, "Why Were the Early Christians Persecuted?" in *Past and Present* 26 (1963), 6f.; "Aspects of the 'Great' Persecution," *Harvard Theological Review* 47,2 (1954), 75–114.

23. Justin, 2 *Apology* 3.

24. R.M. Grant, *Early Christianity and Society,* "Christian Devotion to the Monarchy," 13–43. Professor Grant acknowledges in the introduction to his book (as I do in the introduction to this one) that he did not intend to write a comprehensive history of the early church, but rather "a venture into the reconstruction of early Christian practicality" (ix), which in many ways he has admirably provided.

25. Justin, 2 *Apology* 2.

26. Clement, *Protreptikos Logos* 10,92.

27. *Ibid.,* 11,114.

28. For discussion, see the classical study by L.R. Taylor, *The Divinity of the Roman Emperor* (New York, 1975).

29. Lucian, *Life of Peregrinus* 13.

30. Marcus Aurelius, *Meditations* 2,3–5.

31. For excellent discussions of the political significance of the imperial cult, see J. Beaujeu, *La Religion romaine à l'apogée de l'Empire* (Paris, 1955), and S.R.F. Price, *Rituals and Power* (Cambridge, England, 1984).

32. Beaujeu, *La religion romaine,* 327.

33. S.R.F. Price, *Rituals and Power.*

34. For discussion of pagan views of the imperial cult, see the above; also G.W. Bowersock, "Greek Intellectuals and the Imperial Cult in the Second Century

A.D.," and F. Miller, "The Imperial Cult and the Persecutions," both in W. den Boer, ed., *Le Culte des souverains dans l'empire romain* (Geneva, 1973), 179–211; 145–75.

35. Justin, 2 *Apology* 5.

36. Justin, 1 *Apology* 5.

37. *Ibid.*, 10.

38. *Ibid.*, 5.

39. P. Brown, *The Making of Late Antiquity* (Cambridge, Mass., 1978), 75.

40. Tatian, *Oratione ad Graecis* 22.

41. Athenagoras, *Legatio pro Christianis* 34.

42. Clement, *Protreptikos Logos* 4,60.

43. Suetonius, *The Caesars*, "Tiberius," 44.

44. Clement, *Protreptikos Logos* 2,37.

45. Clement, *Protreptikos Logos* 4,47.

46. Justin, 1 *Apology* 13; cf. R. MacMullen, "The Roman Concept of the Robber-Pretender," *Revue Internationale des Droits de l'Antiquité* 3 (1983), 221–226.

47. Justin, 1 *Apology* 14.

48. Justin, 2 *Apology* 4.

49. Justin, 1 *Apology* 17.

50. *Ibid.*, 12.

51. Justin, 2 *Apology* 4.

52. Justin, 1 *Apology* 17.

53. Justin, 1 *Apology* 12.

54. Irenaeus, AH 5,24,2.

55. Athenagoras, *Legatio pro Christianis* 32.

56. *Ibid.*, 25.

57. Justin, 1 *Apology* 5.

58. *Ibid.*, 9.

59. A. Birley, *Marcus Aurelius* (Boston, 1960), 122.

60. *Acts of the Martyr Justin and His Companions* B,2, in *Acts of the Christian Martyrs*, 49.

61. *Ibid.*, 5,53.

62. Justin, 1 *Apology* 12. As noted above (note 4), see R.M. Grant's argument for Christian patriotism.

63. Tacitus, *The Histories* 5,4.

64. *Ibid.*, 5,5.

65. Tacitus, *Annals* 15,44,3–8.

66. Tertullian, *Apology* 50.

67. *Ibid.*, 39.

68. *Ibid.*

69. Clement, *Protreptikos Logos* 10,98.

70. Clement, *Stromata* 4,8. See the excellent discussion by Walter Burghardt, S.J., *The Image of God in Man According to Cyril of Alexandria* (Washington, D.C., 1957), especially chap. 4, "Freedom," and chap. 5, "Dominion," 40–64.

71. Clement, *Paidagogos* 3,3.

72. Justin, 1 *Apology* 27.

73. Minucius Felix, *Octavius* 30.

74. *Ibid.*, 16.

75. Clement, *Stromata* 4,8.

76. Minucius Felix, *Octavius* 38.

77. E. Gibbon, *The History of the Decline and Fall of the Roman Empire* 3 (New York, 1984), 70. Emphasis added.

78. M. Hammond, *The Antonine Monarchy* (Rome, 1959), 211.

79. N. Lewis, *Life in Egypt Under Roman Rule* (Oxford, 1983), 207.

80. *Ibid.*

81. G.E.M. de Ste. Croix, *The Class Struggle in the Ancient Greek World* (Ithaca, N.Y., 1981), 435.

82. *Ibid.*, 439.

83. See, e.g., Tertullian, *Apology* 10; Minucius Felix, *Octavius* 29.

84. Tertullian, *Apology* 25.

85. *Ibid.*

86. Minucius Felix, *Octavius* 25.

87. See the excellent study by R. MacMullen, *Enemies of the Roman Order: Treason, Unrest, and Alienation in the Empire* (Cambridge, Mass., 1966); G.E.M. de Ste. Croix, *The Class Struggle,* 368.

88. Minucius Felix, *Octavius* 37. Emphasis added.

89. See W.H.C. Frend, *Martyrdom and Persecution in the Early Church* (Oxford, 1965).

90. Tertullian, *Apology,* 28,1. Emphasis added.

# CHAPTER THREE

For a more scholarly and technical discussion of the sources discussed in this chapter, see E. Pagels, "Exegesis and Exposition of the Genesis Creation Accounts in Selected Texts from Nag Hammadi," in *Nag Hammadi, Gnosticism, and Early Christianity,* ed. C. Hedrick and R. Hodgson (Peabody, Mass., 1986), 257–286.

A more general discussion of the gnostic sources appears in E. Pagels, *The Gnostic Gospels* (New York, 1979). For the convenience of nonspecialists, I have listed the Nag Hammadi texts as they appear in the one-volume English translation, ed. J.M. Robinson, *The Nag Hammadi Library in English* (New York, 1977). Students and scholars will probably wish to consult the technical editions of the texts published by Brill Press in Leiden in the Nag Hammadi series.

1. For the term, see M. Smith, "The History of the term 'Gnostikos,' " in *The Rediscovery of Gnosticism (Proceedings of the International Conference on Gnosticism at Yale),* ed. B. Layton (Leiden, 1981), vol. 2, 796–807.

2. Ignatius, *Letter to the Romans* 5,1.

3. Ignatius, *Letter to the Magnesians* 6,1; *Trallians* 3,1; *Ephesians* 5,3. For discussion, see E. Pagels, "The Demiurge and His Archons: A Gnostic View of the Bishop and Presbyters?" in *Harvard Theological Review* 69,3–4 (1976), 301–324.

4. See, for example, H. von Campenhausen, *Ecclesiastical Authority and Spiritual Power,* trans. J.A. Baker (Stanford, 1969), 96–106.

5. Cf. G. Theissen, *The Sociology of Early Palestinian Christianity,* trans. J. Bowden (Philadelphia, 1978).

6. See especially W. Meeks, *The First Urban Christians* (New Haven, 1983).

7. Galen, *De Platonis Rei Publicae Summariis,* ed. Kraus-Walzer, fragment 1. For discussion of various pagan attitudes toward Christians, see R.L. Wilken, *The Christians as the Romans Saw Them* (New Haven/London, 1984).

8. Justin, 1 *Apology* 14.

9. Theodotus, cited in Clement of Alexandria's *Exerpta ex Theodoto* 78,2.

10. The Greek word here translated "mature" (τέλειος), which gnostic Christians frequently used to describe their adherents, can also mean "complete" or even "initiated."

11. For discussion, see E. Pagels, *The Gnostic Gospels,* xviii–xix.

12. Cf. Irenaeus, AH 4,33,7. Here Irenaeus acknowledges that their purpose is to purify and reform the churches, but he charges that in the attempt they are dividing and damaging the church.

13. AH, *Praefatio.*

14. For discussion, see Morton Smith, "The History of the Term 'Gnostikos,'" note 1 above.

15. Tertullian, *Adversus Valentinianos,* 4.

16. Clement of Alexandria, *Stromata* 7,7. For a reconstruction of Valentinian teaching, see G. Quispel, "The Original Doctrine of Valentine," in *Vigiliae Christianiae* 1 (1947), 43–73.

17. For discussion, see E. Pagels, *The Gnostic Gospels,* introduction and passim.

18. Cf. E. Pagels, *The Gnostic Gospels,* xix–xx; 119–141.

19. Justin, 1 *Apology* 61.

20. For a Valentinian view of baptism, see, for example, the *Gospel of Philip* 64,23–40; 74,12–20; E. Pagels, "Valentinian Interpretation of Baptism and Eucharist—and Its Critique of 'Orthodox' Sacramental Theology and Practice," *Harvard Theological Review* 65 (1972), 153–170.

21. Hippolytus, *Refutatio Omnium Haeresium* 6,42.

22. For explication of gnostic exegesis, see E. Pagels, *The Johannine Gospel in Gnostic Exegesis* (Nashville, Tenn., 1973), and *The Gnostic Paul: Gnostic Exegesis of the Pauline Letters* (Philadelphia, 1975); also the fine work of K. Koschorke, *Die Polemik der Gnostiker gegen das kirchliche Christentum* (Leiden, 1978), and one of his more recent articles, "Paulus in den Nag-Hammadi-Texten," in *Zeitschrift für Theologie und Kirche* 78 (1981), 177–185.

23. E. Pagels, *The Johannine Gospel in Gnostic Exegesis,* and *The Gnostic Paul: Gnostic Exegesis of the Pauline Letters.*

24. Tertullian, *De Cultu Feminarum* 1,12. Emphasis added.

25. Tertullian, *De Jejuniis* 3.

26. Tertullian, *De Exhortatione Castitatis* 5.

27. For references and discussion of this type of exegesis see E. Pagels, "Exegesis and Exposition of the Genesis Creation Accounts," cited at the beginning of notes for this chapter.

28. Jerome, *Letter* 22,18.

29. Irenaeus, AH 1,18,1.

30. Irenaeus, AH 3,11,9.

31. Philo, *Opificio Mundi* 66; *Legum Allegoricum* 1,31; 1,90; 3,161.

32. Philo, *Legum Allegoricum* 3,161; 2,2; 2,6.

33. *Philo's Use of the Categories Male and Female* (Leiden, 1970), passim.

34. R.B. Blakney, ed. and trans., *Meister Eckhart* (New York, 1941), 135.

35. *Ibid.*, 14.

36. I owe this formulation to my friend and colleague Professor Theodor H. Gaster, who had in mind, of course, orthodox self-definition. No doubt there were, and are, however, spiritually inclined people from all these traditions who *would* agree with Eckhart on the basis of their own experience and conviction.

37. *Gospel of Philip* 71,35–72,3.

38. *Ibid.*

39. *The Exegesis on the Soul* (or *Interpretation of the Soul*), 133,6–9, in *The Nag Hammadi Library,* ed. J.M. Robinson (New York, 1977), 184.

40. For a further discussion, see the article cited in note 27.

41. *The Hypostasis of the Archons* 89,13–17, published in *The Nag Hammadi Library in English,* 152–160. The same translator, B. Layton, has published the text together with the notes in two articles: "The Hypostasis of the Archons, or the Reality of the Rulers," in *Harvard Theological Review* 67,4 (1974), 351–426; and "Hypostasis of the Archons, Part II," in *Harvard Theological Review* 69,1–2 (1976), 31–102.

42. *The Hypostasis of the Archons* 89,31–90,12.

43. *Thunder: Perfect Mind* 13,16,16,14, in *The Nag Hammadi Library,* 271–277. For discussion of this remarkable text, see G. MacRae, "The Thunder: Perfect Mind," in *The Center for Hermeneutical Studies, Fifth Colloquy* (Berkeley, Calif., 1975), 18, with following discussion by B. Pearson and T. Conley; also the fine and perceptive study by B. Layton, "The Riddle of the Thunder (NHC VI,2): The Function of Paradox in a Gnostic Text from Nag Hammadi," in *Nag Hammadi, Gnosticism, and Early Christianity,* 37–54.

44. *Apocryphon of John* 31,1–6, in *The Nag Hammadi Library,* 98–116.

45. See especially such texts as *The Hypostasis of the Archons, Thunder: Perfect Mind,* and the secondary sources here cited for both. Cf. E. Pagels, *The Gnostic Gospels,* chap. 3, and the articles cited in notes 22, 27, and 43. For more recent studies, see J. Jacobson-Buckley, *Female Fault and Fulfillment in Gnosticism* (Chapel Hill/London, 1986), and the volume forthcoming from the 1985 conference in Claremont, Calif., on "Images of the Feminine in Gnosticism," ed. K. King (Philadelphia, 1988).

46. *Gospel of Philip* 70,10.

47. *Ibid.,* 68,25.

48. Irenaeus, AH 2,27,2.

49. *Testimony of Truth* 45,30–47,10, in *The Nag Hammadi Library,* 406–416.

50. *Ibid.,* 47,15–48,4.

51. *Ibid.,* 33,25.

52. *Ibid.,* 33,21.

53. Irenaeus, AH 1,6,2.

54. *Ibid.*

55. Clement, *Stromata* 3,1.

56. See such passages in the *Gospel of Philip* as 69,1–70,22. For discussion, see R.M. Grant, "The Mystery of Marriage in the Gospel of Philip," in *Vigiliae Christianiae* 15 (1961), 129–50; D.H. Tripp, "The 'Sacramental System' of the Gospel of Philip," in *Studia Patristica,* vol. xvii I, ed. E.A. Livingstone (Oxford, 1982), 251–260.

57. G. Quispel, "Birth of the Child," in *Eranos Lectures* 3, *Jewish and Gnostic Man,* (Princeton, 1966), 22–26.

58. M.A. Williams, " 'Gnosis' and 'Askesis,' " in *Aufstieg und Niedergang der Römischen Welt: Geschichte und Kultur Roms im Spiegel der Neueren Forschung* 2,22.

59. *Gospel of Philip* 53,14–19.

60. *Ibid.,* 53,24; for discussion, see K. Koschorke, "Die 'Namen' im Philippusevangelium," in *Zeitschrift für die neutestamentliche Wissenschaft* 64 (1973), 307–322.

61. *Gospel of Philip* 74,5–12.

62. *Ibid.,* 80,23–81,7.

63. *Ibid.,* 77,20–25.

64. *Ibid.,* 77,25–29.

65. *Ibid.,* 83,18–29. Emphasis added.

66. *Ibid.,* 83,29–84,13.

67. Irenaeus, AH 3,2,2; 3,15,2; 1,13,6.

68. Methodius, *Symposium,* passim; for references and discussion, see chap. 4.

69. Gregory of Nyssa, *De Hominis Opificio* 4,1.

70. Irenaeus, AH 4,37,1.

71. This is suggested in the *Acts of Thomas* (82–83) and stated clearly by John Chrysostom (*De Genesi* 4,1; *Homiliae in Epistolam ad Ephesios* 22,2) and Augustine (*City of God* 19,5).

72. See, in New Testament, Philemon; 1 Corinthians 7:20–24. R.L. Fox, *Pagans and Christians* (New York, 1987), 295–299, and R.M. Grant, *Early Christianity and Society* (New York, 1977), 89–95, both categorically state that Paul opposed social mobility, and specifically any concern to free slaves on the basis of Christian teaching.

73. A literal translation of αὐτός and ἐξουσία.

74. For one Valentinian teacher's view of different paths to salvation and redemption, see E. Pagels, *The Johannine Gospel in Gnostic Exegesis,* 83–97.

75. Irenaeus, AH 1,1,1.

76. *Ibid.,* 1,2,2.

77. *Ibid.,* 1,4–5: for a reconstruction of this teaching, see G. Quispel's "Original Doctrine of Valentine," in *Vigiliae Christianiae.*

78. Irenaeus, AH 1,1,1.

79. *Gospel of Truth* 18,30–35.

80. Irenaeus, AH 3,4,1–3.

81. See E. Pagels, *The Gnostic Gospels,* 48–69.

## CHAPTER FOUR

Sections of this chapter are forthcoming in more technical form as the article " 'Freedom from Necessity': Philosophical and Psychological Dimensions of Christian Conversion," in *Intrigue in the Garden: Genesis 1–3, A History of Exegesis,* ed. G. Robbins (Lewiston/New York, 1988).

1. Marcus Aurelius, *Meditations,* 8,23; 9,23.

2. *Ibid.,* 8,12.

3. As Gregory of Nyssa said: *De Virginitate* 4. The twentieth-century writer Thomas Merton, who "renounced the world" to become a Cistercian monk, described his decision in similar terms: see his introduction to *The Wisdom of the Desert* (New York, 1960), 3–23.

4. The phrase is Jerome's (*Letter* 22,18). At the end of the fourth century a Roman monk argued against this view, and used the Scriptures, starting from Genesis 1, to defend marriage as being as holy as virginity; but his views were denounced by Ambrose, Jerome, and Augustine, and condemned by Pope Siricius as heresy: see above, pp. 91–96, and the classic study by D. Chitty, *The Desert a City* (New York, 1966), passim; also P. Rousseau, *Ascetics, Authority, and the Church in the Age of Jerome and Cassian* (Oxford, 1978).

5. Gregory of Nyssa, *De Virginitate* 12.

6. P. Brown, *The Body and Society* (forthcoming).

7. Matthew 16:26; also Mark 8:36.

8. As P. Brown shows in *The Body and Society* (forthcoming).

9. Matthew 19:21.

10. Athanasius, *Life of Saint Anthony* 2, published and translated in *Early Christian Biographies*, ed. R.J. Deferrari, in *Fathers of the Church* 15 (Washington, D.C., 1952), 133–224.

11. *Ibid.*, 3.

12. *Ibid.*

13. *Ibid.*, 5.

14. *Ibid.*, 4. As P. Rousseau says of the fourth-century Egyptian monks of Tabennesis, "to enroll oneself in the resurrected economy of Tabennesis . . . was not to abandon society, but to transfer one's allegiance . . . from one rural community to another." *Pachomius: The Making of a Community in Fourth-Century Egypt* (Berkeley/Los Angeles/London, 1985), 13.

15. R. MacMullen, *Christianizing the Roman Empire (A.D. 100–400)* (New Haven/London, 1984), 86.

16. G. Dix and many others depict the monastic movement as a reaction against the increasing worldliness of the churches; *The Shape of the Liturgy* (Glasgow, Scotland, 1945).

17. Gregory of Nyssa, *De Virginitate* 4.

18. *Ibid.*, 3.

19. *Ibid.*

20. *Ibid.*, 4.

21. *Ibid.*; on the recovery of the "image of God" as the goal of the contemplative life, see Gregory of Nyssa, *De Hominis Opificio* 4–9.

22. Gregory of Nyssa, *De Virginitate* 8.

23. For discussion of the significance and dynamics of the story of Clement in the *Clementine Homilies*, especially *Homilies* 4–6, see E. Pagels, " 'Freedom from Necessity': Philosophical and Psychological Dimensions of Christian Conversion," in *Intrigue in the Garden: Genesis 1–3, A History of Exegesis*, ed. G. Robbins (Lewiston/New York, 1988).

24. Methodius, *Symposium* 1,1–4.

25. *Ibid.*, 2,1.

26. *Ibid.*, 4,1.

27. *Ibid.*, 7,9.

28. *Ibid.*, 8,13.

29. *Ibid.*, 11,2.

30. *Ibid.*

31. R. Ruether, "Mothers of the Church: Ascetic Women in the Late Patristic Age," in *Women of Spirit: Female Leaders in the Jewish and Christian Traditions*, ed. R. Ruether and E. McLaughlin (New York, 1979), 71–98; see also the excellent studies by E. Clark, in *Ascetic Piety and Women's Faith: Essays on Late Ancient Christianity* (Lewiston/Queenston, 1986). Especially valuable on the present point is her essay "Ascetic Renunciation and Feminine Advancement: A Paradox of Late Ancient Christianity," 175–208. See also R. Kraemer, "The Conversion of Women to Ascetic Forms of Christianity," *Signs* 6 (1980/81), 298–307; A. Rousselle, *Porneia: De la Maîtrise du corps à la privation sensorielle, IIe–IVe siècles de l'ère chrétienne* (Paris, 1983). For a very different viewpoint, see E. Castelli's intriguing essay "Virginity and Its Meaning for Women's Sexuality in Early Christianity," in *Journal of Feminist Studies in Religion* 2,1 (1982), 61–88.

32. *Vita Melaniae Junioris* 1, introduced and translated by E. Clark, in *The Life of Melania the Younger* (Lewiston, N.Y., 1984), 1,27–28.

33. *Ibid.*

34. *Ibid.*, 6.

35. *Ibid.*, 10–12.

36. *Ibid.*, 14.

37. E. Clark, "Ascetic Renunciation and Feminine Advancement," as well as her other essays, cited in note 31.

38. Jerome, *Letter 22, To Eustochium*, 7.

39. *Ibid.*, 24.

40. *Ibid.*, 16.

41. Jerome, *To Paula*, 6.

42. Jerome, *Adversus Jovinianum* 1,41: for a study of Jovinian, see W. Haller, *Iovinianum: Die Fragmente seiner Schriften, die Quellen zu seiner Geschichte, sein Leben und seine Lehre, Texte und Untersuchungen* 17,2 (Leipzig, 1897). Since Jovinian's writings, condemned by the pope, were destroyed, only fragments of his treatises remain in Jerome's polemics against him.

43. Jerome, *Adversus Jovinianum* 1,1.

44. *Ibid.*, 1,5.

45. *Ibid.*, 1,3. I am grateful to Robert Wilkin for referring me to David Hunter's article in *Theological Studies* 48 (1987), "Resistance to the Virginal Ideal in Late-Fourth-Century Rome: The Case of Jovinian," 45–64. Hunter's argument that Jovinian polemicizes against Manichaeans, not against celibates generally, is intriguing.

46. Jerome, *Adversus Jovinianum* 1,5.

47. *Ibid.*, 1,1,12.

48. *Ibid.*, 1,5.

49. *Ibid.*, 1,4.

50. *Ibid.*, 1,34.

51. *Ibid.*

52. *Ibid.*, 1,16. For a fine discussion of Jerome's exegesis, see E. Clark, "Heresy, Asceticism, Adam, and Eve: Interpretations of Genesis 1–3 in the Later Latin Fathers," in *Ascetic Piety and Women's Faith*, 353–385.

53. Jerome, *Adversus Jovinianum* 1,10; 20.

54. After he joined the Montanist movement, Tertullian's views on marriage became far more rigorist and negative. See, for example, D. Barnes's excellent biography, *Tertullian: A Historical and Literary Study* (Oxford, 1971).

55. Jerome, *Adversus Jovinianum* 1,6.

56. *Ibid.*, 1,7.

57. *Ibid.*, 1,40.

58. *Ibid.*, 2,36.

59. Jerome, *Letter 48, To Pammachius,* 2.

60. Yet, as Father William Meninger, Cistercian monk of Saint Benedict's Monastery in Snowmass, Colorado, reminds me, many monastics believe, as he does, that even the most cloistered life of contemplative prayer does, in fact, contribute to the welfare of humankind.

61. T. Merton, *The Wisdom of the Desert* (New York, 1970), 5–6.

# CHAPTER FIVE

For a more technical version of this discussion, see E. Pagels, "The Politics of Paradise: Augustine's Exegesis of Genesis 1–3 Versus that of John Chrysostom," in *Harvard Theological Review* 78, 1–2 (1985), 67–95.

1. *Vita Adae et Evae* 22.1–2; *Jubilees* 2:14; see Jacob Jervell, *Imago Dei: Gen. 1,26f. im Spätjudentum, in der Gnosis, und in den paulinischen Briefen* (Göttingen, 1960), 40–41.

2. Gregory of Nyssa, *De Hominis Opificio* 2,1.

3. *Ibid.*, 4,1. The opposite theme—that of the emperor as sole representative of God's sovereignty on earth, a theme often supported with reference to Romans 13:1—does emerge, however, especially among theologians of the Byzantine era, as G.E.M. de Ste. Croix notes: *The Class Struggle in the Ancient Greek World from the Archaic Age to the Arab Conquests* (Ithaca, N.Y., 1981), 397–400.

4. Gregory of Nyssa, *De Hominis Opificio* 4,1.

5. *Ibid.*, 16,11.

6. Both themes, certainly, appear in the works of patristic theologians; for an overview, see Lewis Spitz, "Man of This Isthmus," in Carl S. Meyer, ed., *Luther for an Ecumenical Age: Essays in Commemoration of the 450th Anniversary of the Reformation* (St. Louis, Mo., 1967), 23–66.

7. For citations and discussion, see below.

8. Cf. C. Baur, *John Chrysostom and His Time,* translated from the French original (1907) by M. Gonzaga (London, 1960). J. Quasten, in *Patrology* (Utrecht/Antwerp, 1960), vol. 3, 424, suggests a date between 344 and 354.

9. Chrysostom, *Homiliae de Statuis ad Populum Antiochenum* 7,3. Hereafter cited as *Hom. ad Pop. Ant.*

10. Gregory of Nyssa, 16, *De Hominis Opificio* 16,17. Emphasis added.

11. Chrysostom, *Hom. ad Pop. Ant.* 7,3.

12. *Ibid.*, 6,1–2.

13. Chrysostom, *Homiliae in Epistolam Secundam ad Corinthios* 17,3.

14. Chrysostom, *Homiliae in Epistolam Primam ad Corinthios* 12,9. Hereafter cited as *Hom. in I Cor.*

15. *Ibid.,* 12,10.

16. Chrysostom, *Homiliae in Epistolam Primam ad Thessalonicos* 5,7.

17. Chrysostom, *Hom. in I Cor.* 12,10.

18. Chrysostom, *Hom. ad pop. Ant.* 6,2.

19. Didymus the Blind eloquently describes how baptism restores us to the original state of our creation: "Through the divine insufflation [cf. Genesis 2:7] we had received the image and likeness of God, which the Scripture speaks of, and through sin we had lost it, but now we are found once more such as we were when we were first made: sinless and masters of ourselves" (*De Trinitate* 2,12).

20. Cf., e.g., Tertullian, *Apology* 4,39; Justin, 1 *Apology* 12,42.

21. Chrysostom, *De sacerdotis* 2,3.

22. *Ibid.* Emphasis added.

23. Chrysostom, *Homiliae in Epistolam ad Ephesios* 11,15–16. Hereafter cited as *Hom. in Eph.* Emphasis added.

24. *Ibid.,* 6,7.

25. Chrysostom, *De sacerdotis,* 3,15.

26. Chrysostom, *Hom in Eph.* 11,15–16.

27. Cf. R.L. Wilken's recent book, *John Chrysostom and the Jews: Rhetoric and Reality in the Late Fourth Century* (Berkeley, 1983), 29–33.

28. Augustine, *Confessiones* 2,2. Translations used here are those of William Watts (1631) in *St. Augustine's Confessions* (Cambridge: Harvard University Press, 1977), 69.

29. *Ibid.,* 2,3.

30. *Ibid.,* 6,12.

31. *Ibid.*

32. Ibid., 6,11. For discussion of the relationships of Augustine's theology with Chrysostom, see Pier Franco Beatrice, *Tradux peccati: Alle fonti della dottrina agostiniana del peccato originale* (Studia Patristica Mediolanensia 8, Milan, 1978), chap. 5: "Crisostomo, Agostino e i pelagiani." On Augustine's change of mind, see Paula Fredricksen Landes, *Augustine on Romans* (California, 1982), ix–xii.

33. Augustine, *Confessiones* 2,7.

34. *Ibid.,* 2,6.

35. See P. Gorday, *Principles of Patristic Exegesis: Romans 9–11 in Origen, John Chrysostom, and Augustine* (New York/Toronto, 1983).

36. Augustine, *Confessiones* 7,3.

37. *Ibid.* Emphasis added.

38. *Ibid.,* 8,5.

39. *Ibid.,* 8,10.

40. *Ibid.* Emphasis added.

41. F. Edward Cranz, "The Development of Augustine's Ideas on Society before the Donatist Controversy," *Harvard Theological Review* 47 (1954), 254–316.

42. Augustine, *De Civitate Dei* 14,15. The translation cited generally follows that of Philip Levine in St. Augustine, *The City of God Against the Pagans* (LCL, 1966).

43. *Ibid.,* 13,21: Lignum scientiae boni et mali proprium voluntatis arbitrium. According to the analysis of M. Harl ("Adam et les deux Arbres du Paradis [Gen.

II–III] chez Philon d'Alexandrie," *Recherches de Science Religieuse* 50 [1962], 321–387), Philo, too, saw human autonomy which exercises choice between good and evil as the alternative—and opposite—of true piety. If so, Philo might agree with Augustine that the result of the fall is "personal control over one's own will." Unlike Augustine, however, Philo regards the daily life of a philosophically inclined person as a constant struggle of ethical decision and action (374), and assumes that humanity has a capacity to choose the good (377).

44. Augustine, *De Civitate Dei* 13,13. Emphasis added.

45. *Ibid.*, 14,15.

46. *Ibid.*, 14,12.

47. *Ibid.*, 14,13.

48. *Ibid.*, 14,15.

49. Augustine, *Confessiones* 7,3.

50. Chrysostom, *Hom. in I Cor.* 17,4.

51. Augustine, *De Civitate Dei* 13,3. Emphasis added.

52. *Ibid.*, 13,14. For discussion of the issue of translation, see chap. 6, note 51.

53. *Ibid.*

54. *Ibid.*

55. Which Augustine did not entirely invent; see, for example, Didymus the Blind, *Contra Manichaeos* 8.

56. Cf. Wilhelm Kamlah, *Christentum und Geschichtlichkeit: Untersuchungen zur Entstehung des Christentums und zu Augustins "Bürgerschaft Gottes"* (2nd ed., Stuttgart, 1951), 322: "Wo Augustin über die politische Herrschaft spricht, verweist er immer sogleich auf diese ursprüngliche Herrschafts- und Schöpfungsordnung und auf die Scheinherrschaft derer, die in der Knechtschaft der *libido dominandi* leben."

57. Augustine, *De Civitate Dei* 2,36.

58. *Ibid.*, 14,15.

59. *Ibid.*, 14,3.

60. *Ibid.*, 14,15.

61. *Ibid.*, 13,13.

62. *Ibid.*, 13,24.

63. Augustine, *De Peccatorum Meritis et Remissione* 2,2; cf. Augustine, *De Civitate Dei* 14,17.

64. Augustine, *De Civitate Dei* 14,19–20.

65. *Ibid.*, 14,16.

66. Augustine, *De Peccatorum Meritis et Remissione* 2,22.

67. Augustine, *De Civitate Dei* 14,26.

68. *Ibid.*, 14,17.

69. Augustine, *Confessiones* 8,5.

70. Augustine, *De Civitate Dei* 14,20. Origen, too, associated intercourse with impurity, although, as Henri Crouzel points out, "the impurity inherent in the exercise of sexuality is no more than an intensification of an even more profound uncleanness, that of the bodily condition" ("Marriage and Virginity: Has Christianity Devalued Marriage?" in idem, *Mariage et divorce, célibat et caractère sacerdotaux dans l'église ancienne: Études diverses* [Torino, 1982], 57).

71. Augustine, *De Civitate Dei* 14,19.

72. *Ibid.*, 14,9. For discussion, see Margaret Ruth Miles, *Augustine on the Body* (American Academy of Religion Dissertation Series 31; Missoula, Mont., 1979), especially 1–98.

73. Augustine, *De Civitate Dei* 15,16; 19,13.

74. *Ibid.*, 14,11.

75. See the excellent discussion by Kari Elizabeth Børrensen, *Subordination and Equivalence: The Nature and Role of Women in Augustine and Thomas Aquinas*, trans. Charles H. Talbot (Washington, D.C., 1981), 15–34.

76. Augustine, *De Civitate Dei* 19,15.

77. *Ibid.*

78. *Ibid.*, 15,1.

79. *Ibid.*, 19,15. Emphasis added.

80. *Ibid.* 19,12.

81. Henrik Berkhof, *Kirche und Kaiser: Eine Untersuchung der Entstehung der byzantinischen und der theokratischen Stattsauffassung im vierten Jahrhundert*, trans. Gottfried W. Locher (Zurich, 1947); Wilhelm Kamlah, *Christentum und Geschichtlichkeit*.

82. Augustine, *De Civitate Dei* 19,12; cf. R.A. Markus, *Saeculum: History and Society in the Theology of St. Augustine* (Cambridge, England, 1970), 22–153.

83. Augustine, *De Civitate Dei* 19,12.

84. For discussion of the image and its history, see R. MacMullen, "The Roman Concept Robber-Pretender," *Revue Internationale des Droits de l'Antiquité,* series 3, 10 (1965), 221–225.

85. Justin Martyr, 1 *Apology* 12.

86. Marcus Aurelius, *Meditations* 10,10.

87. Augustine, *De Civitate Dei* 4,4.

88. As R.A. Markus rightly notes; see his discussion in *Saeculum,* 84–86.

89. Irenaeus, AH 5,24,2.

90. Justin, *Apology* 65.

91. Augustine, *De Civitate Dei* 19,16.

92. See P.R.L. Brown, "Saint Augustine's Attitude to Religious Coercion," *Journal of Roman Studies* 54 (1964), 107–116. For a fascinating account of the incorporation of this image into the Roman liturgy, see G.M. Lukken, *Original Sin in the Roman Liturgy: Research into the Theology of Original Sin in the Roman Sacramentaria and the Early Baptismal Liturgy* (Leiden, 1973).

93. We need only recall how in *Confessiones* 8,12 Augustine describes the instrument of his salvation as, first, the child's voice that, he believes, directed him to "take and read" the Scriptures (a Christian version of the *bath kol*), and then the passage in Romans (13:13) to which the "Apostle's book" fell open when he obeyed God's command mediated through that voice.

94. For a detailed discussion, see Markus, *Saeculum.* According to Markus's reconstruction, Augustine from 390, for ten or fifteen years, "appeared to have joined the chorus of his contemporaries in their triumphant jubilation over the victory of Christianity" (31). "For a decade or more, his historical thinking was dominated by this motif" (32). Yet from 410, Augustine became "much less ready to speak of a Christian empire. . . . he became much more reserved" (36).

95. Markus sees Augustine's theory as admirably balanced: "The Empire is not to be seen either in terms of the messianic image of Eusebian tradition, or of the

apocalyptic image, as the Antichrist of the Hippolytan tradition. The Empire has become no more than an historical, empirical society with a chequered career. . . . It is theologically neutral" (*ibid.*, 559). I believe that Markus overstates his case when he goes further and claims that Augustine also sees the church as "theologically neutral."

96. See, e.g., Hans Joachim Diesner's discussion of Ambrose, in "Kirche und Staat im ausgehenden vierten Jahrhundert: Ambrosius von Mailand," in his *Kirche und Staat im Spätromischen Reich: Aufsätze zur Spätantike und zur Geschichte der Alten Kirche* (Berlin, 1963), especially 28–34.

97. Yet, as the British historian G.E.M. de Ste. Croix observes, "In the late Republic there was a totally different kind of *libertas,* and to those who held it the optimate version of *libertas,* that of Cicero & Co., was *servitus* (slavery, political subjection), while their *libertas* was stigmatized by Cicero as mere *licentia* ('license,' lawlessness)—in a word used also by the Roman rhetorician Cornificius as the equivalent of the standard Greek word for freedom of speech, *parrhesia.*" G.E.M. de Ste. Croix, *Class Struggle,* 368.

98. Minucius Felix, *Octavius* 37,1. Emphasis added.

99. *Ibid.,* 38,1.

100. Tertullian, *Apology* 28.

101. Another favorite Christian slogan, *free will,* bore similar connotations. Many of Augustine's contemporaries, hearing Christians advocate free will (*libero arbitrio*), might associate this with those who advocate revolution, or, at least, resistance to Roman rule. See J.N.L. Myres, "Pelagius and the End of Roman Rule in Britain," *Journal of Roman Studies* 50 (1960), 21–36.

102. Augustine, *De Civitate Dei* 13,21.

103. *Ibid.,* 14,15.

104. Claudian, *Stilicho* 3,113–115. For an informative and incisive discussion of Claudian's point of view, see Alan Cameron, *Claudian: Poetry and Propaganda of the Court of Honorius* (Oxford, 1970).

105. I am grateful to Peter Brown for pointing this out, and for referring me to the discussion of *libertas* in Gerd Tellenbach, *Church, State and Christian Society at the Time of the Investiture Contest,* trans. R.F. Bennett, *Studies in Medieval History* 3 (Oxford, 1959), 14–18.

106. On the dating, see note 8 above.

107. Chrysostom, *Hom. ad pop. Ant.* 3,6.

108. *Ibid.,* 6,6.

109. For a detailed and useful analysis, see Florent van Ommeslaeghe, "Jean Chrysostome et le peuple de Constantinople," *AnBoll* 99 (1981), 329–349: "Il est certain qu'une des raisons de l'attachement du peuple de Constantinople à son chef spirituel fut sa bonté, son amour des pauvres, de nos jours on dirait: son sens social" (348). Also see J.H.W.G. Liebeschutz, "Friends and Enemies of John Chrysostom," in Ann Moffatt, ed., *Maistor: Classical, Byzantine and Renaissance Studies for Robert Browning* (Byzantina Australiensia 5, 1984), 85–111.

110. Otto Seeck, *Geschichte des Untergang der antiken Welt* (6 vols. in 8; Berlin, 1897–1920), 5,336–337.

111. Florent van Ommeslaeghe, "Jean Chrysostome en conflit avec l'impératrice Eudoxie: Le dossier et les origines d'une légende," *AnBoll* 97 (1979), 131–159.

112. Chrysostom, *Epistola* 94.

113. Augustine, *Sermo,* 355,2, as cited in Peter Brown, *Augustine of Hippo* (Berkeley, 1969), 138.

114. *Ibid.,* 225.

115. Augustine, *De Moribus Ecclesiae Catholicae et De Moribus Manichaeorum* 1,30,63.

116. See, for example, the account in F. Cayre, *Manual of Patrology and History of Theology* (Rome, 1935), vol. 1, 625–629. For a recent and comprehensive historical study, see W.H.C. Frend, *The Donatist Church: A Movement of Protest in Roman North Africa* (Oxford, 1952).

117. P. Brown, *Augustine,* 235.

118. Augustine, *De Baptismo* 1,15,23–24.

119. P. Brown, *Augustine,* 358. Emphasis added.


# CHAPTER SIX

1. H.C. Van Eijk, "Marriage and Virginity, Death and Immortality," in *Mélanges Jean Danielou* (Paris, 1972), 209–235.

2. For a different perspective on John Chrysostom and Augustine in the Pelagian controversy, see F.J. Thonnard, "Saint Jean Chrysostome et Saint Augustin dans la Controverse Pélagienne," in *Mélanges Venance Grumel* (Paris, 1967), 189–218. Thonnard concludes that Augustine's view of original sin "ne manque ni de valeur scientifique ni de vraisemblance historique" (217).

3. For a detailed discussion, see G. de Plinval, *Pélage: Ses Ecrits, Sa Vie, et Sa Réforme* (Lausanne, 1943); also the more recent study of O. Wermelinger, *Rom und Pelagius* (Stuttgart, 1975).

4. Cf. N.Q. King, *The Emperor Theodosius and the Establishment of Christianity* (Philadelphia, 1960). Constantine himself, the first Christian emperor, had deferred to the clergy as to his spiritual superiors; some sixty years later, Augustine's revered teacher Ambrose, the powerful bishop of Milan, literally brought the emperor to his knees. Ambrose had denounced Theodosius the Great for ordering a massacre of people in Thessalonica, and refused to allow the emperor to participate in communion until he had publicly repented.

5. See P. Brown, "Pelagius and His Supporters: Aims and Environment," in *Journal of Theological Studies, New Series,* 19,1 (1968), 93–114; and "The Patrons of Pelagius: The Roman Aristocracy Between East and West," in *Journal of Theological Studies, New Series,* 21,1 (1970), 56–72.

6. For discussion of the social and historical events of Pelagius's condemnation, see the sources cited above, especially the studies of Plinval, Wermelinger, and Brown.

7. See the excellent discussions by G.I. Bonner, "*Libido* and *Concupiscentia* in St. Augustine," in *Studia Patristica* 6 (Berlin, 1962), 303–314, and P. Brown, "Sexuality and Society in the Fifth Century A.D.: Augustine and Julian of Eclanum," in *Tria Corda: Scritti in Onore de Arnaldo Momigliano* (Como, 1983), 49–70; also E. Clark, "Vitiated Seeds and Holy Vessels: Augustine's Manichaean Past," in

E. Clark, *Ascetic Piety and Women's Faith: Essays on Late Ancient Christianity* (New York, 1986), 291–352.

8. Didymus the Blind, *De Trinitate* 2,12.

9. de Plinval, *Pélage,* 344.

10. On Julian, see A. Bruckner, *Julian von Eclanum: Sein Leben und Seine Lehre. Ein Beitrag zur Geschichte des Pelagianusmus, Texte und Untersuchungen,* 15,3 (Leipzig, 1897).

11. Augustine, *Opus Imperfectum Contra Julianum,* 4,91. Hereafter cited as *Opus Imperfectum.*

12. *Ibid.* 4,92–93: "Quidquid enim naturale est, voluntarium non esse manifestum est. . . . Istae duae definitiones tam contrariae sibi sunt, quam contrarium est necessitas et voluntas, quarum confirmatio ex mutua negatione generatur. Nam sicut nihil est aliud voluntarium, quam non coactum; ita nihil est aliud coactum, quam non voluntarium." Unlike Bonner, who agrees with de Plinval (*Pélage,* 360) that Julian concerns himself primarily with *libido,* I agree with F. Refoulé, whose excellent article "Julien d'Éclane: Théologien et Philosophe" (in *Recherches de Science Religieuse* 52 [Paris, 1964], 42–74) shows that Julian concerns himself above all with the question of *nature* and *will.* Refoulé states clearly and accurately that "C'est . . . par sa notion de nature que Julien d'Éclane sépare fondamentalement d'Augustin. Toute sa polémique contre l'interprétation d'Augustin du péché originel se fonde sur une distinction rigoureuse entre *nature* et *volunté,* étrangère à Augustin" (67).

13. Augustine, *Opus Imperfectum* 4,40.

14. *Ibid.* 6,30: Non est enim tanti unius meritum, ut universa quae naturaliter sunt instituta perturbet. Emphasis added.

15. *Ibid.* 6,26.

16. *Ibid.* 4,114.

17. *Ibid.* 6,25. Emphasis added.

18. *Ibid.* 6,26.

19. Augustine often returns to this theme, as P. Brown notes in *Augustine of Hippo: A Biography* (Berkeley, 1969), 397; for a few references, see *Contra Julianum* 3,3–6; 9; *Opus Imperfectum* 3,159; 198.

20. Augustine, *Opus Imperfectum* 6,27.

21. *Ibid.*

22. *Ibid.*

23. *Ibid.* 6,30: ". . . potestas vivendi, nec nulla moriendi necessitas."

24. *Ibid.* 6,27.

25. Augustine, *Contra Julianum* 3,3–5.

26. *Ibid.* 3,6.

27. Augustine, *Opus Imperfectum* 6,23,5.

28. Augustine, *Opus Imperfectum* 3,109. For a fine discussion of Augustine's view of divine justice as it relates to original sin, see Y. de Montcheuil, "La Polémique de Saint Augustin contre Julien d'Éclane d'après l'*Opus imperfectum,*" in *Recherches de Science Religieuse* 44,2 (Paris, 1956), 193–218.

29. Augustine, *Opus Imperfectum* 5,22.

30. *Ibid.* 1,1–2.

31. *Ibid.* 1,14.

32. *Ibid.* 6,26.

33. *Ibid.*

34. *Ibid.* 6,29.

35. *Ibid.* 6,26; for Julian's reply, 6,26–29.

36. For a fine and nuanced discussion of Chrysostom's position, see E. Clark, "The Virginal *Politeia* and Plato's *Republic:* John Chrysostom on Women and the Sexual Relation," in E. Clark, *Jerome, Chrysostom, and Friends* (New York, 1971), 1–22.

37. Augustine, *Opus Imperfectum* 6,27.

38. *Ibid.*

39. *Ibid.*

40. *Ibid.* 6,40.

41. *Ibid.* 3,82.

42. *Ibid.* 3,154.

43. *Ibid.* 2,33.

44. Augustine, *Contra Julianum* 3,14.

45. *Ibid.* 3,13. Emphasis added.

46. *Ibid.* Emphasis added.

47. *Ibid.* 3,14. Emphasis added.

48. Augustine, *Opus Imperfectum* 3,109.

49. *Ibid.* 4,92. Emphasis added.

50. *Ibid.* 5,45.

51. For some discussion of the exegetical issues, see G. Bonner, "Augustine on Romans 5,12," in *Studia Evangelica* 2 (Berlin, 1968), 242–247; S. Lyonnet, "Le Péché Originel et l'Exégèse de Rom. 5,12–14," in *Recherches de Science Religieuse* 44,1 (Paris, 1956), 63–84; also by Lyonnet, "Le Sens de ἐφ' ᾧ en Rom. 5,12 et l'Exégèse des Pères Grecs," in *Biblica* 36 (Rome, 1955), 427–456; A. d'Alès, "Julien d'Eclane, Exégète," in *Recherches de Science Religieuse* 6 (Paris, 1916), 311–324; H. Wolfson, "Philosophical Implications of the Pelagian Controversy," in *Proceedings of the American Philosophical Society* 103 (Philadelphia, 1959), 554–562; A. Bruckner, *Julian von Eclanum,* 114–123.

52. P. Gorday, *Principles of Patristic Exegesis,* 1–135.

53. A. Bruckner, *Julian von Eclanum,* 100.

54. *Ibid.,* 123–127. Emphasis added.

55. J. Ferguson, *Pelagius: A Historical and Theological Study* (Cambridge, England, 1966).

56. Augustine, *Opus Imperfectum* 6,35. Emphasis added.

57. *Ibid.* 6,30. "Man had it in his power not to die, had he not sinned."

58. *Ibid.* 6,35. Emphasis added.

59. *Midrash Rabbah,* Numbers 9, 4–10.

60. *Sun Chief: The Autobiography of a Hopi Indian,* ed. Leo W. Simmons (New Haven: Yale University Press, 1942), chap. 1.

61. E.E. Evans-Pritchard, "The Notion of Witchcraft Explains Unfortunate Events," in *Witchcraft, Oracles, and Magic Among the Azande* (Oxford, 1976), 18–32.

62. Luke 13:4–5.

63. *Midrash Rabbah,* Genesis 12,6; 21,3; 24,2, *passim*; L. Ginzberg, *Legends of the Jews* (Philadelphia, 1925), I, 49–101; V, 63–142.

64. I am grateful to Dr. Zephirah Gitay for sharing with me her research on Dürer's depictions of the Paradise story.

65. Augustine, *Opus Imperfectum* 5,49; cf. 3,103.

66. *Ibid.* 3,109. For further references and discussion, see Refoulé, "Julien d'Eclane," 66–72.

67. Augustine, *Opus Imperfectum* 6,40.

# INDEX

# FOR THE BEST IN PAPERBACKS, LOOK FOR THE

In every corner of the world, on every subject under the sun, Penguin represents quality and variety – the very best in publishing today.

For complete information about books available from Penguin – including Pelicans, Puffins, Peregrines and Penguin Classics – and how to order them, write to us at the appropriate address below. Please note that for copyright reasons the selection of books varies from country to country.

---

**In the United Kingdom:** Please write to *Dept E.P., Penguin Books Ltd, Harmondsworth, Middlesex, UB7 0DA*

If you have any difficulty in obtaining a title, please send your order with the correct money, plus ten per cent for postage and packaging, to *PO Box No 11, West Drayton, Middlesex*

**In the United States:** Please write to *Dept BA, Penguin, 299 Murray Hill Parkway, East Rutherford, New Jersey 07073*

**In Canada:** Please write to *Penguin Books Canada Ltd, 2801 John Street, Markham, Ontario L3R 1B4*

**In Australia:** Please write to the *Marketing Department, Penguin Books Australia Ltd, P.O. Box 257, Ringwood, Victoria 3134*

**In New Zealand:** Please write to the *Marketing Department, Penguin Books (NZ) Ltd, Private Bag, Takapuna, Auckland 9*

**In India:** Please write to *Penguin Overseas Ltd, 706 Eros Apartments, 56 Nehru Place, New Delhi, 110019*

**In Holland:** Please write to *Penguin Books Nederland B.V., Postbus 195, NL–1380AD Weesp, Netherlands*

**In Germany:** Please write to *Penguin Books Ltd, Friedrichstrasse 10–12, D–6000 Frankfurt Main 1, Federal Republic of Germany*

**In Spain:** Please write to *Longman Penguin España, Calle San Nicolas 15, E–28013 Madrid, Spain*

**In France:** Please write to *Penguin Books Ltd, 39 Rue de Montmorency, F-75003, Paris, France*

**In Japan:** Please write to *Longman Penguin Japan Co Ltd, Yamaguchi Building, 2–12–9 Kanda Jimbocho, Chiyoda-Ku, Tokyo 101, Japan*

## PENGUIN ARCHAEOLOGY

### The Dead Sea Scrolls in English   G. Vermes

This established and authoritative English translation of the non-biblical Qumran scrolls – offering a revolutionary insight into Palestinian Jewish life and ideology at a crucial period in the development of Jewish and Christian religious thought – now includes the Temple Scroll, the most voluminous scroll of them all.

### Hadrian's Wall   David J. Breeze and Brian Dobson

A penetrating history of the best-known, best-preserved and most spectacular monument to the Roman Empire in Britain. 'A masterpiece of the controlled use of archaeological and epigraphical evidence in a fluent narrative that will satisfy any level of interest' – *The Times Educational Supplement*

### Before Civilization   The Radiocarbon Revolution and Prehistoric Europe
Colin Renfrew

'I have little doubt that this is one of the most important archaeological books for a very long time' – Barry Cunliffe in the *New Scientist*. 'Pure stimulation from beginning to end … a book which provokes thought, aids understanding, and above all is immensely enjoyable' – *Scotsman*

### The Ancient Civilizations of Peru   J. Alden Mason

The archaeological, historical, artistic, geographical and ethnographical discoveries that have resurrected the rich variety of Inca and pre-Inca culture and civilization – wiped out by the Spanish Conquest – are surveyed in this now classic work.

# FOR THE BEST IN PAPERBACKS, LOOK FOR THE 🐧

## PENGUIN HISTORY

### The Germans   Gordon A. Craig

An intimate study of a complex and fascinating nation by 'one of the ablest and most distinguished American historians of modern Germany' – Hugh Trevor-Roper

### Imperial Spain 1469–1716   J. H. Elliot

A brilliant modern study of the sudden rise of a barren and isolated country to the greatest power on earth, and of its equally sudden decline. 'Outstandingly good' – *Daily Telegraph*

### British Society 1914–1945   John Stevenson

A major contribution to the *Penguin Social History of Britain*, which 'will undoubtedly be the standard work for students of modern Britain for many years to come' – *The Times Educational Supplement*

### Montaillou   Cathars and Catholics in a French Village 1294–1324
Emmanuel Le Roy Ladurie

'A classic adventure in eavesdropping across time' – Michael Ratcliffe in *The Times*

### The Penguin History of Greece   A. R. Burn

Readable, erudite, enthusiastic and balanced, this one-volume history of Hellas sweeps the reader along from the days of Mycenae and the splendours of Athens to the conquests of Alexander and the final dark decades.

### A History of Latin America   George Pendle

'Ought to be compulsory reading in every sixth form … this book is right on target' – *Sunday Times*. 'A beginner's guide to the continent … lively, and full of anecdote' – *Financial Times*

## PENGUIN HISTORY

### The Victorian Underworld   Kellow Chesney

A superbly evocative survey of the vast substratum of vice that lay below the respectable surface of Victorian England – the showmen, religious fakes, garrotters, pickpockets and prostitutes – and of the penal methods of that 'most elightened age'. 'Charged with nightmare detail' – *Sunday Times*

### A History of Modern France   Alfred Cobban

Professor Cobban's renowned three-volume history, skilfully steering the reader through France's political and social problems from 1715 to the Third Republic, remains essential reading for anyone wishing to understand the development of a great European nation.

### Stalin   Isaac Deutscher

'The Greatest Genius in History' and the 'Life-Giving Force of Socialism'? Or a tyrant more ruthless than Ivan the Terrible and a revolutionary whose policies facilitated the rise of Nazism? An outstanding biographical study of a revolutionary despot by a great historian.

### A History of Christianity   Paul Johnson

'Masterly … It is a huge and crowded canvas – a tremendous theme running through twenty centuries of history – a cosmic soap opera involving kings and beggars, philosophers and crackpots, scholars and illiterate *exaltés*, popes and pilgrims and wild anchorites in the wilderness' – Malcolm Muggeridge

### The Habsburg Monarchy 1809 – 1918   A. J. P. Taylor

Dissolved in 1918, the Habsburg Empire 'had a unique character, out of time and out of place'. Scholarly and vividly accessible, this 'very good book indeed' (*Spectator*) elucidates the problems always inherent in the attempt to give peace, stability and a common loyalty to a heterogeneous population.

### Industry and Empire   E. J. Hobsbawm

Volume 3 of the *Penguin Economic History of Britain* covers the period of the Industrial Revolution: 'the most fundamental transformation in the history of the world recorded in written documents.' 'A book that attracts and deserves attention … by far the most gifted historian now writing' – John Vaizey in the *Listener*

# FOR THE BEST IN PAPERBACKS, LOOK FOR THE

## PENGUIN RELIGION

### Islam in the World  Malise Ruthven

This informed and informative book places the contemporary Islamic revival in context, providing a fascinating introduction – the first of its kind – to Islamic origins, beliefs, history, geography, politics and society.

### The Orthodox Church  Timothy Ware

In response to increasing interest among western Christians, and believing that a thorough understanding of Orthodoxy is necessary if the Roman Catholic and Protestant Churches are to be reunited, Timothy Ware explains Orthodox views on a vast range of matters from Free Will to the Papacy.

### Judaism  Isidore Epstein

The comprehensive account of Judaism as a religion and as a distinctive way of life, presented against a background of 4,000 years of Jewish history.

### Mysticism  F. C. Happold

What is mysticism? This simple and illuminating book combines a study of mysticism – as experience, as spiritual knowledge and as a way of life – with an illustrative anthology of mystical writings, ranging from Plato and Plotinus to Dante.

### The Penguin History of the Church: 4  Gerald R. Cragg
### The Church and the Age of Reason

Gerald Cragg's elegant and stimulating assessment of the era from the Peace of Westphalia to the French Revolution – a formative period in the Church's history – ranges from the Church life of France under Louis XIV to the high noon of rationalism and beyond.

 ### The Gnostic Gospels  Elaine Pagels

Written over 2,000 years ago and discovered in 1945 buried in the Upper Egyptian desert, the so-called gnostic gospels – revealing unprecedented information about the early Christian Church – are examined in this 'fascinating' (*The Times*) book.